TREASURY
of
DAILY DEVOTIONS

The Ambassador

TREASURY
of
DAILY DEVOTIONS

Compiled by
CHARLES EDWARDS

AMBASSADOR
BELFAST ♦ **GREENVILLE**
NORTHERN IRELAND   SOUTH CAROLINA

TREASURY OF DAILY DEVOTIONS

First published October 1998
Copyright © 1998 Charles Edwards

ISBN 1 84030 033 7

Ambassador Publications
a division of
Ambassador Productions Ltd.
Providence House
16 Hillview Avenue,
Belfast, BT5 6JR
Northern Ireland

Emerald House
1 Chick Springs Road, Suite 203
Greenville,
South Carolina 29609, USA

www.emeraldhouse.com

Day by day manna fell:
O to learn Thy lesson well.
Still by constant mercy fed,
Give me Lord, my daily bread.

Day by day, the promise reads,
Daily strength for daily needs:
Cast foreboding fears away;
Take the manna for today.

Lord! my times are in Thy hand:
All my sanguine hopes have planned,
To Thy wisdom I resign,
And would make Thy treasure mine

JOSIAH CONDER

JANUARY 1

CONSIDER YOUR WAYS

Exhort one another daily.
HEBREWS 3:13

When a traveller passes very rapidly through a country, the eye has not time to rest upon the different objects in it, so that, when he comes to the end of his journey, no distinct impressions have been made upon his mind - he has only a confused notion of the country through which he has travelled.

This explains how it is that death, judgment and eternity, make so little impression upon most men's minds. Most people never stop to think, but hurry on through life, and find themselves in eternity, before they have once put the question, "What must I do to be saved?" More souls are lost through want of consideration than in any other way.

The reason why men are not awakened and made anxious for their souls is, that the devil never gives them time to consider. Therefore God cries, "Stop, poor sinner, stop and think. Consider your ways. Oh that you were wise, that you understood this, that you considered your latter end!" And, again He cries, "Israel doth not know, My people doth not consider."

In the same way does the devil try to make the children of God doubt if there be a Providence. He hurries them away to the shop and market. Lose no time, he says, but make money. Therefore God cries, "Stop, poor sinner, stop and think; " and Jesus says, "Consider the lilies of the field, how they grow; consider the ravens, which have neither storehouse nor barn."

In the same way does the devil try to make the children of God live uncomfortable and unholy lives. He beguiles them away from simply looking to Jesus; he hurries them away to look at a thousand other things, as he led Peter, walking on the sea, to look around at the waves. But God says, "Look here, consider the Apostle and High Priest of your profession; look unto me and be ye saved; run your race, looking unto Jesus; consider Christ, the same yesterday, today and forever."

ROBERT MURRAY McCHEYNE

JANUARY 2

KEPT FOR JESUS

What is man, that thou art mindful of him?
PSALM 8:4

While we have been undervaluing these fractions of eternity, what has our gracious God been doing in them? How strangely touching are the words, "What is man, that ... Thou shouldest set Thine heart upon him, and that Thou shouldest visit him every morning, and try him every moment?" Terribly solemn and awful would be the thought that He has been trying us every moment, were it not for the yearning gentleness and love of the Father revealed in that wonderful expression of wonder, "What is man, that Thou shouldest set Thine heart upon him?" Think of that ceaseless setting of His heart upon us, careless and forgetful children as we have been! And then think of those other words, none the less literally true because given under a figure: "I, the Lord, do keep it; I will water it every moment."

We see something of God's infinite greatness and wisdom when we try to fix our dazzled gaze on infinite space. But when we turn to the marvels of the microscope, we gain a clearer view and more definite grasp of these attributes by gazing on the perfection of His infinitesimal handiwork. Just so, whereas we cannot realise the infinite love that fills eternity, and the infinite vistas of the great future are dark with excess of light even to the strongest telescopes of faith, we see that love magnified in the microscope of the moments, brought very close to us, and revealing its unspeakable perfection of detail to our wondering sight.

But we do not see this as long as the moments are kept in our own hands. We are like little children closing our fingers over diamonds. How can they receive and reflect the rays of light, analysing them into all the splendour of their prismatic beauty, while they are kept shut up tight in the dirty little hands? Give them up! Let our Father hold them for us, and throw His own great light upon them. Then we shall see them full of fair colours of His manifold loving-kindness.

Let Him always keep them for us, and then we shall always see His light and His love reflected in them.

FRANCES R. HAVERGAL

JANUARY 3

CALVARY'S CROSS

... Jesus Christ, and him crucified.
I CORINTHIANS 2:2

The cross means that Christ died for sinners upon the cross, that He made atonement for sinners by His suffering for them on the cross - a complete and perfect sacrifice for sin, which He offered up when He gave His own body to be crucified. This is the meaning in which Paul used the expression, when he told the Corinthians, "The preaching of the cross is to them that perish foolishness." (1 Corinthians 1: 18), and when he wrote to the Galatians, "God forbid that I should glory save in the cross," he simply meant, I glory in nothing but Christ crucified as the salvation of my soul."

This is the subject he loved to preach about.

He was a man who went to and fro on the earth, proclaiming to sinners that the Son of God had shed His own heart's blood to save their souls, that Jesus Christ had loved them and died for their sins upon the cross. Mark how he says to the Corinthians, "I delivered unto you first of all that which I also received, how that Christ died for our sins." (I Corinthians 15: 3). He - a blaspheming, persecuting Pharisee - had been washed in Christ's blood. He could not hold his peace about it. He was never weary of telling the story of the cross.

This is the subject he loved to dwell upon when he wrote to believers.

It is wonderful to observe how full his epistles generally are of the sufferings and death of Christ. He enlarges on the subject constantly. He returns to it continually. It is the golden thread that runs through all his doctrinal teaching and practical exhortation. He seems to think that the most advanced Christian can never hear too much of the cross.

This is what he lived upon all his life, from the time of his conversion. He tells the Galatians, "The life that I now live in the flesh I live by the faith of the Son of God, who loved me and gave himself for me" (Galatians 2:20). What made him so strong to labour, so willing to work, so unwearied in endeavouring to save some, so persevering and patient? The secret of it all was that he was always feeding by faith on Christ's body and Christ's blood. Jesus crucified was the meat and drink of his soul.

J. C. RYLE

JANUARY 4

YOUR ONLY HOPE

But God, who is rich in mercy, for his great love wherewith he loved us.
EPHESIANS 2:4

I know what it is you want. You want the best robe without your Father's giving it to you, and the shoes on your feet of your own procuring. You do not like going in a beggar's suit and receiving all from the Lord's loving hand. But this pride of yours must be given up, and you must get away to God, or perish forever. You must forget yourself, or only remember yourself so as to feel that you are bad throughout and no more worthy to be called God's son. Give yourself up as a sinking vessel that is not worth pumping, but must be left to go down, and get you into the lifeboat of free grace. Think of God your Father and of His dear Son, the one Mediator and Redeemer of the sons of men. There is your hope - to fly away from self and to reach your Father.

Sinner, your business is with God. Hasten to Him at once. You have nothing to do with yourself or your own doings or what others can do for you. The turning point of salvation is "He arose and came to his father." There must be a real, living, earnest, contact of your poor guilty soul with God, a recognition that there is a God and that God can be spoken to, and an actual speech of your soul to Him through Jesus Christ for it is only God in Christ Jesus that is accessible to all. Going thus to God, we tell Him that we are all wrong, and want to be set right; we tell Him we wish to be reconciled to Him and are ashamed that we should have sinned against Him; we then put our trust in His Son, and we are saved.

O soul, go to God; it matters not that the prayer you come with may be a very broken prayer, or even if it has mistakes in it, as the prodigal's prayer had when he said, "Make me as one of thy hired servants"; the language of the prayer will not matter so long as you really approach God. "Him that cometh to me," says Jesus, "I will in no wise cast out"; and Jesus ever liveth to make intercession for them that come to God through Him.

CHARLES H. SPURGEON

JANUARY 5

THE BOOK ABOVE ALL BOOKS

Let the word of Christ dwell in you richly.
COLOSSIANS 3:16

Like many believers, I practically preferred, for the first four years of my divine life, the works of uninspired men to the oracles of the living God. The consequence was that I remained a babe, both in knowledge and grace. In knowledge I say; for all true knowledge must be derived by the Spirit, from the Word. And as I neglected the Word, I was for nearly four years so ignorant that I did not clearly know even the fundamental points of our holy faith. And this lack of knowledge most sadly kept me from walking steadily in the ways of God.

For it is the truth that makes us free (John 8: 31-32), by delivering us from the slavery of the lusts of the flesh, the lust of the eyes, and the pride of life. The Word proves it. The experience of the saints proves it; and also my own experience most decidedly proves it. For when it pleased the Lord in August 1829 to bring me really to the Scriptures, my life and walk became very different. And though ever since that I have very much fallen short of what I might and ought to be, yet, by the grace of God, I have been enabled to live much nearer to Him than before.

If any believers read this who prefer other books to the Holy Scriptures, and who enjoy the writings of men much more than the Word of God, may they be warned by my loss. I shall consider this book to have been the means of doing much good, should it please the Lord, through its instrumentality, to lead some of His people no longer to neglect the Holy Scriptures, but to give them the preference, which they have hitherto bestowed on the writings of men.

My dislike to increase the number of books would have been sufficient to deter me from writing these pages had I not been convinced that this is the only way in which the brethren at large may be benefited through my mistakes and errors, and been influenced by the hope that, in answer to my prayers, the reading of my experience may be the means of leading them to value the Scriptures more highly and to make them the rule of all their actions.

GEORGE MUELLER

TWO KINDS OF PEACE

*The peace of God, which passeth all understanding shall keep your
hearts and minds through Christ Jesus.*
PHILIPPIANS 4:7

There are two kinds of peace mentioned in the New Testament. The first peace, for blood-washed men and women is, "Justified by faith, we have peace with God." That is not something that you gain: it is a gift. It is not a payment. It does not matter what your denomination may be, or whether you have any denomination, or who you are or what you are, if you are saved by God's grace you have peace with God through our Lord Jesus Christ.

But there is another peace mentioned in Scripture, which you find in Philippians 4: 7, "... the peace of God, to garrison your heart and mind in Christ Jesus." Every born-again one has peace *with* God, but it is not every Christian that has the *peace of God*, though he *should* have it. The first peace is determined by your union with the Lord; the second, by your communion with your Lord. If I am walking in the light as He is in the light, we are having fellowship one with the other and I possess the peace of God. "Come unto Me ... and I will give you rest." This is a first call. But beyond it there is something far richer and deeper. "There remaineth a rest for the people of God," and they who enter into this rest have ceased from their own works, and enter into a possession that is peculiar and wonderfully precious - the peace of God.

Peace, perfect peace, in this dark world of sin?
The blood of Jesus whispers peace within.
Peace, perfect peace, by thronging duties pressed?
To do the will of Jesus, this is rest.

W. P. NICHOLSON

JANUARY 7

ASSURANCE FOREVER

*Purge me with hyssop, and I shall be clean: wash me and I
shall be whiter than snow.*
PSALM 51:7

God refuses to compromise His own character for the sake of anyone, much as He yearns to have all men to be saved.

It was this that stirred the soul of Luther, and brought new light and help after long, weary months of groping in the darkness, trying in vain to save himself in conformity to the demands of blind leaders of the blind. As Luther was reading the Latin Psalter, he came across David's prayer, "Save me in thy righteousness." Luther exclaimed, "What does this mean? I can understand how God can damn me in His righteousness, but if He would save me it must surely be in His mercy!" The more he meditated on it, the more the wonder grew. But little by little the truth dawned upon his troubled soul that God Himself had devised a righteous method whereby He could justify unrighteous sinners who came to Him in repentance and received His word in faith.

Isaiah stresses this great and glorious truth throughout his marvellous Old Testament unfolding of the gospel plan. In unsparing severity, the prophet portrays man's utterly lost and absolutely hopeless condition apart from divine grace. "The whole head is sick, and the whole heart faint. From the sole of the foot even unto the head there is no soundness in it; but wounds and bruises and putrifying sores: they have not been closed, neither bound up, neither mollified with ointment." (Isaiah 1: 5-6). It is surely a revolting picture, but nevertheless it is true of the unsaved man as God sees him. Sin is a vile disease that has fastened upon the very vitals of its victim. None can free himself from its pollution or deliver himself from its power.

But God has a remedy. He says, "Come now, and let us reason together, saith the Lord: though your sins be as scarlet, they shall be as white as snow; though they be red like crimson, they shall be as wool" (Verse 18). It is God Himself who can thus purge the leper from all his uncleanness, and justify the ungodly from all his guilt. And He does it, not at the expense of righteousness, but in a perfectly righteous way.

HARRY IRONSIDE

JANUARY 8

GOD'S PURPOSE

I will instruct thee and teach thee in the way which thou shalt go.
PSALM 32:8

There are three possible plannings for human life. We may be guided by our senses - "We like this or do not like that." We may be guided by our own will and choice. But, best of all, we may be guided, as our Lord was, by constantly waiting for the indication of God's purpose. That indication is like a deep-toned bell ringing in our heart-depths, but finally corroborated by circumstances and certainly vindicated by results.

One Sunday morning, I was sitting on the porch of Mr. Moody's home, looking down on the Connecticut River. We were talking of the ways of God, and he recalled a sermon of Dr. Andrew Bonar on the words, repeated five times in Scripture, "See that thou make all things according to the pattern shown thee on the Mount." Dr. Bonar described the tabernacle pattern as woven out of sunbeams; and Moses walked with God from one part to another of the ethereal structure, learning the specific reason for each. When, for instance, they viewed the altar of sacrifice, God explained that in process of time Calvary would bear the weight of the dying Saviour; and, as they looked on the laver, God would explain that the soul, redeemed by the blood of Christ, would always need cleansing. So also the significance of the altar of incense, the veil, the ark, and the mercy-seat. When presently Moses returned to the people, he discovered that for everything that had been revealed in the vision there was exact and adequate provision in the gifts of the people.

This is a most helpful lesson. The first thing for any of us is not to run hither and thither, consulting people or soliciting their help, but to be perfectly assured that we are in the mind of the Lord and that He will supply all our need, according to His riches in glory by Christ Jesus.

It must never be forgotten that none of those that live in God's purposes need ever be ashamed. His delays are not denials. "(From of old), men have not heard, nor perceived by the ear, neither hath the eye seen, O God, beside Thee, what He hath prepared for him that waiteth for Him." (Isaiah 64:4)

F. B. MEYER

JANUARY 9

TRUE HAPPINESS

... Your joy no man taketh from you.
JOHN 16:22

That the world is guilty before God, is not only declared by Scripture, but is also to be seen by the present state of man with regard to happiness. It is obvious to any impartial observer that the human race is *miserable*, even amidst its mirth and dissipation. Men are *seeking* happiness (a proof that they do not have it) from the enjoyment of earthly things, according to their various tastes and appetites; but they find it not. From the highest to the lowest, there is that which *mars* their peace and enjoyment. The very things which the poor regard as evidences of the happiness of the rich, are but so many devices to drive away sorrow. If they would honestly express themselves, the millionaire in his mansion and the king on his throne would declare, *"all* is vanity and vexation of spirit." True happiness is to be found in God alone.

In such a state of guilt and misery is placed the whole human race. It is indeed a melancholy truth, but one which is altogether incontestable. Instead, then, of disputing the Divine testimony, let us inquire from the same authority, whether there be any way of escape. Is the fate of fallen men as hopeless as that of fallen angels? No, blessed be God, it is not. The same Word of Truth which tells of man's ruin, announces the Divine remedy; the same Book which describes human guilt and wretchedness, tells of a way of deliverance therefrom. The One, who, in the exercise of His high sovereignty, reserved the sinning angels in everlasting chains of darkness unto the judgment of the great day, has, in His abounding mercy, provided salvation for undone sinners of Adam's race.

It was down at the feet of Jesus,
O the happy, happy day!
That my soul found peace in believing,
And my sins were washed away.

A. W. PINK

FOR HIS JOY

Herein is my Father glorified, that ye bear much fruit.
JOHN 15:8

W hat a long time it takes us to come to the conviction, and still more to the realisation, that without Christ we can do nothing, but that He must work all our works in us! This is the work of God, that you believe in Him whom He has sent. And no less must it be the work of God that we go on believing and that we go on trusting. Then, dear friends, who are longing to trust Him with unbroken and unwavering trust, cease the effort and drop the burden, and now entrust your trust to him! He is just as well able to keep that as any other part of the complex lives we want Him to take and keep for Himself.

And do not be content with the thought *Yes, that is a good idea, perhaps I should find that a great help*. But, now, then, do it. It is no help to the sailor to see a flash of light across a dark sea, if he does not instantly steer accordingly.

Consecration is not a religiously selfish thing. If it sinks to that, it ceases to be consecration. We want our lives kept, not that we may feel happy, and be saved the distress consequent on wandering, and get the power with God and man, and all the other privileges linked with it. We shall have all this, because the lower is included in the higher, but our true aim, if the love of Christ constrains us, will be far beyond this. Not of "me" at all, but "for Jesus"; not for my comfort, but for His joy; not that I may find rest but that He may see the travail of His soul and be satisfied!

Yes, for Him I want to be kept. Kept for His sake; kept for His use; kept to be His witness; kept for His joy! Kept for Him, that in me He may show forth some tiny sparkle of His light and beauty. By being kept in Him I shall be able to do His will and His work in His own way.

I take Thee, blessed Lord,
I give myself to Thee;
And Thou, according to Thy Word,
Dost undertake for me.

FRANCES R. HAVERGAL

JANUARY 11

OCCUPY TILL I COME

Redeeming the time, because the days are evil.
EPHESIANS 5:16

What is the present duty of all Christ's professing disciples? When I speak of present duty, I mean, of course, their duty between the period of Christ's first and second advents. I find an answer in the words of the nobleman, in the parable, to his servants, "He delivered them ten pounds, and said unto them, Occupy till I come."

Few words are more searching and impressive than these four: "Occupy till I come". They are spoken to all who profess and call themselves Christians. And they address everyone who has not formally turned his back on Christianity. They ought to stir up all hearers of the gospel to examine themselves whether they are in the faith and to prove themselves. For your sake, remember, these words were written: "Occupy till I come".

The Lord Jesus bids you to "occupy". By that He means you are to be "a doer" in your Christianity and not merely a hearer and professor. He wants His servants not only to receive His wages and to eat His bread and dwell in His house and belong to His family - but also to do His work. You are to "let your light so shine before men that they may see your good works". Have you faith? It must not be a dead faith; it must "work by love". Do you love Christ? Prove the reality of your love by keeping Christ's commandments.

Do not forget this charge to "occupy". Beware of an idle, talking, gossiping, sentimental, do-nothing religion. Think not because your doings cannot justify you, or put away one single sin, that therefore it matters not whether you do anything at all. Away with such delusion! Cast it behind you as an invention of the devil. As ever you would "make your calling and election sure", be a doing Christian.

J. C. RYLE

THE LIFE OF OBEDIENCE

... What doth the Lord require of thee, but to do justly, and to love mercy,
and to walk humbly with thy God?
MICAH 6:8

Christ revealed the new law of love to be merciful as the Father in heaven, to forgive just as He does, to love enemies and to do good to them that hate us, and to live lives of self-sacrifice and beneficence. This was the religion Jesus taught on earth.

When we are provoked or ill-used, let us look upon an unforgiving spirit, upon unloving thoughts and sharp or unkind words, upon the neglect of the call to show mercy and do good and bless, all as so much disobedience. As such, our disobedience must be felt and mourned over and plucked out like a right eye; only then can the power of a full obedience be ours.

Christ spoke much of self-denial. Self is the root of all lack of love and obedience. Our Lord called each disciple to deny him - or herself and to take up the cross, forsake self and become the servant of all. Christ issued the call because self - self-will, self-pleasing, self-seeking - is simply the source of all sin.

When we indulge the flesh in such a simple thing as eating and drinking, when we gratify self by seeking or accepting or rejoicing in what indulges our pride, when self-will is allowed to assert itself and we make provision for the fulfilment of its desire, we are guilty of disobedience to His command. This gradually clouds the soul and makes the full enjoyment of His light and peace an impossibility.

Christ claimed for God the love of the whole heart. For Himself He equally claimed the sacrifices of all to come and follow Him. The Christian who has not definitely at heart made this his aim, who has not determined to seek for grace so to live, is guilty of disobedience. There may be much in his religion that appears good and earnest, but he cannot possibly have the joy consciousness of knowing that he is doing the will of his Lord, and keeping His commandments.

ANDREW MURRAY

JANUARY 13

THE "MUST" OF THE DECREASING SELF

... Walk not after the flesh, but after the Spirit.
ROMANS 8:4

Some of us can never forget the hymn composed by the late Pastor Theodore Monod of Paris in his first radiant vision of a life hidden in Christ with God:

All of Self and none of Thee!
Some of Self and some of Thee!
Less of Self and more of Thee!
None of Self and all of Thee!

"Reckon yourselves to be dead indeed unto sin, but alive unto God, through Jesus Christ our Lord."

We must receive more of the grace of the Holy Spirit. In Romans 7, the apostle Paul complains of being tied and bound by the self-life. He is like a caged bird, which beats its breast against the bars of its cage in vain aspirations for liberty. Then suddenly, in Romans 8, he changes his note and cries, "There is now no more of this self-condemnation, for those who are in Christ Jesus, who walk and live after the Spirit, because the law of the Spirit of life, in Christ Jesus, has made them free from the law of sin and death."

Let us stand together on the deck of an ocean-bound steamer and watch the flight of a seagull. There is, of course, the downward pull of gravitation; but, for every pull downwards, there is a stroke of the live bird's wing on the elastic air; and this more than compensates for the downward pull. That stroke, we know, is due to the spirit of life, which throbs in the bird's breast.

So, by the Holy Spirit, who indwells our spirit, there is given to each one of us the very life of our glorious Saviour. The regularity, immediacy, and quality of the Christ-life are more than sufficient to counteract the downward pull of sin. At the first slight suggestion of sin, the Holy Spirt resists the self-life, so that we may not do the things that we otherwise would; nor shall we fall into those sins of will and thought and act, which were once natural to us. "If we live by the Spirit, by the Spirit let us walk." (see Galatians 5: 16-26). The Spirit will lust against the flesh and obtain absolute victory, which will fill our hearts with joy. Indeed, temptation may even promote a stronger character by making Jesus a more living reality.

F. B. MEYER

POWER RELIGION

Ye shall receive power, after that the Holy Ghost is come upon you.
ACTS 1:8

We boast about our religion that it is a religion of power. We glory in the Cross of Chirst "towering o'er the wrecks of time". It is the marvellous power in Christ and in this Gospel that is our boast. We cannot boast of that too much; but there is a difference between what you read today in the Bible and its manifestation in your life. The world is concerned more about the power in your life than about what you say. They have a right to know and see the expression of that power in your life and mine. The Lord told His disciples "Ye shall receive power". Are you living the powerless or paralysed life? Is your life full of Divine energy? or is it a life where the paramount thing is weakness? Here is what the Word of God says, and here is how I live: Do they correspond? Is my life a life of power or of paralysis? Am I being wheeled around like a paralytic invalid? or am I a mighty man helping on the work of Christ in the strength of God? Is the life full of Divine energy or of human weakness? is it a life of failure or of victory? Are you triumphing in Christ, or are the devil and the world triumphing over you?

Come, Holy Spirit, heavenly dove,
With all Thy quickening powers;
Kindle a flame of sacred love
In these cold hearts of ours.

W. P. NICHOLSON

THE VERACITY OF GOD

God is not a man, that he should lie.
NUMBERS 23:19

In the past eternity the Father made definite promises to the Mediator. From these we may cite the following: "I the Lord have called thee in righteousness, and will hold thine hand, and will keep thee, and give thee for a covenant of the people, for a light of the Gentiles; To open the blind eyes, to bring out the prisoners from the prison" (Is. 42: 6,7). "In the Lord *shall* all the seed of Israel (namely "the Israel of God" Gal. 6: 16) be justified, and shall glory" (Isa. 45: 25). "Thus saith the Lord, the Redeemer of Israel, his Holy One, to him whom man despiseth, to him whom the nation abhorreth, to a servant of rulers, Kings shall see and arise, princes also *shall* worship, because of the Lord that is *faithful*" (Isa. 49: 7). "He *shall* see of the travail of his soul, and be satisfied: by his knowledge *shall* my righteous servant justify many: for he shall bear their iniquities. Therefore will I divide him a portion with the great, and he *shall* divide the spoil with the strong" (Isa. 53: 11,12). "Ask of me, and I *shall give* thee the heathen for thine inheritance, and the uttermost parts of the earth for thy possession" (Psa. 2:8). In view of these promises, Christ had a joy "set before him", for which joy he endured the Cross and despised the shame (Heb. 12: 2).

Now if one man enters into a solemn engagement with another which is duly ratified, signed, sealed and witnessed to, for him to attempt to break it would be to violate his honour, forfeit his good name, and make him an object of contempt to all righteous people. But the man who is honourable and upright, respects his pledges: his word is his bond. Infinitely more so does all this hold good of Him who is the God of Truth.

A. W. PINK

JANUARY 16

OPEN THOU MY LIPS

... That with all boldness they may speak thy word.
ACTS 4:29

Yes, it is true enough that we should show forth His praise not only with our lips but in our lives; but with very many Christians the other side of the prayer wants praying - they want rousing up even to wish to show it forth not only in their lives but with their lips. I wonder how many, even of those who read this, really pray, "O Lord, open Thou my lips, and my mouth shall show forth Thy praise!"

And when opened, oh, how much one does want to have them so kept for Jesus that He may be free to make the most of them, not letting them render second-rate and indirect service when they might be doing direct and first-rate service to His cause and kingdom. It is terrible how much less is done for Him that might be done, because we think that if what we are doing or saying is not bad, we are doing good in a certain way, and therefore may be quite easy about it. People are not converted by this sort of work; at any rate I never met or heard of anyone.

"He thinks it better for his quiet influence to tell!" said an affectionately excusing relative of one who had plenty of special opportunities of soul winning, if he had only used his lips as well as his life for his Master.

"And how many souls have been converted to God by his quiet influence all these years?" was my reply. And to that there was no answer. For the silent shining was all very beautiful in theory, but not one of the many souls placed specially under his influence had been known to be brought out of darkness into marvellous light. If they had, they must have been known, for such light can't help being seen.

When one has even a glimmer of the tremendous difference between having Christ and being without Christ; when one gets but one shuddering glimpse of what eternity is and what it may mean without Christ; when one gets but a flash of realisation that all these neighbours of ours, rich and poor alike, will have to spend that eternity either with Him or without Him, - it is hard, very hard, indeed, to understand how a man or woman can believe these things at all and make no effort for anything beyond the temporal elevation of those around.

FRANCES R. HAVERGAL

JANUARY 17

SUPPLIED FOR TODAY

My God shall supply all your need.
PHILIPPIANS 4:19

August 3rd, 1844. Saturday - with the twelve shillings we began the day. My soul said: "I will now look out for the way in which the Lord will deliver us this day again; for He will surely deliver. Many Saturdays, when we were in need, He helped us and so He will do this day also." Between nine and ten o'clock this morning I gave myself to prayer for means, with three of my fellow-labourers, in my house. I gave myself to prayer, there was a knock at my room door, and I was informed that a gentleman had come to see me. When we had finished prayer, it was found to be a brother from Tetbury, who had brought from Barnstable one pound, fourteen shillings, six pence for the orphans. Thus we have one pound, two shillings, six pence with which I must return the letter-bag to the orphan houses, looking to the Lord for more.

August 6th - Without one single penny in my hands the day began. The post brought nothing, nor had I yet received anything, when ten minutes after ten this morning the letter bag was brought from the orphan houses for the supplies of today. Now see the Lord's deliverance! In the bag I found a note from one of the labourers in the orphan houses, enclosing two sovereigns, which she sent for the orphans, stating that it was part of a present she had just received unexpected for herself. Thus we are supplied for today.

September 4th - Only one farthing was in my hand this morning. Pause a moment, dear reader! Only one farthing in hand when the day commenced. Think of this and think of nearly 140 persons to be provided for. You poor brothers, who have six or eight children and small wages, think of this; and you, my brothers, who do not belong to the working classes, but have, as it is called, very limited means, think of this! May you not do what we do under your trials? Does the Lord love you less than He loves us? Does He not love all His children with no less love than that with which He loves His only begotten Son, according to John 17: 20-23? Or are we better than you?

GEORGE MUELLER

DELIVERANCE FROM SINNING

Sin shall not have dominion over you.
ROMANS 6:14

Salvation would be a sadly incomplete affair if it did not deal with this part of our ruined estate. We want to be purified as well as pardoned. Justification without sanctification would not be salvation at all. It would call the leper clean and leave him to die of his disease; it would forgive the rebellion and allow the rebel to remain an enemy to his king. It should remove the consequences but overlook the cause, and this would leave an endless and hopeless task before us. It would stop the stream for a time, but leave an open fountain of defilement, which would sooner or later break forth with increased power. Remember that the Lord Jesus came to take away sin in three ways: he came to remove the penalty of sin, the power of sin, and, at last, the presence of sin. "We know that he was manifested to take away our sins".

The angel said of our Lord, "Thou shalt call his name Jesus, for he shall save his people from their sins." Our Lord Jesus came to destroy in us the works of the devil. That which was said at our Lord's birth was also declared in His death; for when the soldier pierced His side forthwith came there out blood and water, to set forth the double cure by which we are delivered from the guilt and the defilement of sin.

If, however, you are troubled about the power of sin and about the tendencies of your nature, as you well may be, here is a promise for you. Have faith in it, for it stands in that covenant of grace that is ordered in all things and sure. God, who cannot lie, has said in Ezekiel 36: 26: "A new heart also will I give you, and a new spirit will I put within you: and I will take away the stony heart out of your flesh, and I will give you an heart of flesh."

CHARLES H. SPURGEON

NOT ASHAMED

Separated unto the gospel of God.
ROMANS 1:1

Most people are ashamed of the gospel of Christ. *The wise* are ashamed of it, because it calls men to believe and not to argue; *the great* are ashamed of it because it brings all into one body; *the rich* are ashamed of it, because it is to be had without money and without price; *the gay* are ashamed of it, because they fear it will destroy all their mirth; and so the good news of the glorious Son of God having come into the world a Surety for lost sinners, is despised, uncared for - men are ashamed of it. Who are not ashamed of it? A little company, those whose hearts the Spirit of God has touched. They were once like the world, and of it; but He awakened them to see their sin and misery, and that Christ alone was a refuge, and now they cry, "None but Christ! none but Christ! God forbid that I should glory save in the Cross of Christ." He is precious to their heart - He lives there; He is often on their lips; He is praised in their family; they would fain proclaim Him to all the world. They have felt in their own experience that the gospel is the power of God unto salvation, to the Jew first, and also to the Greek. Dear friends, is this your experience? Have you received the gospel not in word only, but in power? Has the power of God been put forth upon your soul along with the word? Then this word is yours: I am not ashamed of the gospel of Christ.

I'm not ashamed to own my Lord,
Or to defend His cause;
Maintain the honour of His Word,
The glory of His cross.

ROBERT MURRAY McCHEYNE

I WILL COME AGAIN

The time is short.
I CORINTHIANS 7:29

The words of the angels shall have a complete fulfilment: "This same Jesus, which is taken up from you into heaven, shall so come in like manner as ye have seen him go into heaven" (Acts 1: 11). As His going away was a literal going away, so his return shall be a literal return. As He came personally the first time with a body, so He shall come personally the second time with a body. As He came visibly to this earth and visibly went away, so when he comes the second time He shall visibly return. And then, and not till then, the complete kingdom of Christ shall begin. He left His servants as "a nobleman"; He returns to His servants as "a king".

Then He intends to cast out that old usurper the devil, to bind him for a thousand years, and to strip him of his power.

Then He intends to make a restitution of the face of creation. It shall be the world's jubilee day. Our earth shall at last bring forth her increase. The King shall at length have His own again. At last the ninety-seventh psalm shall be fulfilled, and men shall say, "The Lord reigneth: let the earth rejoice!"

Then He intends to fulfil the prophecies of Enoch, John the Baptist, and St. Paul, "To execute judgement upon all the ungodly" inhabitants of Christendom - "to burn up the chaff with unquenchable fire" - and "in flaming fire to take vengeance on them that know not God, and obey not the gospel."

Then He intends to raise His dead saints and gather His living ones, to gather together the scattered tribes of Israel, and to set up an empire on earth in which every knee shall bow to Him and every tongue confess that Christ is Lord.

When, how, where, in what manner, all these things shall be, we cannot say particularly. Enough for us to know that they shall be.

J. C. RYLE

JANUARY 21

BEAUTIFUL FEET

*Inasmuch as ye have done it unto one of the least of these my brethren,
ye have done it unto me.*
MATTHEW 25:40

Our Lord has many uses for what is kept for Himself. How beautiful are the feet of them that bring glad tidings of good things! That is the best use of all, and I expect the angels think those feet beautiful, even if they are cased in muddy boots or galoshes.

Once the question was asked, "Wherefore wilt thou run, my son, seeing that thou hast no tidings ready?" So if we want to have these beautiful feet, we must have the tidings ready which they are to bear. Let us ask Him to keep our hearts so freshly full of His good news of salvation that our mouths may speak out of their abundance. If the clouds be full of rain, they empty themselves upon the earth. May we be so filled with the Spirit that we may have much to pour out for others.

Besides the privilege of carrying water from the wells of salvation, there are plenty of cups of cold water to be carried in all directions; not to the poor only - ministries of love are often as much needed by a rich friend. But the feet must be kept for these; they will be too tired for them if they are tired out for self-pleasing. In such services we are treading in the blessed steps of Christ, who went about doing good.

Then there is literal errand-going - just to fetch something that is needed for the household or something that a tired relative wants, whether asked or unasked. Such things should come first instead of last, because these are clearly our Lord's will for us to do, by the position in which He has placed us; what seems more direct services may be after all not so directly apportioned by Him.

Take my hands, and let them move,
At the impulse of Thy love;
Take my feet, and let them be,
Swift and beautiful for Thee.

FRANCES R. HAVERGAL

JANUARY 22

THE THINGS CONCERNING HIMSELF

The Lord hath laid on him the iniquity of us all.
ISAIAH 53:6

The Old Testament types supply incontrovertible evidence that the Gospel was no novel invention of New Testament times. When the risen Saviour would make known to His disciples the meaning of His death, we read that, "Beginning at Moses and all the prophets, he expounded unto them in all the scriptures the things concerning himself" (Luke 24:27). So far from the evangel of the apostle's being any (absolutely) new thing, every element in it was revealed long centuries before their birth, not only in words, but in visible representations: there was both a wondrous anticipation of the preparation for the Gospel. Thus a reverent contemplation of the types supplies a blessed confirmation of faith, for they attest the Divine authorship of both Testaments. Moreover, they stimulate adoration; even when we know a person, we enjoy looking at his picture; so here. It is *Christ* that is before us in them.

The *Divine* origin of sacrifice is self-evident. Whoever would have dreamed of the device of offering animal sacrifices to God as a method of acceptable worship? That Abel should have "brought of the firstlings of his flock and of the fat thereof". (Gen. 4:4) can only be satisfactorily accounted for on the ground that he knew this was what God required from him. And this is precisely what the New Testament affirms: Hebrews 11:4 declares that it was "by faith" that Abel offered his sacrifice, and Romans 10:17 says, "faith cometh by hearing, and hearing by the word of God." Thus, Abel had received a revelation from God, and believing what he had "heard", acted accordingly.

The great sacrifice of Christ was foreshadowed from the beginning. The lamb was "foreordained before the foundation of the world" (I Peter 1:20).

A. W. PINK

LEAVE IT THERE

Delight thyself also in the Lord; and he shall give thee the desires of thine heart.
PSALM 37:4

How can you find "rest for your soul"? One way is by *faith*. "We which have *believed* do enter into rest" (Heb. 4: 3 italics added).

The point there is that faith has two hands. With one hand faith is always handing over, and with the other she is always reaching down - ours is the up and the down life. The angels went up on the ladder carrying Jacob's worries, and they came down the ladder bringing God's help. You have the two directions in your life. Send them up, and let them come down.

Do you know what it is when you are worried to kneel down and say to God: "Father, take this," and by one definite act to hand over the worry to God and leave it there? I heard a lady say that she had been in the habit of kneeling by her bedside and handing things over to God, and then jumping into her bed and by a strong pull pulling in all the things after her. Now that is not the best way. When you really trust God, you put a thing into His hands, and then you do not worry yourself or Him.

If there is one thing that annoys me more than another, it is for a man to say to me: "Will you do this?" And I say, "Certainly", and then he keeps sending postcards or letters to me all the time to work me up. I say, "That man does not trust me." So when I have really handed a thing over to God I leave it there, and I dare not worry for fear it would seem as if I mistrusted Him. But I keep looking up to Him - I cannot help doing that - and say, "Father, I am trusting."

My dog at home has such trust. He used to worry me very much to be fed at dinner, but he never got any food that way. But lately he has adopted something that always conquers me. He sits under the table and puts one paw on my knee. He never barks, never leaps around, never worries me, but he sits under the table with that one paw on my knee, and that conquers me. I cannot resist the appeal. Although my wife says I must never do it, I keep putting little morsels under the table.

That is the way to live - with your hand on God's knee. Say, "My God, I am not going to worry; I am not going to fret but there is my hand, and I wait until the time comes, and Thou shalt give me the desires of my heart."

F. B. MEYER

JANUARY 24

EXCEPT YE ABIDE

Without me ye can do nothing.
JOHN 15:5

If I am to be a true branch, if I am to bear fruit, if I am to be what Christ as the Vine wants me to be, my whole existence must be as exclusively devoted to abiding in Him as that of the natural branch is to abiding in its vine (see John 15).

Abiding is to be an act of the will and the whole heart. Just as there are degrees in seeking and serving God, "not with a perfect heart," or "with the whole heart", so there may be degrees in abiding. In regeneration the divine life enters us but does not all at once master and fill our whole being. This comes as a matter of command and obedience. There is unspeakable danger of our not giving ourselves with our whole heart to abide. There is unspeakable danger of our giving ourselves to the work of God and to bear fruit, with but little of the true abiding, the whole-hearted losing of ourselves in Christ and His life. There is unspeakable danger of much work with but little fruit, for lack of this one thing needful. We must allow the words "not of itself", "except it abide", to do their work of searching and exposing, of pruning and cleansing, all that there is of self-will and self-confidence in our life; that will deliver us from this great evil, and so prepare us for His teaching, giving the full meaning of the word in us: "Abide in me, and I in you."

Our blessed Lord desires to call us away from ourselves and our own strength to Himself and His strength. Let us accept the warning and turn with great fear and self-distrust to Him to do His work. "Our life is hid with Christ in God!" That life is a heavenly mystery, hid from the wise even among Christians, and revealed unto babes. The childlike spirit learns that life is given from heaven every day and every moment to the soul that accepts the teaching: "not of itself", "except it abide", and seeks its all in the Vine. Abiding in the Vine then comes to be nothing more nor less than the restful surrender of the soul to let Christ have all and work all, as completely as in nature the branch knows and seeks nothing but the vine.

ANDREW MURRAY

IT IS GOD WHO JUSTIFIES

Being justified by his grace ... made heirs according to the hope of eternal life.
TITUS 3:7

D o you not see - for I want to bring this out clearly, what a splendid thing it is - that none but God would think of justifying the ungodly, and none but God could do it? See how the apostle puts the challenge: "Who shall lay anything to the charge of God's elect? It is God that justifieth" (Romans 8:33).

If God has justified a man it is well done, it is rightly done, it is justly done, it is everlastingly done. I read the other day in a print that is full of venom against the gospel and those who preach it that we hold some kind of theory by which we imagine that sin can be removed from men. We hold no theory, we publish a fact. The grandest fact under heaven is this - that Christ by His precious blood does actually put away sin and that God, for Christ's sake, deals with men on terms of divine mercy, forgives the guilty and justifies them, not according to anything that He sees in them, or foresees will be in them, but according to the riches of His own mercy. This we have preached, do preach and will preach as long as we live. "It is God that justifieth" - that justifieth the ungodly; He is not ashamed of doing it, nor are we of preaching it.

The justification that comes from God Himself must be beyond question. If the Judge acquits me, who can condemn me? If the highest court in the universe has pronounced me just, who shall lay anything to my charge? Justification from God is a sufficient answer to an awakened conscience. The Holy Spirit by His means breathes peace over our entire nature, and we are no longer afraid. With this justification we can answer all the roarings and railings of Satan and ungodly men. With this we shall be able to die: with this we shall bodily rise again and face the last great judgement.

Friend, the Lord can blot out all your sins. I make no shot in the dark when I say this. "All manner of sin and of blasphemy shall be forgiven unto men." Though you are steeped up to your throat in crime, He can with a word remove the defilement and say, "I will, be thou clean." The Lord is a great forgiver.

"I believe in the forgiveness of sins." Do you?

CHARLES H. SPURGEON

JANUARY 26

KEPT IN PEACE

Thou wilt keep him in perfect peace, whose mind is stayed on thee.
ISAIAH 26:3

Sometimes all has been dark, exceedingly dark, with reference to my service among the saints, judging from natural appearance. Indeed, at those times I should have been overwhelmed in grief and despair had I looked at things after the outward appearance. At such times I have sought to encourage myself in God, by laying hold in faith on His mighty power, His unchangeable love, and His infinite wisdom. During those times I have said to myself: *God is able and willing to deliver me, if it be good for me*; for it is written: "He that spared not his own Son, but delivered him up for us all, how shall he not with him also freely give us all things?" (Romans 8: 32).

When, through His grace, I believed this, my soul kept in peace. Further, when in connection with the orphan houses, day schools, etc., trials have come upon me that were far heavier than the means; when lying reports were spread that the orphans had not enough to eat, or that they were cruelly treated in other respects, and the like; or when other trials, still greater, but which I cannot mention, have befallen me in connection with this work - at such times my soul was stayed upon God.

Even at times when I was almost a thousand miles absent from Bristol and had to remain absent week after week, I believed His word of promise was applicable to such cases. I poured out my soul before God and arose from my knees in peace, because the trouble that was in the soul was cast upon God in believing prayer.

Thus I was kept in peace, though I saw it to be the will of God to remain far away from work. Further, when I needed houses, fellow labourers, carers for the orphans or for the day schools, I have been able to look for all to the Lord and trust in Him for help. Dear reader, I may seem to boast; but, by the grace of God, I do not boast in this speaking. From my inmost soul I do ascribe it to God alone that He has enabled me to trust in Him and that hitherto He has not suffered my confidence in Him to fail.

GEORGE MUELLER

THE SON REVEALED

The glory which shall be revealed in us.
ROMANS 8:18

When it pleased God, who separated me from my mother's womb, and called me by His grace, to reveal His Son in me, that I might preach Him among the heathen, immediately I conferred not with flesh and blood" (Galatians 1: 15-16). Paul wrote that "it pleased God to reveal His Son in me." Now, "to reveal" means "undrape". There is a statue, covered with a veil. It is there, but it's hidden. I take off the veil, and you see it. When you were generated, Christ came unto you: that is what regeneration means - Christ born into your spirit. But Christ came in as a veiled figure, and you who are regenerate but who have never seen the Christ as He truly is behold Him as a veiled figure, even though He is in you. When Jesus died, the veil of the temple was rent in two from the top to the bottom; and when the soul appreciates the death of Christ at its own death to sin, the veil is rent in two from the top to the bottom, and the Holy Ghost reveals Jesus as the substitute for the self-life.

"It pleased God to reveal His Son in me." O, my God, I thank Thee that Thou hast revealed Thy Son as the Alpha, the pivot, the fountain, the origin of my life! May it be so with us all!

A friend of mine was staying near Mont Blanc. He had been there for a fortnight, but had not seen the "monarch of the Alps", for the thick clouds held it behind a veil. Nearly out of heart with waiting, he was preparing to leave. Going up to dress for dinner, he passed a window and saw that the monarch was still veiled in mist. Having dressed, he came downstairs, passing the window again. Every vestige of mist now parted, and Mont Blanc stood revealed from base to snow-clad peak. So now there shall come upon you a breath of the Holy Ghost, before which the misconceptions of your life shall pass, and to you God will reveal His Son in you as the centre of your life.

For a moment, think about Colossians 1: 27, a favourite passage of mine: "To whom God would make known what is the riches of the glory of this mystery among the Gentiles; which is Christ in you, the hope of glory."

F. B. MEYER

JANUARY 28

OUR MISSION

I love my master ... I will not go out free.
EXODUS 21:5

In which way ought we to give to Christ Jesus? I fear many, many give as if they were free to give what they choose, what they think they can afford. The believer to whom the right, which the purchase price of the blood has acquired, has been revealed by the Holy Spirit, delights to know that he is the bond slave of redeeming love, and to lay everything he has at his Master's feet, because he belongs to Him.

Have you ever wondered that the disciples accepted the great command so easily and so heartily? They came fresh from Calvary, where they had seen the blood. They had met the risen one, and He had breathed His Spirit into them. During the forty days "through the Holy Ghost he had given his commandments unto them". Jesus was to them Saviour, Master, Friend, and Lord. His word was with divine power; they could not but obey. Oh, let us bow at His feet and yield to the Holy Spirit to reveal and assert His mighty claim, and let us unhesitatingly and with the whole heart accept the command as our one life-purpose: the gospel to every creature!

The last great command has been so prominently urged in connection with foreign missions that many are inclined exclusively to confine it to them. This is a great mistake. Our Lord's words, "Make disciples of all nations; teaching them to observe all things whatsoever I have commanded you," tell us that our aim is to be nothing less than to make every man a true disciple, living in holy obedience to all Christ's will.

What a work there is to be done in our Christian churches and our so-called Christian communities ere it can be said that the command has been carried out! And what a need that the whole church, with every believer in it, realise that to do this work is the sole subject of its existence! The gospel brought fully, perseveringly, savingly to every creature: this is the mission, this ought to be the passion, of every redeemed soul. For this alone is the Spirit and likeness and life of Christ formed in you.

ANDREW MURRAY

DOING OUR PART

Go work today in my vineyard.
MATTHEW 21:28

A re we also doing our part to hasten on His coming? And is it habitually our prayer that the Lord will be pleased to hasten the fulfilment of events yet to be fulfilled before that day comes?

One thing remains to be considered, namely, the practical effect this truth should have upon our hearts. If it be really received and entered into, the child of God will say, "What can I do for my blessed Saviour before He comes again? How can I most glorify Him? His will concerning me is that I should occupy 'until He comes'. How then can I best use for Him the talents with which I am entrusted, my physical strength, my mental powers? How can my sight, my tongue, all my faculties of mind and body, be best devoted to His praise? How should my time, my money, all that I am and have, be used for Him? How can my whole spirit, soul and body be best consecrated to His service?"

These are deeply important, practical questions that all believers in the Lord Jesus should ask themselves, seeing that we are not our own, but are bought with a price, even with His precious blood. Instead of indulging in inactivity and listlessness on account of the evil state of things around us, we should pray and work, and work and pray, as if it were in our power to stem the torrent of abounding iniquity. Who can say how much good one single child of God, who is thoroughly in earnest, may accomplish, and how greatly he may glorify God by walking in entire separation from all that is hateful to Him? We must especially also guard against the temptation of slackening our efforts for the conversion of sinners, because the world will not be converted before Jesus comes. Rather we should say, "the time that He shall delay His coming may be short; what therefore can I do to warn sinners and to win souls for Him?"

O come, let us go and find them,
In the paths of death they roam;
At the close of the day, 'twill be sweet to say:
I have brought some lost ones home.

GEORGE MUELLER

WHAT IF YOU DON'T "FEEL" DIFFERENT?

By grace are ye saved through faith.
EPHESIANS 2:8

It is a remarkable fact that the word "feel" is found only once in the King James Version of the New Testament, and that is in Paul's sermon to the Athenians (Acts 17). There he rebukes the Greeks for imagining the God-head to be like unto silver and gold and shows that the true God is the Creator of all things, "and hath made of one blood all nations of men for to dwell on all the face of the earth, and hath determined the times before appointed, and the bounds of their habitation; that they should seek the Lord, if haply they might feel after him, and find him, though he be not far from every one of us; for in him we live and move, and have our being; as certain also of your own poets have said, For we are also his offspring" (Verses 26-28).

The word *feel* appears in the very midst of this passage, but it has nothing to do with the gospel, but rather with the heathen groping in the dark: "if haply they might feel after God". We, however, are not in their ignorant condition. We have heard the gospel. We know of the one living and true God. We are not told to feel anything but to believe His record.

Then it may interest you to know that the word *feeling* is only found twice in the New Testament and never has anything to do with the message of salvation. In Ephesians 4: 19 the Spirit of God describes the state of certain unbelieving Gentiles in these words: "Who being past feeling have given themselves over unto lasciviousness, to work all uncleanness with greediness". This is what continual indulgence in sin does for people. They become insensate - "past feeling" - and so conscience ceases to register, as they plunge into one excess and enormity after another.

The only other place where we read of *feeling* is in a very different connection. In Hebrews 4: 15 our blessed Lord Himself is described as having empathy for our infirmities: "For we have not an high priest which cannot be touched with the feeling of our infirmities; but was in all points tempted like as we are, yet without sin."

Nowhere else do we read of feeling in all the New Testament! But oh, how many times we read of believing, of faith, of trust, of confidence! Yes, these are the words for us. Ignore your feelings altogether, and tell the Lord Jesus now that you will trust Him and confess Him before men.

HARRY A. IRONSIDE

JANUARY 31

ACCORDING TO PROMISE

... he remembered his holy promise.
PSALM 105:42

The Lord is prompt to the moment in carrying out His gracious engagements. The Lord has threatened to destroy the world with a flood, but He waited the full time of respite until Noah had entered the ark; and then, on the selfsame day, the fountains of the great deep were broken up. He had declared that Israel should come out of Egypt, and it was so: "And it came to pass at the end of the four hundred and thirty years, even at the selfsame day it came to pass, that all the hosts of the Lord went out from the land of Egypt". (Exodus 12: 41). According to Daniel, the Lord numbers the years of His promise and counts the weeks of His waiting. As for the greatest promise of all, namely, the sending of His Son from heaven, the Lord was not slow in that great gift, "but when the fullness of the time was come, God sent forth His Son, made of a woman". Beyond all question, the Lord our God keeps His Word to the moment.

When we are in need, we may be urgent with the Lord to come quickly to our rescue, even as David pleaded in the seventieth psalm, "Make haste, O God, to deliver me; make haste to help me, O Lord" (Verse 1). "I am poor and needy; make haste unto me, O God: thou art my help and my deliverer; O Lord, make no tarrying" (Verse 5). The Lord even condescends to describe Himself as making speed to carry out His gracious engagements: "I the Lord will hasten it in his time" (Isaiah 60:22). But we must not pray in this fashion as though we had the slightest fear that the Lord could or would delay or that He needed us to quicken His diligence. No. "The Lord is not slack concerning his promise, as some men count slackness" (2 Peter 3:9). Our God is slow to anger, but in the deeds of grace "his word runneth very swiftly" (Psalm 147:15) Sometimes His speed to bless His people outstrips time and thought: as, for instance, when He fulfils that ancient declaration, "It shall come to pass, that before they call, I will answer; and while they are yet speaking, I will hear. (Isaiah 65:24).

CHARLES H. SPURGEON

FEBRUARY 1

THE MAJESTY OF LOVE

Being rooted and grounded in love.
EPHESIANS 3:17

There are times when something comes into our lives which is charged with love in such a way that it seems to open the Eternal to us for a moment, or at least some of the Eternal Things, and the greatest of these is love.

It may be a small and intimate touch upon us or our affairs, light as the touch of the dawn-wind on the leaves of the tree, something not to be captured and told to another in words. But we know that it is our Lord. And then perhaps the room where we are, with its furniture and books and flowers, seems less "present" than His Presence, and the heart is drawn into that sweetness of which the old hymn sings.

Or is it the dear human love about us that bathes us as in summer seas and rests us through and through. Can we ever cease to wonder at the love of our companions? And then suddenly we recognise our Lord in them. It is His love that they lavish upon us. O love of God, made manifest in Thy lovers, we worship Thee!

"That ye ... may be able to comprehend ... what is the breadth, and length and depth and height; and to know the love of Christ, which passeth knowledge" (Ephesians 3:17-19). The words are too great for us. What do we comprehend, what do we know? Confounded and abased, we enter into the Rock and hide us in the dust before the glory of the Majesty of love - the love whose symbol is the Cross. And a question pierces then: What do I know of Calvary love?

Thou, Lord, hast borne for me
More than my tongue can tell
Of bitterest agony
to rescue me from hell.
Thou sufferedst all for me:
What have I borne for Thee?

AMY CARMICHAEL

RADIANT SERVICE

Fill the waterpots with water. And they filled them up to the brim.
And he saith unto them, Draw out now.
JOHN 2:7-8

The servants' part in this miracle was important; they had to carry the water and fill the vessels, and then draw out and bear the wine to the guests. They became co-workers with Christ in His miracle. So our Lord always calls His people to be His helpers in blessing the world. We cannot do much. The best we can bring is a little of the common water of earth; but if we bring that to Him, He can change it into the rich wine of heaven, which will bless weary and fainting ones. If we take simply what we have and use it as He commands, it will do good. Moses had only a rod in his hand, but with this he accomplished great wonders. The disciples had only five barley loaves, but these, touched by Christ's hand, made a feast for thousands. So the common water carried by these servants, under the Master's blessing, became wine for the wedding.

Christ passes the gifts of His love and grace through human hands to others. The redemption is divine, completed by Christ alone, but the priesthood that mediates is human; human hands must distribute the blessings. Gifts of mercy can get to the lost only through those who have been saved. Then how striking is the other side of this truth: the servants carried only common water from the spring, but with Christ's blessing the water became good wine. So it always is when we do what Christ bids us to do - our most mundane work produces heavenly results.

No labour is in vain which is completed in the Lord. Our most common work amid life's trivialities, in business, or in the household, which seems only like carrying water to be emptied out again, is transformed into radiant service, like angelic ministry, and leaves glorious results behind. The simplest things we do at Christ's bidding may become immortal blessings to other souls or to our own!

J.R. MILLER

FEBRUARY 3

GOD'S PATH

Jacob went on his way, and the angels of God met him.
GENESIS 32:1

It is in the path where God has bade us walk that we shall find the angels around us. We may meet them, indeed, on paths of our own choosing, but it will be the sort of angel that Balaam met, with a sword in his hand, mighty and beautiful, but wrathful too; and we had better not affront him! but the friendly helpers, the emissaries of God's love, the apostles of His grace, do not haunt the roads that we make for ourselves.

Walk quietly -
When evening shadows lie against the hill -
In the hush of twilight, when the word is still.
And the balm of peace soothes every ill -
Walk quietly.

Walk quietly -
And know that He is God.
Let your life be governed by His guiding hand
E'en though it varies from the way you planned,
Bow your head in sweet submission and
Walk quietly.

ALEXANDER MACLAREN

WHAT THE WORLD NEEDS

Ye shall be witnesses unto me ... unto the uttermost part of the earth.
ACTS 1:8

Men are questioning now, as they never have questioned before, whether Christianity is indeed the true religion which is to be the salvation of the world. Christian men, it is for us to give our bit of answer to that question. It is for us, in whom the Christian church is at this moment partially embodied, to declare that Christianity, that the Christian faith, the Christian manhood can do that for the world which the world needs.

You ask, "What can I do?"

You can furnish one Christian life. You can furnish a life so faithful to every duty, so ready for every service, so determined not to commit every sin that the great Christian church shall be the stronger for your living in it, and the problem of the world be answered, and a certain great peace come into this poor, perplexed, phase of our humanity as it sees that new revelation of what Christianity is.

Send forth Thy gospel, Holy Lord!
Kindle in us love's sacred flame;
Love giving all and grudging naught
For Jesus sake, in Jesus' name.

Send forth the Gospel! Tell it out!
Go, brothers, at the Master's call;
Prepare His way, who comes to reign
The King of kings and Lord of all.

PHILLIPS BROOKS

FEBRUARY 5

ROOTLESS GRACES

Some fell upon stony places.
MATTHEW 13:5

There is a thin covering of soil on the rock. The seed sinks in a little way, and the heat radiating from the rock causes it to shoot up at once. This represents a class of people whose religion is emotional. At first they give great promise. They are easily moved by any appeal. The feelings work immediately to the surface. Such persons always seem most affected by sorrow. They repent ardently, but their grief is soon over. In the same way they appear to be most deeply affected by religious appeals. They begin a Christian life with an earnestness that puts older Christians to shame. They attend all meetings; they weep as they sing and pray; they talk of Christ to their friends; their zeal is wonderful. "Immediately it sprang up, because it had no depth of earth."

But such quick growth lacks root and cannot endure the heat of summer. The sun soon scorches such plants, and they wither. In spiritual life, also, the analogy applies. Emotional religion is not apt to be permanent. It bursts up into great full flower today, but we are not sure that it will be found tomorrow in a deeper life. Too often the enthusiasm is only temporary. In the heat of trials, temptation, toil, or sorrow, the rootless graces wilt and die.

Usually the religious life that is most permanent is that which springs up naturally and grows slowly to strength and beauty. It has good soil, and the roots go down deep into the earth and are unaffected by the frequent changes in temperature, by heat or cold, by rain or drought. If anyone finds that his spiritual graces are rootless and that there is a hard rock in his heart underneath the surface, he should seek at once to have the rock broken by penance and prayer, that the plants of righteousness in him may have opportunity to grow.

J.R. MILLER

IN THE SHADOWS OF GETHSEMANE

I have finished the work which thou gavest me to do.
JOHN 17:4

Was the work of the Master indeed done? Was not its heaviest task yet to come? He had not yet met the dread hour of death. Why did He say that His work was done? It was because He knew that, when the will is given, the battle is ended. He was only in the shadows of the garden; but to conquer these shadows was already to conquer all. He who has willed to die has already triumphed over death. All that remains to him is but the outer husk, the shell.

The cup which our Father giveth us to drink is a cup for the will. It is easy for the lips to drain it when once the heart has accepted it. Not on the heights of Calvary but in the shadows of Gethsemane is the cup presented; the act is easy after the choice. The real battlefield is in the silence of the spirit. Conquer there, and thou art crowned.

Go to dark Gethsemane
Ye that feel the tempter's power;
Your Redeemer's conflict see
Watch with Him one bitter hour!
Turn not from His grief away;
Learn of Jesus Christ to pray.

GEORGE MATHESON

PERFECT LIKENESS

Now are we the sons of God, and it doth not yet appear what we shall be;
but we know that when he shall appear, we shall be like him,
for we shall see him as he is.
1 JOHN 3:2

"Now are we the sons of God." That is the pier upon one side of the gulf. "It doth not yet appear what we shall be, but when he shall appear we shall be like him." That is the pier on the other. How are the two to be connected? There is only one way by which the present sonship will blossom and fruit into the future perfect likeness: If we throw across the gulf, by God's help day by day, the bridge of growing likeness to Himself, and purity therefrom.

Behold, what love, what boundless love
The Father hath bestowed
On sinners lost, that we should be
Now called the sons of God!

What we in glory soon shall be,
It doth not yet appear;
But when our precious Lord we see,
We shall His image bear.

ALEXANDER MACLAREN

CLEAN UP OUR HABITS

Let us lay aside every weight, and the sin which doth so easily beset us.
HEBREWS 12:1

Think, as you sit here, of anything that you are doing that is wrong, of any habit of your life, of your self-indulgence, or of that great pervasive habit of your life which makes you a creature of the present instead of the eternities, a creature of the material earth instead of the glorious skies. Ask yourself of any habit that belongs to your own personal life, and bring it face-to-face with Jesus Christ.

Give me the strength to stand for the right.
When other folks have left the fight,
Give me the courage of a man
Who knows that, by God's help, he can.
Teach me to see in every face
The good, the kind and not the base.

Make me sincere in word and deed;
Blot out from me all sham and greed;
Help me to guard my troubled soul
By constant, active self-control
Clean up my thought, my speech, my play
Lord, keep me pure from day to day.

PHILLIPS BROOKS

FEBRUARY 9

PASSING BY

*By chance there came down a certain priest that way: and when he saw him,
he passed by on the other side.*
LUKE 10:31

We must not suppose that all priests were cold and heartless. Ministers are generally warm-hearted men; they should all be so; they ought to set the people an example of kindness and sympathy; they ought to be like Christ - and He was always ready to help anybody in trouble. No doubt many of the Jewish priests were kind and generous; but here was one who was not. This shows us that being a priest or a minister does not make anyone tender-hearted; one may hold a very sacred office and yet have a cold and hard heart. But it is very sad when it is so.

This priest did not even stop to look at the sufferer, or to ask him how he came to be injured, or to inquire what he could do for him. He kept as far to the other side of the road as he could get; perhaps he even pretended not to see the wounded man. No doubt he had excuses ready in his own mind. He was in a great hurry, or he was very tired, or he could not do anything for the poor man if he should stop, or he was sensitive and could not bear to look on blood.

No matter about his motives; it is more important to avoid repeating his fault. Do we never pass by human wants that we know well we ought to stop to relieve? Do we never keep out of the way of those whose needs strongly appeal to us? Do we never have trouble conjuring up excuses to satisfy our own insistent consciences because we passed by someone we ought to have helped? Some people look the other way when they are passing a blind man on the wayside. Ministers have refused to go to see sick people because they were weary. Persons have stayed away from church because there was to be an appeal for money for a needy cause. This verse is an ugly mirror, isn't it? It shows us blemishes that we didn't know we had.

J.R. MILLER

GOD'S PURPOSE FOR US

But the Comforter, which is the Holy Ghost ... shall teach you all things.
JOHN 14:26

"What does God do all day?" once asked a little boy ... Unfortunately most of us are not even boys in religious intelligence, but only very unthinking babes. It no more occurs to us that God is engaged in any particular work in the world than it occurs to a little child that its father does anything except be a father.

The first great epoch in a Christian's life, after the awe and wonder of its dawn, is when there breaks into his mind some sense that Christ has a purpose for mankind, a purpose beyond him and his needs ... a purpose which embraces every kindred and nation formed, which regards not their spiritual good alone, but the welfare in every part, their progress, their health, their work, their wages, their happiness in this present world.

HENRY DRUMMOND

FEBRUARY 11

MORNING AND EVENING

In the daytime ... he led them with a cloud, and all the night with a light of fire.
PSALM 78:14

My day is my prosperity; it is the time when the sun of fortune is bright above me, and therefore it is the time when I need a shade. If my sunshine were not checkered I would forget Thee, O my God.

But I have nights to meet as well as days. The night is my adversity; it is the time when the sun of fortune has gone down behind the hills, and I am left alone, and then it is, O my Father, that I need the light of Thy fire! My light of fire for the night is the vision of Calvary - the vision of Thy love in the Cross. I need the light of Thy fire "*all the night*".

Begin the day with God!
He is thy sun and day;
He is the radiance of the dawn,
To Him address the day.

Your last transaction be
With God Himself above;
And so through all the years of life
You'll know the Father's love.

GEORGE MATHESON

FEBRUARY 12

NO OTHER ROCK

The stone which the builders rejected, the same is become the head of the corner.
MATTHEW 21:42

Those to whom Christ first came did not think Him suitable to be their Messiah. So they refused to accept Him and nailed Him on a cross instead. But now what do we see? That same Jesus whom they thought unfit to be their king God has made King of glory, Lord of heaven and earth. All things are in His hands, all power, all mercy, all judgment. The very rulers who rejected Him and demanded His crucifixion, when they awake on the judgment morning, shall see as their Judge the same Jesus whom they thus despised and condemned to die.

A great many people now think Christ unsuitable to be their Master. They do not consider it an honour to be called Christians. They are embarrassed at His name or to include themselves among His followers. They do not care to model their life on His holy and perfect life. All these should remember that Christ has highest honour in heaven. No angel is ashamed to speak His name. Redeemed spirits praise Him day and night. God the Father has exalted Him to the throne of eternal power and glory. Why, then, should sinful men be ashamed to claim Him as Lord?

They should remember, also, that God has made Him the cornerstone of the whole building not made with hands. No life that is not built on Him can stand. There is no other rock on which to rest their hope. If they ever are saved it must be by this same Jesus whom they are now rejecting.

How can they live who, sinning, never seek
To have their sins forgiven;
Who, knowing that the strongest yet are weak,
Ask not thy grace and never know thy peace -
The gift unspeakable of thy release,
The pardon sealed in heaven?

J.R. MILLER

FEBRUARY 13

EVERYDAY RELIGION

Christ in you, the hope of glory.
COLOSSIANS 1:27

Religion is not the simple fire escape that you build in anticipation of a possible danger, upon the outside of your dwelling, and leave there until danger comes. You go to it some morning when a fire breaks out in your house, and the poor old thing that you built up there, and thought that you could use someday, is so rusty and broken, and the weather has so beaten upon it and the sun so turned its hinges, that it will not work.

That is the condition of a man who has built himself what seems a creed of faith, a trust in God in anticipation of the day when danger is to overtake him, and has said to himself, "I am safe, for I will take refuge in it then." But religion is the house in which we live, it is the table at which we sit, it is the fireside at which we draw near, the room that arches its graceful and familiar presence over us; it is the bed on which we lie and think of the past, and anticipate the future, and gather our refreshment.

My faith has found a resting-place,
Not in device or creed;
I trust the Ever-living One
His wounds for me shall plead.

My heart is leaning on the Word,
The written Word of God,
Salvation by my Saviour's name,
Salvation through His blood.

PHILLIPS BROOKS

A THIRST ONLY GOD CAN FILL

Blessed are they which do hunger and thirst after righteousness.
MATTHEW 5:6

What meaneth this restlessness of our nature?... What mean those unmeasurable longings which no gratification can extinguish, and which still continue to agitate the heart of man, even in the fullness of plenty and of enjoyment? If they mean anything at all, they mean that all which this world can offer is not enough to fill up his capacity for happiness - that time is too small for him and he is born for something beyond it - that the scene of his earthly existence is too limited and he is formed to expiate in a wider and a grander theatre - that a nobler destiny is reserved for him - and that to accomplish the purpose of his being he must soar above the littleness of the world and aim at a loftier prize.

I want in this short life of mine,
As much as can be pressed
Of service true for God and man:
Make me to be Thy best.

THOMAS CHALMERS

HEAVEN'S GATE

Surely the Lord is in this place, and I knew it not.
GENESIS 28:16

"Surely the Lord was in this place, and I knew it not." My soul, this is also thine experience! How often hast thou said in thy sorrow, "Verily thou art a God that hidest Thyself!" How often hast thou slept for very heaviness of heart, and desired not to wake again! And when thou didst wake again, lo, the darkness was all a dream! Thy vision of yesterday was a delusion. God had been with thee all the night with that radiance which has no need of the sun.

O my soul, it is not only after the future thou must aspire; thou must aspire to see the glory of thy past. Thou must find the glory of that way by which thy God has led thee, and be able even of thy sorrow to say, "This was the gate of heaven!"

Lo, God is here! Let us adore,
And own how holy is this place!
Let all within us feel His power,
And silent bow before His face;
Who knows His power, His grace who prove,
Serve Him with awe, with reverence love.

GEORGE MATHESON

GOD'S BEST

Full of [satisfied with] years.
GENESIS 25:8

Scaffoldings are for buildings, and the moments and days and years of our earthly lives are scaffolding. What are you building inside it? What kind of a structure will be disclosed when the scaffolding is knocked away? Days and years are ours, that they may give us what eternity cannot take away - a character built upon the love of God in Christ, and moulded into His likeness.

Has your life helped you to do that? If so, you have gotten the best out of it, and your life is completed, whatever may be the number of its days. Quality, not quantity, is the thing that determines the perfectness of a life. Has your life this completeness?

Let my hands perform His bidding,
Let my feet run in His ways,
Let my eyes see Jesus only,
Let my lips speak forth His praise;

Worldlings prize their gems of beauty,
Cling to gilded toys of dust,
Boast of wealth and fame and pleasure;
Only Jesus will I trust.

ALEXANDER MACLAREN

THE WALK TO EMMAUS

While they communed together and reasoned, Jesus himself drew near.
LUKE 24:15

These two friends, as they walked along with heavy hearts, had only one theme: they were talking of their heavy loss and of Him whom they had lost. They were so intensely absorbed in their sorrow as they talked of it that they were not aware of the near approach of a stranger until He had drawn up to them and joined them. Jesus always draws near today when His friends are talking of Him. In the Old Testament it was said that when the Lord's people come together and speak of sacred things, the Lord listens and keeps a book of remembrance.

There is something more to this. Two of Christ's friends talk of Him, and He comes and joins them. How much those Christian people miss who meet and pass time together, if they have no theme of conversation but the silly gossip of society, filled with backbiting and bits of malicious criticism and mischievous scandal, but without one single word about Christ! Does anyone suppose that the Lord hearkens to such conversation or puts it down in His book of remembrance? Of course He hears every word of the talk, and every word goes down in the book of remembrance, and we must give account for every idle word. But He does not listen and record the conversation in the sense the prophet meant, with loving pleasure. Does anyone think Christ will draw near and become one of any such group of Christians as often gather in homes, deliciously feeding on every bit of fresh gossip, but with never a word about their Redeemer?

What a blessing every hour of conversation would bring if we would only talk together of Christ and His kingdom! He would then draw near and join us, adding the joy of His presence to our hearts. Shall we not talk together more of our Lord?

J.R. MILLER

FEBRUARY 18

CALVARY LOVE

Walk worthy of the vocation wherewith ye are called.
EPHESIANS 4:1

If I have not compassion on others even as my Lord had pity on me, then I know nothing of Calvary love. If I belittle those whom I am called to serve, talk of their weak points in contrast perhaps with what I think of as my strong points; if I adopt a superior attitude, forgetting "Who maketh thee to differ ... and what hast thou that thou didst not receive?" (I Corinthians 4:7), then I know nothing of Calvary love.

If I can write an unkind letter, speak an unkind word, think an unkind thought without grief and shame, then I know nothing of Calvary love.

If, in dealing with one who does not respond, I weary of the strain and slip from under the burden, then I know nothing of Calvary love.

If I cast up a confessed, repented and forsaken sin against another, and allow my remembrance of that sin to colour my thinking and feed my suspicions, then I know nothing of Calvary love.

If I am afraid to speak the truth, lest I lose affection, or lest the one concerned should say, "You do not understand," or because I fear to lose my reputation for kindness; if I put my own good name before the other's highest good, then I know nothing of Calvary love.

If I am content to heal a hurt slightly, saying, "Peace; and there was no peace" (Ezekiel 13:10); if I forget the poignant word "Let love be without dissimulation" (Romans 12:9), and blunt the edge of truth, speaking not right things but smooth things, then I know nothing of Calvary love.

If I hold on to choices of any kind, just because they are my choice; if I give any room to my private likes and dislikes, then I know nothing of Calvary love.

If I am soft and slide comfortably into the voice of self-pity and self-sympathy; if I do not, by the grace of God, practice fortitude, then I know nothing of Calvary love.

AMY CARMICHAEL

HIS SOVEREIGN WILL

Into thine hand I commit my spirit.
PSALM 31:5

Some desire to live that they may see more of that glorious work of God for His church, which they believe He will accomplish. So Moses prayed that he might not die in the wilderness, but go over Jordan, and see the good land.

Paul knew not clearly whether it were not best for him to abide a while longer in the flesh on this account … But no man can die cheerfully or comfortably who lives not in a constant resignation of the time and season of his death unto the will of God, as well as himself with respect unto death itself.

Our times are in His hand, at His sovereign disposal, and His will in all things must be complied withal. Without this resolution, without this resignation, no man can enjoy the least solid peace in this world.

My times are in Thy hand;
I'll always trust in Thee;
And, after death, at Thy right hand
I shall for ever be.

JOHN OWEN

EAGLE'S WINGS

*They shall mount up with wings as eagles; they shall run, and
not be weary; and they shall walk and not faint.*
ISAIAH 40:31

This, my soul, is the triumph of thy being - to be able to *walk* with God! Flight belongs to the young soul; it is the *romance* of religion. To run without weariness belongs to the *lofty* soul; it is the *beauty* of religion. But to walk and not faint belongs to the *perfect* soul; it is the *power* of religion.

Canst thou walk in white through the stained thoroughfares of men? Canst thou touch the vile and polluted ones of earth and retain thy garments pure? Canst thou meet in contact with the sinful and be thyself undefiled? *Then* thou hast surpassed the flight of the eagle!

*God wills not that His people
By sin enthralled should be,
But that their lives, as ransomed
Be lives of victory;
And so at our disposal
He places all His power,
That we from its resources
May draw in danger's hour.*

GEORGE MATHESON

FIXED ON HIM

He staggered not at the promise of God through unbelief.
ROMANS 4:20

Those who mind Christ's glory, He mindeth their salvation. He is interceding for you in heaven when you are glorifying Him on earth; He is doing your business in heaven when you are doing His business in the world; He is your advocate, and you are His bailiffs and factors: Matthew 10:32, "Whosoever therefore shall confess me before men, him will I confess also before my Father which is in heaven." When you own Christ in the world, and avow His name and truth in the world, you shall lose nothing. When you come to pray, Christ will own you: Father, hear him, this is one of mine. You cannot honour Christ so much as He will honour you.

The work which his goodness began
The arm of His strength will complete;
His promise is Yea and Amen,
And never was forfeited yet.

THOMAS MANTON

TELL JESUS

The apostles gathered themselves together unto Jesus, and told him all things.
MARK 6:30

That is just what we should always do when we have been trying to do any service for our Lord. We should do it as well as we can, and then go and tell Him what we have done. At the close of each day we should go to Him and tell Him of all that we have done or tried to do during the day. We should tell Him how we have lived, how we have done our work, how we have endured temptations, how we have treated our friends and those with whom we have been associated, how we have performed our mission as His servants, what words we have spoken for Him, what efforts we have made to do good or to give comfort or help, and how we have met the calls upon us for sympathy and aid.

We must not forget to tell him about the day's failures. Did we lose our patience? Did we yield to temptation? Did we neglect to speak the word for the Master that we ought to have spoken? Were we unkind to anyone? We must tell Him of the effort to do good which seemed to come to nothing. Oftentimes we are like the disciples who had toiled all the night and caught nothing. At many a setting sun we come, weary and sad, with empty hands. Then sometimes we are tempted to stay away form the Master and make no report; what have we to report? Nothing but a fruitless day. But we should not keep away from Him who sent us out. Jesus had days in His own life that seemed fruitless, and He can understand our sadness when we come with no sheaves.

So let us tell Him everything. That is the kind of evening solitary prayer that will bless us. It will make us very watchful all day if we remember that we must report to Jesus all we say, or do, or fail to do; it will keep us in more intimate relations with Him. Then His sympathy will strengthen us for better service each day.

J.R. MILLER

PEACE IN THE MIDST OF THE STORM

Jesus constrained His disciples to get into a ship.
MATTHEW 14:22

Jesus *constrained* them to go! One would think that if ever there was the certain promise of success in a mission, it was here. Surely here, if anywhere, a triumphant issue might have been confidently predicted; and yet here, more than anywhere, there was seeming failure. He sent them out on a voyage, and they met such a storm as they had never yet experienced.

Let me ponder this, for it has been so with me, too. I have sometimes felt myself impelled to act by an influence which seemed above me - constrained to put to sea. The belief that I was constrained gave me confidence, and I was sure of a calm voyage. But the result was outward failure. The calm became a storm; the sea raged, the winds roared, the ship tossed in the midst of the waves, and my enterprise was wrecked ere it could reach the land.

Was then my divine command a delusion?

Nay; nor yet was my mission a failure. He did send me on that voyage, but He did not send me for *my* purpose. He had one end and I had another. My end was the outward calm; His was my meeting with the storm. My end was to gain the harbour of a material rest; His was to teach me there is a rest even on the open sea.

So while here the cross I'm bearing,
Meeting storms and billows wild.
Jesus for my soul is caring,
Naught can harm His Father's child.

GEORGE MATHESON

DEATH OF JOHN THE BAPTIST

And he sent, and beheaded John in the prison.
MATTHEW 14:10

This seems a sad end for this glorious man's life. After a few months of faithful preaching he was cast into a dungeon, where he lay for a year and where he was beheaded as a criminal. To us it is very mysterious. Why did God permit such a fate to come upon so faithful and noble a servant? Our Lord Himself said that no greater man ever lived than John. Why then was his life allowed to go out in such darkness?

We know, first, that it was no accident. There are no accidents in this world over which our loving Father presides. John would not have chosen such a destiny for himself, so brief, with such a tragic ending; few of us would choose just the life we live in this world. There are no chances, no accidents. Our ways are those of the Lord's choosing - ways sadder, perhaps, but safer; rougher, perhaps, but surer; narrower, perhaps, but better than those of our own dreaming.

John finished his work. If there had been anything further for him to do, he would not have been left to die so shamefully to gratify the revenge of a wicked woman. His work was done when Christ began to preach. Then when he died, it was for faithfulness to the truth. It is not long years that make a complete life. A life is complete, whether long or short, that fulfils the purpose of its creation. And the longest life is incomplete and a failure if it does not do the work for which it was made. It is better to die in youth with a life unspotted than to live on to old age in sin and crime. It was a thousand times better every way to die as John died than to live on as Herod and Herodias lived.

He liveth long who liveth well -
All else is being flung away;
He liveth longest who can tell
Of rue things truly done each day.

J.R. MILLER

OUR HOME, HIS HOUSE

By faith Noah ... prepared an ark to the saving of his house.
HEBREWS 11:7

What a humble, what a modest sphere for the exercise of faith! One would have said that the purpose was quite disproportionate to the work. The ark was a great undertaking, but what was it undertaken for? To save his own family. Is so narrow a sphere worthy to be the object of faith? Is so commonplace a scene as the life of the family circle fit to be a temple for the service of God? ...

My soul, when thou hast finished thy prayers and ended thy meditations, do not say that thou hast left the house of God. God's house shall to thee be everywhere, and thine own house shall be a part of it. Thou shalt feel that all the duties of this place are consecrated; that it is none other than the house of God and one of the gates to heaven. Thou shalt feel that every one of its duties is an act of high communion.

Therefore be it thine to make thy house *His* house. Be it thine to consecrate each word and look and deed in the social life of home. Be it thine to build thine ark of refuge for the wants of common day; verily, thy labour of love shall be called an act of faith.

A home is sweet, though rich or poor,
If Jesus dwells within -
Abiding in our heart and lives
And overcoming sin;
Then bringing Heaven's sunshine down
To cheer us on our way,
And lead us thro' this toilsome world
To Heaven's golden day.

GEORGE MATHESON

FEBRUARY 26

THE LIFE OF GOD

Work out your own salvation with fear and trembling.
PHILIPPIANS 2:12

The old Puritan writer who defined salvation as "the life of God in the soul of man" was entirely right. Only do not fail to bear in mind that the man in whom He dwells is not himself passive ... Indolent activity, even in the name of orthodox belief, can never hold fellowship with essential energy - which is what God is. Yes, there are hands unseen working with our hands. There is a will omnipotent energising our wills. There is a wisdom ineffable informing our minds ... There is a strength untold directing our members. There is a divine craftsman repeating Himself in us. And all in such a manner that our individuality is not thereby destroyed but developed. We are ourselves workers together with Him, pledged to do our part, though always aware that without Him we are nothing.

Take Thou my love, O Lord, and consecrate it,
Burn out the dross and make it all Thine own;
Save me from self and all of earth's ambitions
Till self has died and Thou doest reign alone.

J. STUART HOLDEN

FEBRUARY 27

AT THE FOOT OF THE CROSS

Let this mind be in you, which was also in Christ Jesus.
PHILIPPIANS 2:5

If the moment I am conscious of the shadow of self crossing my threshold, I do not shut the door, and in the power of Him Who works in us to will and to do, keep that door shut, then I know nothing of Calvary love.

If I say, "Yes, I forgive, but I cannot forget", as though the God, who twice a day washes all the sands on all the shores of all the world, could not wash away such memories from my mind, then I know nothing of Calvary love (Psalm 103:12; Micah 7:19).

If monotony tires me, and I cannot stand drudgery; if stupid people fret me and little ruffles set me on edge; if I make much of the trifles of life, then I know nothing of Calvary love.

If there be any reserve in my giving to Him Who so loved that He gave His Dearest for me; if there be a secret "but" in my prayer, "anything but that, Lord," then I know nothing of Calvary love.

If I avoid being "ploughed under", with all that such ploughing entails of rough handling, isolation, uncongenial situations, strange tests, then I know nothing of Calvary love.

If I refuse to be a corn of wheat that falls to the ground and dies ("is separated from all in which it lived before") then I know nothing of Calvary love (John 12:24).

If I ask to be delivered from trial rather than for deliverance out of it, to the praise of His glory, if I forget that the way of the Cross leads to the Cross and not to the bank of flowers; if I regulate my life on these lines, or even unconsciously my thinking, so that I am surprised when the way is rough, and think it strange though the word is "Think it not strange … Count it all joy", then I know nothing of Calvary love (I Peter 4:1-2; James 1:2).

If the ultimate, the hardest, cannot be asked of me; if my fellows hesitate to ask it and turn to someone else, then I know nothing of Calvary love.

If I covet any place on earth but the dust at the foot of the Cross, then I know nothing of Calvary love. That which I know not, teach Thou me, O Lord, my God.

AMY CARMICHAEL

FEBRUARY 28

HIS FOR EVER

And this is the Father's will ... that of all which he hath
given me I should lose nothing.
JOHN 6:39

We have Christ always for us in heaven; He hath a part of His office to perform there. His absence doth not hinder us from having a right to Him, or a spiritual possession of Him. He is ours, and He hath His residence in heaven, and hath power to open it to us and give us entrance.

His high honour doth not hinder Him from the discharge of His office to do us good. He is at God's right hand, and yet a minister of the sanctuary ... Many forget their poor friends when advanced; Christ regardeth his poor church as much as ever ... Hebrews 4:15, "We have not a high priest which cannot be touched with the feeling of our infirmities." His heart is not changed by His honour; but He is in a greater capacity to do us good.

THOMAS MANTON

NOT THE GIFT, BUT THE GIVER

Ye servants of the Lord, which by night stand in the house of the Lord ...
PSALM 134:1

If I would know the love of my friend, I must see what it can do in the winter. So with the divine love. It is very easy for me to worship in the summer sunshine, when the melodies of life are in the air and the fruits of life are on the trees. But let the song of the bird ease, and the fruit of the tree fall; and will my heart still go on to sing? Will I stand in God's house by night? Will I love Him in His own night? Will I watch with Him even one hour in His Gethsemane? Will I help to bear His cross up the Via Dolorosa?

My love has come to Him in His humiliation. My faith has found Him in His lowliness. My heart has recognised His majesty through His mean disguise, and I know at last that I desire not the gift, but the Giver. When I can stand in His house by night, I have accepted Him for Himself alone.

Thou hast given so much to me,
Give one thing more - a grateful heart:
Not thankful when it pleaseth me,
As if thy blessings had spare days,
But such a heart whose pulse may be Thy praise.

GEORGE MATHESON

MARCH 1

A TIME TO LISTEN

Be still, and know that I am God.
PSALM 46:10

Prayer among evangelical Christians is always in danger of degenerating into a glorified "gold rush." Almost every book on prayer deals with the "get" element mainly. How to get things we want from God occupies most of our space.

Christians should never forget that the highest kind of prayer is never the making of requests.

Prayer at its holiest moment is the entering into God to a place of such blessed union as makes miracles seem tame and remarkable answers to prayer appear something very far short of wonderful, by comparison.

We should be aware that there is a kind of school where the soul must go to learn its best eternal lessons. It is the school of silence. "Be still and know," said the psalmist.

It might well be a revelation to some Christians if they were to get completely quiet for a time - a time to listen in the silence for the deep voice of the Eternal God!

Be still, my soul: The Lord is on thy side;
Bear patiently the cross of grief or pain;
Leave to thy Lord to order and provide;
In every change He faithful will remain.
Be still, my soul: Thy rest thy heavenly Friend
Through thorny ways leads to a joyful end.

A. W. TOZER

MARCH 2

RUNNING OVER

Thou preparest a table before me in the presence of mine enemies:
thou anointest my head with oil; my cup runneth over.
PSALM 23:5

Turn your eyes upon Jesus, and wells of joy will rise from the Fountain of Life and literally surge through your whole being. Keep your face to the sun, and the shadows will be behind you. That is true optimism. Look at your circumstances through the eyes of faith, as from the "heavenly places." Everything earthly is small when looked at from the heights. Did you ever hear of the two buckets, one joyous and the other gloomy? The pessimist said, "I never go away from this well full but I return again empty." Said the optimistic bucket, "I never come to the well empty but I go away again full." You see it all depends upon the point of view. Are you heavy-hearted and discouraged? Does the midnight seem dark and dreary? Cheer up! Jesus is on the throne. He doeth all things well. Look up, and sing the song of faith. Claim the promise; you will sing, "My cup runneth over." Refuse even your feelings, if necessary; and even though it demand an almost cold-blooded faith, sing a midnight carol. Sing, my brother, my sister; *sing!* He will put music in your heart, lighten your darkness, take your heavy load, and haunting melodies will resound through the gloom of midnight. "Cry out and shout, thou inhabitant of Zion." Take the "three cheers" He freely offers: first, *His forgiveness*; second, *His fortitude*; third, *His fullness*.

Upward, ever upward,
Toward the radiant glow,
Far above the valley
Where the mist hangs low;
On, with songs of gladness,
Till the march shall end
Where ten thousand thousand
Hallelujahs blend.

REGINALD WALLIS

MOVING FORWARD

Create in me a clean heart, O God; and renew a right spirit within me.
PSALM 51:10

The Christian life is never static. One must either grow in grace, or there will be backsliding and deterioration. "The backslider in heart shall be filled with his own ways" (Proverbs 14: 14). He who does not go on with God, but allows himself to drift, is almost sure to lose the joy of his salvation. Examine yourself as to this matter, and if you find that you have been careless in regard to the study of your Bible, careless as to your prayer life, careless as to the proper use of the means of grace, confess all this to God and give diligence to walk with Him in days to come, that you may develop a stronger Christian character.

Last of all, let me remind you that any known sin condoned in your life will rob you of the joy and assurance of your salvation. "If I regard iniquity in my heart, the Lord will not hear me." Many believers have gone on happily with Christ for some time, but, through toying with sin, have become ensnared and entrapped into something that has so grieved the Spirit of God that they have lost their sense of acceptance in Christ. See to it that there is no unconfessed sin in your life. Be sure that you are not tolerating any secret sin that is draining you of spiritual power and hindering your communion with God.

Worldliness, carnal indulgence of any kind, unfaithfulness as to your Christian responsibilities, the harbouring of malice or ill-will toward others - all or any of these things are calculated to destroy your sense of assurance. If guilty of any of them, face things honestly in the presence of God, remembering that He has said, "If we confess our sins, he is faithful and just to forgive us our sins, and to cleanse us from all unrighteousness."

Do not accept the suggestion of the tempter that you are powerless to break away from evil habits. Remember, it is not a question of your own power, but when you honestly repent of the wrongdoing and turn to the Lord for divine help to overcome your besetting sin, He will undertake for you. As you reckon yourself to be dead indeed unto sin, but alive unto God through Jesus Christ our Lord, the Holy Spirit will work in you and through you. He will cause you to triumph over tendencies toward evil and enable you to live victoriously to the glory of the God who has saved you.

HARRY IRONSIDE

HOW DO YOU KNOW?

All that the father giveth me shall come to me;
and him that cometh to me I will in no wise cast out.
JOHN 6:37

There was a day in my life when, if my old mother had said to me, or if you had said to me: "Is honey sweet?" I would have said: "Why, certainly, honey is sweet."

"How do you know?"

"My mother told me."

But there came a day when I stuck my finger in the honey-pot, then into my mouth. Then if you had said to me: "Is honey sweet?" and had asked me: "How do you know?" after I had said: "Yes," I would have told you, in addition to saying: "My mother told me; I read it in a book," "I have tasted the honey for myself, so that not only have I second-hand knowledge, but I have first-hand knowledge, that honey is sweet."

If you had said to me: "Does fire burn?" I would have said: "Why, certainly, fire burns."

"How do you know?"

"Well, my mother told me. Many a skelping I got for bothering with the fire, and poking at it. I was told to keep back from the fire."

But there came a day when I was seriously burnt, and I have the scar of that burn upon my arm to this day.

You now say to me: "Does fire burn?"

"Why, certainly, fire burns."

"How do you know?"

"Why, my mother told me; I read it in a book; but now I have experienced it, and I know that it burns."

You say to me: "Is the 37th verse of the 6th chapter of the Gospel according to St. John true?"

"Why, certainly, it is true. It is God's Word."

"How do you know?"

"I have experienced it. Hallelujah!"

W. P. NICHOLSON

MARCH 5

SOMETHING TO SING ABOUT

Sing, O barren.
ISAIAH 54:1

Though we have brought some fruit to Christ, there are times when we feel barren. Prayer is lifeless, love is cold, faith is weak, and each grace in the garden of our heart is like a languishing, drooping flower in the hot sun. We need a refreshing shower.

In this condition, what can we do? Our text supplies the answer. "Sing, O barren ... break forth into singing and cry aloud." But what can I sing about? I cannot talk about the present, and even the past looks bleak. Ah, I can sing of Jesus Christ. I can talk of visits the Redeemer has made to me. I can magnify His great love, when He came from the heights of heaven for His people's redemption.

I will go to the cross again. Come, my heavily-laden soul. You once lost your burden there; go to Calvary again. Perhaps the cross that gave you life will give you fruitfulness.

What is my barrenness but the platform for His fruit-creating power? What is my desolation but the black velvet setting for the sapphire of His everlasting love? I will go to Him in poverty, I will go in helplessness, I will go in all my shame and backsliding. I will tell Him that I am still His child, and with confidence in His faithful heart, even I, the barren one, will sing.

Sing, believer, it will cheer your heart and the hearts of other desolate ones. Sing on, for now that you are really ashamed of being barren, you will soon be fruitful. Now that God has made you loath to be without fruit, He will cover you with clusters.

The experience of barrenness is painful, but the Lord's visitations are delightful. A sense of our own poverty drives us to Christ, and that is where we need to be. In Him our fruit is found.

Jesus, confirm my heart's desire
To work, and speak, and sing for Thee;
Still let me guard the holy fire,
And still stir up Thy gift in me.

CHARLES H. SPURGEON

MARCH 6

HE WHOM THOU LOVEST IS SICK

This sickness is not unto death, but for the glory of God.
JOHN 11:4

A certain man was sick named Lazarus. Lazarus was evidently a child of God, and yet Lazarus was sick.

Learn not to judge others because of affliction. Job's three friends tried to show him that he must be a hypocrite and a bad man, because God afflicted him. They did not know that God afflicts His own dear children. Lazarus was sick; and the beggar Lazarus was full of sores; and Hezekiah was sick, even unto death; and yet all were peculiarly dear to Jesus.

God's children should not doubt His love when He afflicts. Christ loved Lazarus peculiarly, and yet He afflicted him very sore. A surgeon never bends his eye so tenderly upon his patient, as when he is putting in the lancet, or probing the wound to the very bottom. And so with Christ; He bends His eye most tenderly over His own at the time He is afflicting them.

Do not doubt the holy love of Jesus to your soul when He is laying a heavy hand upon you. Jesus did not love Lazarus less when He afflicted him, but rather more - "even as a father correcteth a son in whom he delighteth" (Proverbs 3: 12). A goldsmith when he casts gold into the furnace looks after it.

Christ was far more glorified than if Lazarus had not been sick and died.

So in all the sufferings of God's people. Sometimes a child of God says: "Lord, what wilt Thou have me to do? I will teach - preach - do great things for Thee." Sometimes the answer is: "Thou shalt suffer for My sake."

It shows the power of Christ's blood - when it gives peace in an hour of trouble - when it can make happy in sickness, poverty, persecution and death. Do not be surprised if you suffer, but glorify God.

It brings out graces that cannot be seen in a time of health. It is the treading of the grapes that brings out the sweet juices of the vine; so it is afflictions that draws forth submission, weanedness from the world, and complete rest in God. Use afflictions while you have them.

ROBERT MURRAY McCHEYNE

GOOD CHRISTIANS IN BAD TIMES

Thou, Lord, hast not forsaken them that seek thee.
PSALM 9:10

I have often thought that the best Christians are found in the worst of times: and I have thought again, that one reason why we are no better, is because God purges us no more. I know these things are against the grain of the flesh, but they are not against the graces of the Spirit.

Noah and Lot, who so holy as they, in the day of their affliction? Noah and Lot, who so idle as they in the day of their prosperity? I might have put in David too, who, while he was afflicted, had ways of serving God that were special; but when he was enlarged, he had ways that were not so good.

Wherefore for conclusion, as we are to receive with meekness the engrafted Word of God, so also we are with patience to bear what God, by man, shall lay upon us.

Who would true valour see,
Let him come hither;
One here will constant be,
Come wind, come weather;
There's no discouragement
Shall make him once relent
His first avowed intent
To be a pilgrim.

JOHN BUNYAN

MARCH 8

MAN PUT GOD ON THE CROSS

And when they were come to the place, which is called Calvary,
there they crucified him.
LUKE 23:33

Oh what a revelation! Man hating God, and hating most when God is loving most! Man acting as a devil and taking the devil's side against God! You say, "What have I to do with the cross, and what right have you to identify me with the crucifiers? Pilate did it, Caiaphas did it, the Jew did it, the Roman did it; I did it not." Nay, but you did, you did. You did it in your representatives - the civilised Roman and the religious Jew - and until you come out from the crucifying crowd, disown your representatives and protest against the deed, you are truly guilty of that blood.

"But how am I to sever myself from these crucifiers and protest against their crime?" By believing in the name of the crucified one. For all unbelief is approval of the deed and identification with the murderers. Faith is man's protest against the deed, and the identification of himself, not only with the friends and disciples of the crucified one, but with the crucified one Himself.

The cross, then, was the public declaration of man's hatred of God, man's rejection of His Son, and man's avowal of his belief that he needs no Saviour. If anyone denies the ungodliness of humanity and pleads for the native goodness of the race, I ask, what means the cross? Of what is it the revealer and interpreter? Of hatred or of love? Of good or of evil?

Besides, in this rejection of the Son of God, we have also man's estimate of Him. He had been for thirty years despised and rejected. He had been valued and sold for thirty pieces of silver, a robber had been preferred to Him; but at the cross, this estimate comes out more awfully, and there we see how man undervalued His person, His life, His blood, His word. His whole errand from the Father.

"What think ye of Christ?" was God's question. Man's answer was, "The cross!" Was not that as explicit as it was appalling?

As the cross reveals man's depravity, so does it exhibit his foolishness. His condemnation of Him in whom God delighted to show this. His erection of the cross shows it still more. As if he could set at naught Jehovah and clear the earth of Him who had come down as the doer of His will! Man's attempt to cast shame on the Lord of Glory is like a child's efforts to blot out or discolour the sun.

HORATIUS BONAR

MARCH 9

A GLORIOUS STANDARD

Repent, and do the first works.
REVELATION 2:5

S atan knew what was the secret of the great success of those early disciples. It was their whole-hearted devotion, their absorbing love to Christ, their utter abnegation of the world. An enthusiastic religion had swallowed them up and made them willing to become wanderers and vagabonds on the face of the earth - for His sake to dwell in dens and caves, to be torn asunder, and to be persecuted in every form. Before this degree of devotion Satan saw he had no chance. Such people, as these, he knew, must ultimately subdue the world.

Therefore the arch-enemy said, *"What must I do? I shall lose my supremacy as the god of this world."* No use to bring in a gigantic system of error which everybody would see to be error. That has never been Satan's way; his plan has been to get hold of a good man here and there who shall creep in, as the apostle said, unawares and preach another doctrine, and who shall deceive, if it were possible, the very elect. And he did it! He accomplished his design. He gradually lowered the standard of Christian life and character, and though, in every revival, God has raised it to a certain extent, we have never got back thoroughly to the simplicity, purity, and devotion set before us in the Acts of the Apostles.

There it is, a glorious standard put before us. The power is proffered, the conditions are laid down, and we can all attain to it - a real, living, self-sacrificing, hardworking, triumphing religion, and the world will be influenced by it.

CATHERINE BOOTH

A MIDNIGHT CHORUS

At midnight Paul and Silas prayed, and sang praises unto God:
and the prisoners heard them.
ACTS 16:25

*T*he scene - a prison in Philippi. *The time* - midnight. *The music* - a chorus of praise. *The singers* - two evangelists with bleeding backs and their feet fast in the stocks. *The crime* - preaching the gospel and casting out demons. How would *you* have felt, and what would *you* have done in their circumstances? Had they not been faithful to their Lord? Why this merciless and unjust retribution? Yes, the whole situation seems to constitute a gross violation of justice. As natural men, they have every reason to be offended. Why should their noble and courageous testimony be rewarded with the stripes and cruel hardship of a Roman dungeon? Has God forgotten them?

The fact is, however, that they are not natural men. They are spiritual. They have learned the secret of an unwavering trust, even in the darkness, and God gives them a midnight chorus instead of a midnight groan. No protest emanates from these blameless prisoners. They are among "the blessed un-offended." No spirit of revolt mars their fellowship with the Most High. Nocturnal darkness in the physical realm mingles with a meridian glory in the spiritual. Dark shadows cast rays of gloom in the jail, but bright sunshine still glows within the heart. Stripes first, then a song! "They looked *unto Him*, and were *radiant*."

Their bodies are confined to the dismal precincts of the penitentiary, but their spirits are liberated into the joy of "heavenly places." The lash has wounded their bodies, but their spirits are untouched. Divine glory ever penetrates human gloom. God always gives a midnight song to His suffering faithful ones.

Through all the changing scenes of life,
In trouble and in joy,
The praises of my God shall still
My heart and tongue employ.

REGINALD WALLIS

MARCH 11

PRAYER AND GOD'S WORK

By their fruits ye shall know them.
MATTHEW 7:20

We cannot wonder that so little is accomplished in the great work in the world which God has in hand. The fact is that it is surprising so much has been done with such feeble, defective agents. *"Holiness to the Lord"* needs again to be written on the banners of the church. Once more it needs to be sounded out in the ears of modern Christians: *"Follow peace with all men, and holiness, without which no man shall see the Lord."* (Hebrews 12:14).

Let it be stated and reiterated that this is the divine standard of religion. Nothing short of this will satisfy the divine requirement. O the danger of deception at this point! How near one can come to being right and yet be wrong! Some men can come very near to pronouncing the test word, "Shibboleth," but they miss it. *"Many will say unto me in that day, Lord, Lord,"* says Jesus Christ, but He further states that then He will say unto them, *"I never knew you; depart from me, ye that work iniquity"* (Matthew 7:22-23).

Men can do many good things and yet not be holy in heart and righteous in conduct. They can do many good things and lack the spiritual quality of heart called holiness. How great the need of hearing the words of Paul guarding us against self deception in the great work of personal salvation:

"Be not deceived; God is not mocked: for whatsoever a man soweth, that shall he also reap." (Galatians 6:7)

O may I still from sin depart;
A wise and understanding heart,
Jesus, to me to be given;
And let me through Thy Spirit know
To glorify my God below,
And find my way to heaven.

E. M. BOUNDS

THE GROWING CHRISTIAN

*Grow in grace, and in the knowledge of our
Lord and Saviour Jesus Christ.*
2 PETER 3:18

Grow in the grace. Grow not just in one grace, but in all grace. Grow in that root grace: faith. Believe the promises. Let faith increase in fullness, consistency, and simplicity.

Grow also in love. Ask that your love be more extended, more intense, more practical, influencing your every thought, word, and deed.

Grow likewise in humility. Listen to know more of your own nothingness. Grow downward in humility and grow upward with a closer approach to God in prayer and a more intimate fellowship with Jesus.

May God the Holy Spirit enable you to "grow in the grace and knowledge of our Lord and Saviour." If you do not grow in the grace and knowledge of Jesus you are refusing to be blessed. To know Him is "life eternal," and "to grow in the grace and knowledge" of Him is to increase your happiness. If you have no desire to learn more about Christ, you know nothing of Him.

Whoever has sipped this wine will never be thirsty. Christ satisfies, yet it is a satisfaction that never fills, but stimulates the appetite. If you know the love of Jesus, "as the deer pants for the water brooks" (Psalm 42: 1), you will long for deep drinks of His love. If you don't want to know Him better, then you don't love Him. Absence from Christ is hell. But the presence of Jesus is heaven.

Do not rest until you have increased your acquaintance with Jesus. Learn more of Him in His divine nature, in His human relationship, in His finished work, in His death, in His resurrection, in His present glorious intercession, and in His second coming.

An increase of our love for Jesus and a more perfect concept of His love for us is one of the best ways to grow in grace.

CHARLES H. SPURGEON

VAIN REGRETS

If our heart condemn us, God is greater than our heart,
and knoweth all things.
1 JOHN 3:20

I do indeed sympathise with you and I think I can divine a little as to the nature of your trials. I wish I were near to comfort and help you - such help as it is I have to offer. The only way of comfort I see for you is to try and walk *alone*, shutting your eyes to what you cannot help.

It is useless to harrow ourselves up about the past, or to waste time in vain regrets. It is past now, and can never be altered. But we can cast it under the blood, and go on praying Him to avert the consequences, and maybe He will stoop to answer us. Do your own part in witnessing for God and truth, and hope that at some future time it will produce its effect.

Comfort yourself in the Lord. He is very pitiful and of tender mercy, and when He sees us truly penitent for our mistakes and failures He delights to pardon us. Do not perplex yourself about the experiences of others. I am more than ever satisfied that God looks more propitiously on those who are striving and struggling to do right and to please Him, even in fear and despondency, than on those who make light of sin and yet make their boast in Him. I fear there are sadly too many who can rejoice when they ought to weep, while some who can never forgive themselves, weep when they ought to rejoice. Perhaps these latter are amongst those who, though they mourn now, *"shall be comforted"* hereafter.

Not a burden we bear,
Not a sorrow we share,
But our toil He doth richly repay:
Not a grief nor a loss,
Not a frown nor a cross,
But is blest if we trust and obey.

CATHERINE BOOTH

MARCH 14

TWO ASPECTS OF PEACE

Peace from God our Father and the Lord Jesus Christ.
ROMANS 1:7

Sometimes people use expressions that will not always bear the test of Scripture. Let me give an instance of this: A number of years ago an earnest young Christian and I went to a mission in San Francisco. At the close of the meeting, a kind, motherly woman came to me and asked, "Are you a Christian, sir?"

I replied immediately, "Yes, I am."

"Thank God," she said, and then turning to my friend, she asked, "And have you made your 'peace with God,' sir?"

Rather to my astonishment, he answered, "No, madam, I have not."

I knew he was a Christian, and I wondered at his replying in that way.

She said to him rather severely, "Well, if you don't make your 'peace with God,' you will be lost forever."

With a bright, happy smile on his face, he replied, "Madam, I can never make my 'peace with God,' and I never expect to try; but I am thankful that the Lord Jesus Christ has settled that for me, and through what He did for me I shall be in heaven for all eternity."

He then put the question to her, "Have you never read that remarkable passage, 'Having made peace by the blood of his cross'?"

As he went on to explain it to her, the truth gripped my own soul. I saw then, and have realised it ever since, that sinners are saved through the "peace" that He made at the cross. And so we read in Romans 5:1, "Therefore being justified by faith, we have peace with God through our Lord Jesus Christ." This peace He made as we accept by faith the testimony of His Word.

But we also read, "My peace I give unto you." What does the Lord Jesus mean by this? It is another aspect of peace altogether. It is that quiet rest of soul that was ever His in the midst of the most trying circumstances. He shares His peace with us. It is of this we read in Philippians 4: 6-7: "Be careful for nothing [or, in nothing be anxious,]; but in every thing by prayer and supplication with thanksgiving let your requests be made known unto God. And the peace of God, which passeth all understanding, shall keep your hearts and minds through Christ Jesus."

HARRY IRONSIDE

NO COMPROMISE

*This is life eternal, that they might know thee the only true God,
and Jesus Christ, whom thou hast sent.*
JOHN 17:3

The Lord save us in these days from compromise with the world, the flesh and the devil! "God divided the light from the darkness." His principles are unchanging. The divine purpose of the age is the *calling out* of a Heavenly people for Himself. Note in conclusion, that lovely touch at the close of verse five. "The evening and the morning were the first day." Were this a human narrative, it would bear the human order - morning and evening. Man's day always terminates in midnight. God's day always finishes in the morning. Praise His Holy Name for ever! One great advantage that the believer possesses over the man of the world is that it is always better on ahead! The Church of God is awaiting the dawn of an eternal day from which the sun will never wester.

Let us ask ourselves if we have had a *day one*? Have we begun to *live*? Have we met Him whom to know is *Life* Eternal? If not, or should there be any doubt about it, God grant that this may be the hour and moment of definite choice. If by grace we are in the Heavenly family, let us reopen all the doors and windows of our redeemed beings today to the advent of the Glory light. Thus shall desolation be turned into the beauty of holiness, the desert shall be made to blossom as the rose, and the wilderness and the solitary place shall evermore rejoice.

"And God saw the light, that it was good" - and every true believer echoes "Amen" with a glad heart. What a wonderful thing to be saved! This is the "day one" of spiritual life. There can be no actual possession, or experimental enjoyment, of the marvellous "things that accompany salvation" (blessedly typified in the following days' creative operations) until the sphere of divine life is entered by second birth. "Day one" is the Alpha of Christian life and experience. It is necessary in these days to emphasise the fact that *no one can live the Christian life until he has received the Christian life to live*. There *must* be a *"day one"*. George Whitefield was asked by his parishioners why he so repeatedly preached on the text, "Ye must be born again." His reply was, "For one simple reason, because ye *must* be born again!" This is old-fashioned theology, but it is also the eternal truth of God and remains inviolate today.

REGINALD WALLIS

STANDING STILL

Quench not the Spirit.
I THESSALONIANS 5:19

Why is it that so many of our churches today are standing where they were, with nothing accomplished, with nothing being done? I believe, dear friends, that that is the secret of it. They have got to the place where God couldn't show them anything different; where, if God began to work in a different way, in an unusual manner or in accordance with unusual methods, they would begin to carp with and criticise God, and question God for His working along such lines. So, dear friends, we want to be warned here; we want to have open minds and hearts; to say: "Lord, it is Thy work, it is not ours. You are the Worker; we are not the workers."

I believe it is an awful calamity when a child of God tries to do God's work. God never asked you to do His work. We would simply make a mug of it and a mess of it, and that is why there is such a mess of it abroad just now. God wants to do His own work, but He wants you and me through whom to do it. We are the instruments, we are the channels, that He may use; but the worst of it is that so many people imagine that by our skill and by our knowledge and by our training and by our experience we can do God's work.

We say: "God help me, and I will do the work." Oh, no! I have been for 30 years in the work of the Lord, since the Lord saved me, and the danger of my life, as it is of yours, dear friend, is that I would imagine that I knew how the work should and must be done. When you get there you have got to the place where the Spirit of God ceases to move and to work. What we want is this, that we shall allow the Spirit of God, who is the Worker, to take us, the channels, and us, the instruments, to do His own work through, and to do it in His own way; not in our way, but in His own way; and when we allow His freedom to operate as He likes, thank God, He will move mightily in our midst. But we must be warned. The danger is that we may quench Him simply by our conservativeness, by our stiffness, by our rigidity, and by the getting into a state of mind, as a people, in which we think that ours is the only way in which the work can be done.

W. P. NICHOLSON

CHRIST RECEIVES SINNERS

A Prince and a Saviour, for to give repentance ...
and forgiveness of sins.
ACTS 5:31

What a gracious thing for us that Jesus Christ never thinks about what we have been. He always thinks about what we are going to be! The Saviour who is our Lord cares absolutely nothing about your moral case history. He forgives it and starts from there as though you had been born one minute before.

The woman of Samaria met our Lord at the well and we ask, "Why was Jesus willing to reveal so much more about Himself in this setting than He did in other encounters during His ministry?"

You and I would never have chosen this woman with such a shadow lying across her life, but Jesus is the Christ of God, and He could sense the potential within her innermost being. He gave her the secret of His Messiahship and the secret of the nature of God. Her frankness and humility appealed to the Saviour as they talked of man's need and the true worship of God by the Spirit of God.

In Jesus' day, His critics said in scorn: "This man receives sinners!" They were right - and He lived and died and rose again to prove it. The blessed part is this: He is still receiving sinners!

Sinners Jesus will receive:
Sound this word of grace to all
Who the heavenly pathway leave,
All who linger, all who fall,

Come, and He will give you rest;
Trust Him, for His Word is plain
He will take the sinfulest;
Christ receiveth sinful men.

A. W. TOZER

MARCH 18

THE LOVE OF JESUS

Now Jesus loved Martha, and her sister, and Lazarus.
JOHN 11:5

These are the words of John. He knew what was in the heart of Christ, for the Holy Spirit taught him what to write, and he leaned upon Jesus' bosom, and knew the deepest secrets of Jesus' heart. This, then, is John's testimony: *"Jesus loved Martha, and Mary and Lazarus."*

You remember they had sent this message to Jesus: *"He whom thou lovest is sick."* Some would have said, that was a presumptuous message to send. How did they know that Lazarus was really converted? - that Jesus really loved him? But here you see John puts his seal upon their testimony. It was really true, and no presumption in it: *"Jesus loved Martha, and Mary, and Lazarus."*

How is it saints know when Jesus loves them? The method: Christ has ways of telling His own love peculiar to Himself. *"The secret of the Lord is with them that fear him."*

How ridiculous is it to think that Christ cannot make known his love to the soul! I shall mention one way - By drawing the soul to himself: *"Yea, I have loved thee with an everlasting love, therefore with loving-kindness have I drawn thee"* (Jer. 31:3).

"No man can come to me, except the Father ... draw him" (John 6:44).

Now when the Lord Jesus draws near to a dead, carnal sinner, and reveals to him a glimpse of His own beauty - of His face fairer than the sons of men - His precious blood - of the room that there is under His wings; and when the soul is drawn away from its old sins, old ways - away from its deadness, darkness, and worldliness, and is persuaded to forsake all, and flow toward the Lord Jesus - then that soul is made to taste the peace of believing, and is made to know that Jesus loves him.

Thus Lazarus knew that Christ loved him. I was a worldly, careless man - I mocked at my sisters when they were so careful to entertain the Lamb of God - I often was angry with them; but one day He came and showed me the way of salvation by Him - He drew me, and now I know that Jesus has loved me.

ROBERT MURRAY McCHEYNE

SUFFER FOR RIGHTEOUSNESS' SAKE

Call to remembrance the former days, in which, after ye were illuminated,
ye endured a great fight of afflictions.
HEBREWS 10:32

Dost thou suffer for righteousness' sake? Why then, thy righteousness is not diminished, but rather increased by thy sufferings. Righteousness thriveth best in affliction, the more afflicted, the more holy man; the more persecuted, the more shining man.

The prison is the furnace, thy graces are the silver and the gold; wherefore, as the silver and the gold are refined by the fire, and so made more to show their native brightness, so the Christian that hath and that loveth righteousness, and that suffereth for its sake, is by his sufferings refined and made more righteous, and made more Christian, more godly.

Some indeed, when they come there, prove lead, iron, tin, and the best, but the dross of silver; and so are fit for nothing, but there to be left and consumed.

A life of overcoming,
A life of ceaseless praise,
Be this thy blessed portion
Throughout the coming days,
The victory was purchased
On Calvary's cross for thee,
Sin shall not have dominion,
The Son hath made thee free

And would'st thou know the secret
Of constant victory?
Let in the Overcomer
And He will conquer thee!
Thy broken spirit, taken
In sweet captivity
Shall glory in His triumph
And share His victory.

JOHN BUNYAN

THE SIGNIFICANCE OF THE CROSS

The offence of the cross.
GALATIANS 5:11

From the day of Christ's crucifixion the cross became a power in the earth - a power which went forth like the light, noiselessly yet irresistibly - smiting down all religions alike, all shrines alike, all altars alike; sparing no superstition or philosophy; neither flattering priesthood nor succumbing to statesmanship; tolerating no error, never refusing to draw the sword for truth; a power superhuman, yet wielded by human, not angelic hands; "the power of God unto salvation."

This power still remains in its mystery, its silence and its influence. This cross had not become obsolete; the preaching of the cross has not ceased to be effectual. There are men among us who would persuade us that in this late age the cross is out of date and out of fashion, time-worn, not time-honoured; that Golgotha witnessed only a common martyr scene; that the great sepulchre is but a Hebrew tomb; that the Christ of the future and the Christ of the past are widely different. But this shakes us not. It only leads us to clasp the cross more fervently and to study it more profoundly, as embodying in itself that gospel that is at once the wisdom and the power of God.

Yet the cross is not without its mysteries or, as men would say, its puzzles, its contradictions. It illuminates, yet it darkens; it interprets, yet it confounds. It raises questions, but refuses to answer all that is raised. It solves difficulties, but it creates them too. It locks as well as unlocks. It opens, and no man shuts; it shuts, and no man opens. It is life, and yet it is death. It is honour, yet it is shame. It is wisdom, but also foolishness. It is both gain and loss; both pardon and condemnation; both strength and weakness; both joy and sorrow; both love and hatred; both medicine and poison; both hope and despair. It is grace, and yet it is righteousness. It is law, yet it is deliverance from law. It is Christ's humiliation, yet it is Christ's exaltation. It is Satan's victory, yet it is Satan's defeat. It is the gate of heaven and the gate of hell.

Let us look at the cross as the divine proclamation and interpretation of the things of God; the key to His character, His Word, His ways, His purposes; the clue to the intricacies of the world's and the church's history.

HORATIUS BONAR

MARCH 21

OUR PHYSICIAN

Simon's wife's mother lay sick of a fever, and anon they tell him of her.
MARK 1:30

This is an interesting little look into the home of an apostolic fisherman. We immediately see that household joys and cares are not a hindrance to the full work of the ministry. As a matter of fact, they furnish an opportunity for personally witnessing the Lord's gracious work on one's own family. They may even instruct the teacher better than any other earthly disciple could. True Christianity and household life go well together.

Peter's house was probably a poor fisherman's hut. Yet the Lord of Glory entered it, lodging there, and worked a miracle in it. If this morning I am speaking to someone who lives in a humble dwelling, let this fact encourage the residents to seek the company of King Jesus, who is more often in little huts than in rich palaces.

Jesus is looking around your room now. He is waiting to be gracious. Sickness had entered Simon's house. Fever in a deadly form had prostrated his mother-in-law. When Jesus came, they told Him of her affliction and He hastened to the patient's bed.

Is there any sickness in your home this morning? You will find Jesus is the best physician. Go to Him. Tell Him all about the problem. Immediately lay the case before Him. It concerns one of His people, therefore it is not trivial to Him. Observe that immediately the Saviour restored the sick woman. No one can heal like Jesus.

We may not be sure that the Lord will at once remove all disease from those we love. We do know, however, that believing prayer for the sick is often followed by restoration. (James 5:15)

If the person is not healed, we must bow to Him who determines life and death. The tender heart of Jesus waits to hear our griefs. Let us pour them into His patient ear.

There is no sorrow, Lord too light
To bring in prayer to Thee;
Nor is there any care too slight
To wake Thy sympathy.

CHARLES H. SPURGEON

COME FORTH

I am the resurrection, and the life.
JOHN 11:25

When Jesus first heard that Lazarus was sick, He abode two days in the place where He was. Slowly and calmly He moved toward Bethany, so that when He arrived beneath its fig-trees, the passing villager told Him that Lazarus had lain in the grave four days already.

Still Jesus did not hurry, but waited till He had drawn forth the unbelief of Martha and Mary - waited till He had manifested His own tender, compassionate heart - waited till He had given public thanks to the Father, to show that He was sent of God. *"And when he thus had spoken he cried with a loud voice, Lazarus come forth."*

His time is the right time. So in giving life to Israel. Israel, like Lazarus, have been lying in their graves eighteen hundred years. Their bones are dry and very many. Since He spake against them, He earnestly remembers them still; and there is a day coming when He will pour the Spirit of life upon them, and make them come forth, and be life to the dead world. But this in His own time.

"He cried with a loud voice, Lazarus, come forth." And he that was dead came forth, bound hand and foot with grave-clothes. What a strange scene was here! It was a retired part of the narrow ravine in which Bethany lies, and the crowd were standing beside the newly-opened sepulchre of Lazarus. It was a huge cave cut in the rock, and the huge stone that had been rolled to the door was now rolled back.

It pierced down into the deep cave, and through the close damp napkin into the dead ear. The heart began suddenly to beat, and the warm current of life to flow though the dead man's veins. The vital heat and the sense of hearing came back. It was a well-known voice. *"The voice of my Beloved,"* he would say, *"he calls my name."* So he arose: *"And he that was dead came forth, bound hand and foot, with grave-clothes."*

How simple, and yet how glorious! Jehovah speaks, and it is done. *"The voice of the Lord is powerful, the voice of the Lord is full of majesty; the voice of the Lord breaketh the cedars, yea, the Lord breaketh the cedars of Lebanon."*

Now were the words of Christ fulfilled: *"This sickness is not unto death, but for the glory of God, that the Son of God may be glorified thereby."*

ROBERT MURRAY McCHEYNE

THE SPIRIT OF HOLINESS

Behold, what manner of love the Father hath bestowed upon us.
I JOHN 3:1

The apostles trusted the gospel with the sinner, and the sinner with the gospel, so unreservedly, and (as many in our day would say) unguardedly. "To him that worketh not, but *believeth* ... his faith is counted for righteousness" (Romans 4:5) was a bold statement. It's a statement by one who had great confidence in the gospel that he preached; who had no misgivings as to its holy tendencies, if men would but give it fair play. He himself always preached it as the one who believed it to be the power of God unto holiness no less than unto salvation.

That this is the understanding of the New Testament, the "mind of the Spirit," requires no proof. Few would in words deny it to be so; only they state the gospel so timorously, so warily, so guardedly, with so many conditions, terms and reservations, that by the time they have finished their statement they have left no good news in what they had once announced as "the gospel of the grace of God."

The more fully that gospel is preached, in the grand old apostolic way, the more likely is it to accomplish results similar to those in apostolic days. The gospel is the proclamation of free love, the revelation of the boundless charity of God. Nothing less than this will suit our world; nothing else is so likely to touch the heart, to go down to the lowest depths of depraved humanity, as the assurance that the sinner has been loved - loved by God with a righteous love and with a free love that makes no bargain as to merit or fitness or goodness.

"Herein is love, not that we loved God, but that he loved us," declares the apostle John in his first letter. With nothing less than this free love will the Lord trust our fallen race. He will not trust them with law or judgment or terror (though these are well in their place); but He will trust them with His love! Not with a stinted or conditional love; with half pardons or an uncertain salvation or a doubtful invitation or an all but impracticable amnesty. With these He will not mock the weary sons of men. He wants them to be holy, as well as safe; and He knows that there is nothing in heaven or earth so likely to produce holiness, under the teaching of the Spirit of holiness, as the knowledge of His own free love.

HORATIUS BONAR

OUTSIDE THE CAMP

He is despised and rejected of men.
ISAIAH 53:3

Just as Christ's place in glory is our place, so His place on earth is our place, as we go through this sinful world. What is His place down here? It is the place of rejection, for "He came unto His own, and His own received Him not." These two expressions of "His own" are not absolutely the same in the original. The first is the neuter; the second is personal. Thus the passage may be rendered: "He came unto His own things and His own people received Him not."

Think of it, He came to His own city, Jerusalem, the city of the great King. If there was any place on earth where he might have expected to be received with gladness and acclaim, it was Jerusalem. He came unto His own temple; every whit of it uttered His glory, the very veil spoke of His perfect humanity, and every piece of furniture pictured Him. There was the altar, the laver, the candlestick, the table of showbread, and everything spoke of Him; but as He came to His own things, the very priests in the temple joined in the cry "Away with Him, away with Him, crucify Him!" and they led Him outside the gate, the rejected One.

There were two candidates that day, Christ and Barabbas. The people chose the murderer and rejected the Saviour. He accepted the place they gave Him, and with lowly grace allowed them to lead Him outside the city, away from the temple, away from the palace, outside the gates, unto the place called Calvary.

As far as the world is concerned, it has never reversed that judgment. He is still the rejected One, and the place the world has given Him should determine the place that you and I will take. He was rejected, not merely by the barbarian world, not merely by those who were living low, degraded lives, but also by the literary world, the cultured world, the religious world. It was the religious leaders of the people who demanded His death, and all the world acquiesced. The world still continues to do so. It has its culture, its refinements, its civilisation (often mistaken for Christianity), its religion (one that has no place for the cross of Christ or the vicarious atonement or His glorious resurrection), but our blessed Lord is apart from it all, and the word to us is this: "Let us go forth therefore unto him without the camp, bearing His reproach."

HARRY IRONSIDE

PRAYER AND HUMILITY

He that humbleth himself shall be exalted.
LUKE 18:14

To be humble is to have a low estimate of one's self. It is to be modest, lowly, with a disposition to seek obscurity. Humility retires itself from the public gaze. It does not seek publicity nor hunt for high places, neither does it care for prominence. Humility is retiring in its nature. Self-abasement belongs to humility. It is given to self-depreciation. It never exalts itself in the eyes of others nor even in the eyes of itself. Modesty is one of its most prominent characteristics.

In humility there is total absence of pride, and it is at the very farthest distance from anything like self-conceit. There is no self-praise in humility. Rather it has the disposition to praise others. *"In honour preferring one another"* (Romans 12:10). It is not given to self-exaltation. Humility does not love the uppermost seats and aspire to the high places. It is willing to take the lowliest seat and prefers those places where it will be unnoticed. The prayer of humility is after this fashion:

Never let the world break in,
Fix a mighty gulf between;
Keep me humble and unknown,
Prized and loved by God alone.

Humility does not have its eyes on self, but rather on God and others. It is poor in spirit, meek in behaviour, lowly in heart. *"With all lowliness and meekness, with longsuffering, forbearing one another in love"* (Ephesians 4:2).

The parable of the Pharisee and publican is a sermon in brief on humility and self-praise. The Pharisee, given over to self-conceit, wrapped up in himself, seeing only his own self-righteous deeds, catalogues his virtues before God, despising the poor publican who stands afar off. He exalts himself, gives himself over to self-praise, is self-centred, and goes away unjustified, condemned and rejected by God.

The publican sees no good in himself and is overwhelmed with self-depreciation. Far removed from anything which would take any credit for any good in himself, he does not presume to lift his eyes to heaven; but with downcast countenance he smites himself, crying out, *"God be merciful to me, a sinner"* (Luke 18:13).

E. M. BOUNDS

MARCH 26

A LONELY PATH

All the disciples forsook him, and fled.
MATTHEW 26:56

The possession of divine charity often necessitates walking a lonely path. Not merely in opposition and persecution but *alone* in it, and here again, Jesus who was the personification of divine love, stands out as our great example. He was emphatically alone and of the people there was none with Him. Even the disciples whom He had drawn nearest to Him, and to whom He had tried to communicate most of His thought and spirit, were so behind that He often had to reprove them, and to lament their obtuseness and want of sympathy. *"Ye shall leave me alone."*

In the greatness of His love He had to go forward into the darkness of Gethsemane. He was alone while they slept, and then he went all alone, through ribaldry, scorn and sarcasm, to the judgment hall. He stood alone before Pilate. On the cross he hung unaccompanied! - *alone.*

It was so with Paul. *"At my first answer no man stood with me,"* and it has commonly been so with those whom God has called to extraordinary paths. Must John have a revelation of things shortly to come to pass? He must go alone to the Isle of Patmos. Must Paul hear unspeakable words, not at that time lawful for a man to utter? He must go alone into the third heaven and not be allowed even to communicate what he saw and heard when he came down.

> *Jesus is standing in Pilate's hall,*
> *Friendless, forsaken, betrayed by all.*
> *Hearken! what meaneth the sudden call:*
> *What will you do with Jesus?*
>
> *Jesus, I give you my heart today!*
> *Jesus, I'll follow you all the way!*
> *Gladly obeying Him, will you say:*
> *"This will I do with Jesus."*

CATHERINE BOOTH

MARCH 27

JESUS CHRIST, MY RIGHTEOUSNESS

*They which receive abundance of grace and of the gift of righteousness
shall reign in life by one, Jesus Christ.*
ROMANS 5:17

One day, as I was passing in the field, and that too with some dashes on my conscience, fearing lest yet all was not right, suddenly this sentence fell upon my soul, *Thy righteousness is in heaven*; and me-thought withal, I saw, with the eyes of my soul, Jesus Christ at God's right hand ... So when I came home, I looked to see if I could find that sentence, *Thy righteousness is in heaven*, but could not find such a saying; wherefore my heart began to sink again; only that was brought to my remembrance, "He is made unto us of God wisdom, and righteousness, and sanctification and redemption"; by this word I saw the other sentence true. For by this Scripture I saw that the Man Christ Jesus ... is our righteousness and sanctification before God.

Jesus, my great High-Priest,
Offered His blood and died,
My guilty conscience seeks
No sacrifice beside;
His powerful blood did once atone,
And now it pleads before the throne.

JOHN BUNYAN

OUT OF THE PIG-STY

I will arise and go to my father, and will say unto him,
Father, I have sinned.
LUKE 15:18

When Jesus told the story of the Prodigal Son, He was giving our lost society a graphic picture of more than a wilful son or a backslidden man.

Years ago I spent time alone with God, in prayer and supplication, asking the Spirit of God to aid me in the comprehension of the parable of the Prodigal Son. I have relied upon the understanding which I believe God gave me.

I believe the Prodigal Son is God's clear-cut picture to us of the entire human race that went out to the pig-sty in Adam - and came back to the Father in Christ!

The most telling part of the parable is the fact that the errant son "came to himself" - and that speaks to us of the reality and necessity of repentance. He could repent and turn and seek forgiveness because he knew that his Father had not changed. He knew the character of his Father. Except for that knowledge, he could never have said: "I will arise and go to my Father!"

Brethren, all of us who have come back to God by faith in our Lord Jesus Christ have found, as did the prodigal, that the Father in heaven has not changed at all!

Vile and sinful though my heart may be,
Fully trusting, Lord, I come to Thee;
Thou hast power to cleanse and make me free;
I am coming home.

Precious blood of Jesus, may its flow
Cleanse from evil, wash me white as snow;
There is hope alone in Thee, I know;
I am coming home.

A. W. TOZER

THE DARKNESS DEEPENS

God is light, and in him is no darkness at all.
I JOHN 1:5

The Gospel has been preached for nearly two millenniums, but men and nations are devising more appalling and venomous means of destruction than ever. Dark counsels are inspiring the spirit of hate and greed among the peoples of the world. Ominous movements of a vile conspiracy are discernible through the shadows. An appalling proportion of the world's population is still in the darkness of heathendom, and even civilised lands are enshrouded in darkness. Many churches of Christendom, beautiful in architectural adornment, with all that music, refinement, and wealth can give them, are functioning in the gloom of a dead formality. Thousands of pulpits are enveloped in darkness. They never radiate light. "Death is in the pot." The light is extinguished. Tens of thousands of pews, perhaps regularly occupied, are destitute of spiritual light. The blind are leading the blind, and both are falling into the dark, muddy ditch. In spite of the advances of culture and civilisation, crime is admittedly on the increase. Dark lawlessness prevails. Sombre defiant fists are being shaken in the very face of God. Heavy shadows of infidelity have fallen upon Christendom with almost stupefying effect. "The whole world lieth in wickedness." It is fast ripening for the dark vials of divine judgment. There is no star to shine in the sodden sky. Such is the inevitable result of rebellion against the Most High, the Creator of the world.

Yet there is light in the world, though men and demons have nothing to do with it - except to try to put it out! Jesus said, "I am the Light," and where He is acknowledged in heart and life there the darkness is dispelled. Where Jesus is, there is glory. He brings peace into the restless heart. He brings joy into a world of sorrow; rest amid the turmoil; love instead of lust. Heaven will be all light, for Jesus reigns there. No speck of sin will ever mar its radiance, for God hates the damnable thing too much, and loves His people too well. Where Jesus is *not*, that is night.

REGINALD WALLIS

MARCH 30

JUST AS I AM

What must I do to be saved?
ACTS 16:30

Take what Christ offers you. "Lord, I accept Thee as my Saviour, I trust Thee with my soul," and as surely as God is in His sky above, you are a saved man or woman. "What things soever ye desire when ye pray, believe that ye receive them, and," says, God, "I will see that you have them." You say to a child, or your daughter or son, "When Christmas comes I'm going to give you a present," and the child has as good as got it, and says, "My father is going to give me a beautiful doll, or a wheelbarrow, or a cricket bat." You pledge yourself to keep your word. "What things soever ye desire when ye pray, believe that ye receive them, and ye shall have them." Take that for granted, and you will not be long on the road until in your heart you will know you have the grace of God and salvation.

Charlotte Elliot had been brought into the fellowship of the Church at Easter time. Her godly minister thought she was truly converted and that her soul rested on Christ. One day he was going past where she lived, and she was coming out of her house dressed for a ball and stepped into a carriage. The old man nearly dropped on seeing that, and he went quickly before the carriage door was closed, and said, "Charlotte, are you saved?" She banged the door and got away from the old man, but she did not get away from his question. Instead of dancing till daylight, she was home before midnight, and for a long week her pride was dying. At last she could stand it no more, and she started to seek the minister. As she was making her way to where he lived, she met him on the street, and she said, "I am delighted to see you. I was making my way to your home, and I have come for two things. First, I apologise to you for my rudeness." "That's all right, Charlotte; I understand it." "Sir, how am I to answer that question you asked me?" "Charlotte," he said, "just as you are, come to Christ." Just as she was she came to Christ, and sometime afterwards she wrote these beautiful words which have been the means of leading thousands to Him:-

> Just as I am - without one plea,
> But that Thy blood was shed for me,
> And that Thou bidd'st me come to Thee,
> O Lamb of God, I come.

W. P. NICHOLSON

MARCH 31

NEVER ALONE

And, lo, I am with you alway,
even unto the end of the world. Amen.
MATTHEW 28:20

Men without God suffer alone and die alone in times of war and in other circumstances of life. All alone!

But it can never be said that any true soldier of the Cross of Jesus Christ, no man or woman as missionary or messenger of the Truth has ever gone out to a ministry alone!

There have been many Christian martyrs - but not one of them was on that mission field alone. Jesus Christ keeps His promise of taking them by the hand and leading them triumphantly through to the world beyond.

We can sum it up by noting that Jesus Christ asks us only to surrender to His Lordship and obey His commands. When the Spirit of God deals with our young people about their own missionary responsibility, Christ assures them of His presence and power as they prepare to go: "All power is given unto Me! I am no longer in the grave. I will protect you. I will support you. I will go ahead of you. I will give you effectiveness for your witness. Go, therefore, and make disciples of all nations - I will never leave you nor forsake you!"

Fear not, I am with thee, O be not dismayed!
I am thy God, and will still give thee aid:
I'll strengthen thee, help thee, and cause thee to stand,
Upheld by My righteous, omnipotent hand.

A. W. TOZER

APRIL 1

JOY IN HEAVEN

And he spake this parable unto them ...
LUKE 15:3

These three wonderful stories which Jesus used, as recorded in the 15th chapter of St Luke's gospel, were specifically used by Him to teach two things: first, that God is seeking His own and wants to find His own; and second, that when His own have sense enough to come and confess their sin there is joy in heaven.

That is the great moving truth of the stories. You remember that when Jesus was receiving the publicans and sinners the Pharisees said: "This man receiveth sinners and eateth with them."

And Jesus said, that any man who would submit his life and soul and heart to the will of God, and turn from sin to God would be saved. That is the substance of these stories. When the sheep went astray a man went after it - the owner - and he sought it till he found it. When the silver went astray, a woman went after it - when the son went away, nobody went after him, because there is a difference between a sheep and a man; there is a difference between a piece of silver and the soul of a man that has to live for ever.

The sheep isn't responsible, or a piece of silver isn't responsible, but a man is. The man is a moral agent; he has a free will; he has a privilege of choice; he has a power to say "No" and the power to say "Yes." He may be lifted to heights ineffable or he can descend to depths unutterable.

When the sheep went away, the owner went after it. When the silver got lost the woman searched for it. Jesus told the story, remember. He told it perfectly, and He is teaching that repentance of the New Testament kind is such a beautiful thing that when a man does repent there is joy in heaven.

GIPSY SMITH

SHINE ON US

Out of Zion ... God hath shined.
PSALM 50:2

I greet Thee, who my sure Redeemer art,
My only Trust and Saviour of my heart,
Who pain didst undergo for my poor sake;
I pray Thee from our hearts all cares to take.

Thou art the King of mercy and of grace,
Reigning omnipotent in every place:
So come, O King, and our whole being sway;
Shine on us with the light of Thy pure day.

Thou art the life, by which alone we live,
And all our substance and our strength receive;
Sustain us by Thy faith and by Thy power,
And give us strength in every trying hour.

Thou hast the true and perfect gentleness,
No harshness hast Thou and no bitterness:
O grant to us the grace we find in Thee,
That we may dwell in perfect unity.

Our hope is in no other save in Thee;
Our faith is built upon Thy promise free;
Lord, give us peace, and make us calm and sure,
That in Thy strength we evermore endure.

JOHN CALVIN

RENDER AN ACCOUNTING

Every one of us shall give account of himself to God.
ROMANS 14:12

There are some in this world who are debtors to the people, and the time comes when each of them must render an accounting.

Let it still be remembered that the Scriptures declare, "To him that knoweth to do good, and doeth it not, to him it is sin." So, some people are bigger sinners than they appear. The amount of my light determines the amount of my responsibility and the amount of my sin, if the light be not lived up to. If people sin in the face of light which shows them the right way, then their condemnation is all the greater.

The debtors of the people are its leaders. I wonder what would happen if the strongest men and women in the city would set the example of Christian living. I mean those strongest in an educational, financial and social way; those who are looked upon as the prominent ones in the city. If those will only conduct their lives with a clear conscience so they can take their stand and lead also in the spiritual world, what would happen?

No one can estimate the good that would be done if these pivotal people consecrated themselves to the service of Jesus Christ. After all, culture, money and breeding do count - people do look up to those fortunate enough to possess these qualities. And the holders should feel their responsibility to those less fortunate. For the God of love who sits on the throne is also the God of justice.

Some day He's coming back to this old earth, and Jesus is coming, coming back to claim His own. He will ask what the man of culture did with his learning, what the man of wealth did with his riches, what those of social position did with their opportunities and powers. We all have to render an accounting.

GIPSY SMITH

THE HEAVENLY CITY

He looked for a city which hath foundations, whose builder and maker is God.
HEBREWS 11:10

A man can be in the land of promise, and yet not feel at home. "He sojourned in the land of promise as in a strange country." But why these feelings of the vagrant? Why this sense of homelessness in the promised land? In the verse which precedes the text we are told that in the land of promise Abraham dwelt in tents; and the shifting tenure made the country appear perpetually strange. Tent-life gave him the consciousness of a changing and uncertain possession. He pitched his tent here today, and for a few short hours he tasted the delights of possession. But on the morrow the tents had to be moved again, and there rushed back into the patriarch's soul all the restless uncertainties of a vagrant. His inheritance was shifting, movable, and transient. He was possessor only by spasms. There was no rich, unbroken, continuous life, to create in his soul the settledness of home.

And yet, what was the voice which Abraham had heard? "To thee will I give the land." That was the promise, and Abraham knew that the promises of the Lord God are not honeycombed with uncertainties. He knew that the promised lands and possessions of the Lord God are not to be held on precarious tenure. If tent-life gave him only a shifting possession, then he knew that the promise was not yet fully matured, and "he looked for a city," a city "which hath foundations, whose builder and maker is God."

We must emphasise the contrast between the city and the tent. The patriarch lived in the tent: he looked for the city. The tent has no foundations. Its holdfasts are only for transient usage. They are made to be easily changed. The city has foundations. It is stable, fixed, and permanent. The tent is the symbol of vagrancy: the city is the symbol of home. The tent is associated with the evanescent and changing: the city is associated with the continuous and the abiding. Abraham dwelt in the land of promise in tents, but "he looked for a city". He longed for settledness. He yearned for the abiding.

J.H. JOWETT

APRIL 5

HE KEEPS THE KEY

We have thought of thy lovingkindness, O God.
PSALM 48:9

C an we not look back and see that some of the hours that throbbed with agony were the most blessed of all the hours of life? ... That affliction was my key to strength, that grave the prelude to resurrection power, that disappointment my finding His appointment, that lonely hour the one in which I found *Jesus only.*

Is there some problem in your life to solve,
Some passage seeming full of mystery?
God knows, Who brings the hidden things to light.
He keeps the key.

Is there some door closed by the Father's hand
Which widely opened you had hoped to see?
Trust God and wait - for when He shuts the door,
He keeps the key.

Is there some earnest prayer unanswered yet,
Or answered not as you had thought 'twould be!
God will make clear His purpose by-and-by.
He keeps the key.

Have patience with your God, your patient God,
All wise, all knowing, no longer tarrier He,
And of the door of all thy future life
He keeps the key.

Unfailing comfort, sweet and blessed rest,
To know every door He keeps the key.
That He at last when just He sees 'tis best,
Will give it thee.

G. CAMPBELL MORGAN

THE WRONG CHOICE

And Lot lifted up his eyes.
GENESIS 13:10

Lot's mistake and the consequent loss of his wife and possessions and family followed when he pitched his tent toward Sodom. You remember that interview with his uncle Abraham. They were living together and their stock and herdsmen were becoming too many to live together peaceably. Lot was the younger of the two and should have revered the opinions of his old uncle. Abraham said unto him, "Choose." He gave him the choice of the watering-places and fertile grazing fields. Why didn't Lot say to his uncle, as he should have said, "Uncle, give me your advice; you are an older man than I"? But he didn't do that - he settled it himself. He looked toward the well-watered plains of Sodom and selfishly chose them. He pitched his tent toward Sodom, and in that way lay danger.

Don't pitch your tent toward Sodom - the next step you will be in Sodom. No man who professes to believe in Jesus Christ can go into Sodom without one of two things happening: either you must make Sodom better or Sodom will make you worse. You can settle that once and for ever. Either you will uplift Sodom or Sodom will lead you far from the path in which you can walk and talk with Jesus.

And to begin with, if you are a Christian, you have no right in Sodom unless you go there to preach the gospel - unless you go there to preach and interpret God's mind and word.

But that was not Lot's purpose in going to Sodom. He went there because his heart was there. He liked the way of the people of Sodom. He liked the glitter and the flash and the sparkle of society there. The Bible calls Lot righteous later on. If he is called righteous, it is because when God forgives a sin, he does it wholly and completely. Lot showed very little of virtue in Sodom. He did not hurt himself trying to make it a better city.

If you take your family to the Devil, do not be surprised if the Devil damns them. Don't tear God from the hearts of your children and be surprised some day if the Devil gets the vacant place.

GIPSY SMITH

APRIL 7

THE WALK TO EMMAUS

Jesus Himself drew near, and went with them.
LUKE 24:15

It happened, on a solemn eventide,
Soon after He that was our surety died,
Two bosom friends, each pensively inclined,
The scene of all those sorrows left behind,
Sought their own village, busied, as they went,
In musings worthy of the great event:
They spake of Him they loved, of Him whose life,
Though blameless had incurred perpetual strife,
Whose deeds had left, in spite of hostile arts,
A deep memorial graven on their hearts.
The recollection, like a vein of ore,
The farther traced, enriched them still the more;
They thought Him, and they justly thought Him, one
Sent to do more than He appeared t'have done;
To exalt a people, and to place them high,
Above all else, and wondered He should die.
Ere yet they brought their journey to an end,
A Stranger joined them, courteous as a friend,
And asked them, with a kind engaging air,
What their affliction was, and begged a share.
Informed, He gathered up the broken thread,
And, truth and wisdom gracing all He said,
Explained, illustrated, and searched so well
The tender theme on which they chose to dwell,
That reaching home, "The night," they said, "is near,
We must not now be parted, sojourn here."
The new acquaintance soon became a guest,
And, made so welcome at their simple feast,
He blessed the bread, but vanished at the word,
And left them both exclaiming, "Twas the Lord!
Did not our hearts feel all He deigned to say,
Did they not burn within us by the way?"

WILLIAM COWPER

APRIL 8

PEACE MOVEMENT

The mighty God, The everlasting Father, The Prince of Peace.
ISAIAH 9:6

Whichever way one turns, unrest, confusion, chaos and wild passions possess the breasts of multitudes. Jealousy, hatred and envy are reigning supreme in the minds of men.

We read in the Scriptures of one person who had seven devils in her, and one man had enough in him to drown two thousand hogs when they were cast out of him. Nations are like that, and they can be saved only by casting out the devils.

As we look across the face of the globe today and see the conflict as manifested, what is there beneath all that we don't see? What about the inward rumblings that only ears divine listen to, and the seething unrest which the human eye cannot detect?

But, ah, every honest, intelligent man knows just a little about it if he will look within his own poor, distracted heart.

And as I sit here this morning and think of these things, I cannot help but ask who is sufficient to the task? Is there anybody that can step in amidst the dark confusion and world misery and still its storm and hush its tempest?

And my heart leaps up with a great bound, saying "Yes, Jesus, who stood on the Galilean lake and lifted His hand amidst the tempest and said, 'Peace be still,' and the wind and waves obeyed and crept away in silence to lick His feet."

If the world would but invite Him to enter its life and its sorrows, He would come and point a way out. He would bring peace because He would still the storm of sin. That's the cause of all the confusion and strife.

Wherever Jesus is listened to, obeyed and enthroned, men become as brothers. What is true of individuals, homes, hamlets and cities, is true also of nations and would be true of the world, and it only needs to be given a trial.

Peace doesn't follow the munition train; it follows in the wake of the Prince of Peace. That's the way to brotherhood.

GIPSY SMITH

THE RENEWED LIFE

Only let your conversation (citizenship) be as it becometh the gospel of Christ.
PHILIPPIANS 1:27

L et your citizenship be worthy of the gospel of Christ." That is the true relationship of Church and State. The Church is to bring into the State an ideal citizenship. The Church is to control the State by the all-pervasive influence of a lofty and distinctive character. Her dominance is to be the dominance of a compact, irresistible, superior life. Ye Christians of Philippi, living there at the crowded meeting-place of nations, surrounded by the pomp of a proud empire, experiencing the breathless rush of material ambition, exposed to all the corruptions which fasten upon a severe militarism and a bloated commercialism; let your influence pervade the huge sickly mass like currents of uncontaminated air; bring into it a life mighty because of its separateness; "let your citizenship be as becometh the gospel of Christ."

"As becometh the gospel of Christ." There is a central pith in the gospel of Christ which is also the central pith of an ideal citizenship. The heart of the one is the heart of the other. The proposition is this, that if we take the gospel of Christ, and dig away to its core, and if we take an ideal citizenship, and dig away to its core, we shall arrive at corresponding treasure, at the same essential and eternal wealth.

Now what is the heart of the gospel of Christ? If we can grip that, we shall have discovered what ought to be the secret energy of all Christian citizenship. Take the life that stretches between Bethlehem and Olivet: what is its consistent and all-inclusive revelation? Mass together the gloomy desolations of Gethsemane, and the appalling abandonments of Calvary; what is the great pulsing purpose that beats within the gloom? It is this - a Saviour seeking the justification of His brethren by the offering of Himself. That is the heart of the gospel - the life and righteousness of all men sought through the unspeakable sacrifice of One.

J.H. JOWETT

APRIL 10

OUR HOPE

Hope thou in God, for I shall yet praise Him.
PSALM 42:5

We live in the springtime of spiritual things, because Jesus died and rose. The summer and the autumn are not yet. The sunlit glory and golden fruitage are our hope, but they come through this awakening of the spring. Our winter is over. It has its place and value, that long, dreary stretch of the centuries, in which for the earth at least the only colour was that of prophetic pictures and the singing of that constrained and imprisoned psalmist.

I have caught a glimpse of glory
Never seen by mortal eyes,
Just beyond the blue horizon
Of evening's transient skies;
But the ear of hope has heard it
And the eye of faith can see
Sound and sign of heaven's nearness
Just beyond mortality.

I have caught a glimpse of glory,
Of that bright eternal day,
When the mists of Time have lifted
And we lay aside his clay;
Then shall be the consummation
Of our longing and desire,
For we'll sing the Song of Ages
In the resurrection choir!

I have caught a glimpse of glory
Just beyond the brink of Time,
And I travel toward the sunrise
Of a better land and clime.
Soon I'll trade this earth for heaven
And inside some golden door
I shall greet the ones I've cherished
Safe with Jesus evermore.

G. CAMPBELL MORGAN

APRIL 11

FROM THE CROSS TO THE THRONE

And said, Behold, I see the heavens opened, and the Son of man
standing on the right hand of God.
ACTS 7:56

When believing souls seek for peace and joy in believing, they do very generally confine their view to Christ upon the earth. They remember Him as the good Shepherd seeking the lost sheep, they look to Him sitting by the well of Samaria, they remember Him saying to the sick of the palsy: "Be of good cheer, thy sins are forgiven thee." But they too seldom think of looking where Stephen looked - to where Jesus is now; at the right hand of God.

Now, my friends, remember, if you would be whole Christians, you must look to a whole Christ. You must lift your eye from the cross to the throne, and you will find Him the same Saviour in all, "the same yesterday, and today, and for ever." I have already observed, that wherever Christ is mentioned as being at the right hand of God, He is spoken of as seated there upon His throne; here, and here only, are we told that He is standing. In other places He is described as enjoying His glory, and entered into His rest; but here He is described as risen from His throne, and standing at the right hand of God.

He rises to intercede: "He is able to save to the uttermost all that come unto God by Him, seeing He ever liveth to make intercession for them."

How often would a believer be a castaway, if it were not for the great Intercessor! How often faith fails! - "flesh and heart faint and fail"; but see here, Christ never fails. On the death-bed, often the mind is taken off the Saviour, by pains of body and distress of mind; but, oh! happy soul that has truly accepted Christ. See here, He rises from His throne to pray for you, when you cannot pray for yourself. Look up to Him with the eye of faith, and cry: "Lord Jesus, receive my spirit."

ROBERT MURRAY McCHEYNE

APRIL 12

READ, PONDER AND DIGEST

Order my steps in thy word.
PSALM 119:133

B rush the dust off your Bible. Half the sorrows of the world come about because people don't read their Bible. They simply don't know and can't understand the great truths it contains.

Everyone likes to hear a secret, and the divine confidences and revelations are fascinating from every point of view.

Jesus once said to the people, "Search the Scriptures; for in them ye think ye have eternal life: and they are they which testify of Me."

In that wonderful walk which He had with His disciples to Emmaus, after the resurrection, He said, after they had expressed their unbelief: "Oh, fools, and slow of heart to believe all that the prophets have spoken: ought not Christ to have suffered these things, and to enter into His glory?" The next verse tells us much: "And beginning at Moses and all the prophets, He expounded unto them in all the Scriptures, the things concerning Himself."

These two men, after it was all over, said: "Did not our hearts burn within us while He talked with us by the way?" Now, then, all He had done was to make the Scriptures live.

Many really good people, anxious to do what's right, fall into all kinds of blunders, and some are led away by popular heresies which are easy to the flesh, simply because they don't read and ponder and inwardly digest the living, abiding words of the Lord.

If we only will read our Bible and listen to its echo within us, we will not fail to bow to righteousness, take off our hats to truth, and, like Moses, our shoes as well, feeling that we are standing on holy ground.

GIPSY SMITH

APRIL 13

THE JOURNEY HOME

Glorious things are spoken of thee, O city of God.
PSALM 87:3

Every one that comes to Christ has a journey to perform in this world. Some have a long, and some a short one. It is through a wilderness. Still Christ prays that at the end you may be with Him. Every one that comes to Christ hath his twelve hours to fill up for Christ. "I must work the works of Him that sent me, while it is day." But when that is done, Christ prays that you may be with Him. He means that you shall come to His Father's house with Him ... You are never very intimate with a person till you see them in their own house - till you know them at home. This is what Christ wants with us - that we shall come to be with Him, at His own home. He wants us to come to the same Father's bosom with Him: "I ascend to My Father and your Father."

What no human eye hath seen,
What no mortal ear hath heard,
What on thought hath never been
In its noblest flights conferred -
This hath God prepared in store
For His people evermore!

Jesus reigns, the life, the sun
Of that wondrous world above;
All the clouds and storms are gone,
All is light, and love.
All the shadows melt away
In the blaze of perfect day!

ROBERT MURRAY McCHEYNE

ENOUGH TO MAKE AN
UNDERTAKER WEEP

*For ye shall go out with joy ... the mountains and the hills shall break
forth before you into singing.*
ISAIAH 55:12

Religion is never a killjoy. All God means to kill is the ugly, the mean, and the sinful. Yet many think the sadder they are, the safer. They go around with faces as long as a wet week. But sanctimoniousness is not sanctity.

There is more religion in a hearty laugh than in a grouch. Let there be more joy and less jaw.

I remember seeing in a religious weekly in England a few years ago an advertisement by a lady and a gentleman who were going to take a trip around the world. She wanted to engage a companion, "Christian woman preferred, but she must be joyful."

Can you imagine anything more ironical than this - and the sadness of it? One chief characteristic of a true Christian is happiness, smiles, laughter. "The joy of the Lord is your strength," and "Then was our mouth filled with laughter."

There are far too many briars and thorns in this life. People don't draw close enough together for fear of getting scratched. What religion is meant to do is to take the scratch out of us. Less briars, more roses, more violets, lilies of the valley and perfume of the beauty of the Lord.

I say this in spite of the fact that I know that there is no real Christian life without its sorrows and its suffering. Through my life God means to bring refreshment and inspiration to those about me. After the storm we see the rainbow of hope, and He takes the sorrow out of the heart by removing the curse of sin.

Religion was never meant to make an undertaker weep. Let there be joy!

GIPSY SMITH

THIS STRANGE SWEET CALM

The Lord will bless his people with peace.
PSALM 29:11

Is this the grace of God, this strange sweet calm?
The weary day is at its zenith still,
Yet 'tis as if beside some cool, clear rill,
Through shadowy stillness rose an evening psalm,
And all the noise of life were hushed away,
And tranquil gladness reigned with gently soothing sway.

It was not so just now. I turned aside
With aching head, and heart most sorely bowed;
Around me cares and griefs in crushing crowd,
While inly rose the sense, in swelling tide,
Of weakness, insufficiency, and sin,
And fear, and gloom, and doubt in mighty flood rolled in.

That rushing flood I had no power to meet,
Nor power to flee: my present, future, past,
Myself, my sorrow, and my sin I cast
In utter helplessness at Jesu's feet:
Then bent me to the storm, if such His will.
He saw the winds and waves, and whispered,
"Peace, be still!"

And there was calm! O Saviour, I have proved
That thou to help and save art really near:
How else this quiet rest from grief and fear
And all distress? The cross is not removed,
I must go forth to bear it as before,
But, leaning on thine arm, I dread its weight no more.

FRANCES RIDLEY HAVERGAL

APRIL 16

THE SUPREMACY OF DUTY

At even my wife died; and I did in the morning as I was commanded.
EZEKIEL 24:18

These words in themselves constitute a powerful sermon. The text carries its interpretation upon the surface. It is full of practical and pathetic suggestions. "At even my wife died." The light of the home went out. Darkness blurred over the face of every familiar thing. The trusted companion, who had shared all the changes of the ever-changing way, was taken from my side. The light of our fellowship was suddenly extinguished, as by some mysterious hand stretched forth from the unseen. I lost "the desire of mine eyes." I was alone. "At even my wife died … and in the morning -" Aye, what about the next morning, when the light broke almost obtrusively upon a world which had changed into a cemetery containing only one grave? "In the morning I did as I was commanded." And what was the command? Perhaps it was something peculiarly appropriate and soothing, something that would not jar upon the most sensitive grief. What was the command? It was a command to go out and awake a morally torpid and filthy city. The prophet had to bestir himself, and proclaim divine indignation and judgment against a city whose life, both civic and personal, was like foul and poisonous scum. "Woe to the bloody city … in thy filthiness is lewdness … according to thy doings shalt thou be judged, saith the Lord God."

That was the prophet's message. The command had been laid upon him in the days before his bereavement. When his home-life was a source of inspiring fellowship, he had laboured to discharge the burdensome task. In the evening-time he had turned to his home, just as weary, dust-choked pilgrims turn to a bath; and, immersed in the sweet sanctities of wedded life, he had found such restoration of soul as fitted him for the renewed labour of the morrow. But "at even my wife died" The home was no longer a refreshing bath, but part of the dusty road; no longer an oasis, but a repetition of the wilderness.

J.H. JOWETT

CONQUERED BY A CONQUEROR

Keep thyself pure.
I TIMOTHY 5:22

We constantly attempt to comfort our hearts with the idea that we can manipulate the results of sin so as to make then less hard to bear, and then have to prove through long and bitter experience that it is not so. There is only one moment in which we can save ourselves from sin, that is before we commit it.

What now, my Soul, and hast thou sinned again,
Thou deeply sinful, desperately wicked Soul?
Wilt thou of sinning never have an end?
Wilt never let thy Maker make thee whole?
Thou seemest bound by strong iniquity,
When thou should'st be, once and for ever, free!

And yet, O sinful Soul, thou knowest well,
That I have struggled hard against thy reign;
As often as I've sinned, I have resolved,
That thou should'st never rule o'er me again;
Alas, deceitful Soul, I did not see,
That, spite of struggle, thou could'st master me!

What can I do, my Soul? Thou art myself;
I cannot 'scape thy presence, nor thy power;
Turn where I will, I feel thy close embrace;
Thou pressest hard upon me, hour by hour;-
Oh, that a Master Man might rise in me;
Then, I should be the man I long to be!

G. CAMPBELL MORGAN

THE TENDER YEARS

Train up a child in the way he should go.
PROVERBS 22:6

It has been said that the hand that rocks the cradle rules the world. Next to the mother in influence comes the school teacher, whose task it is to train the mind of the future generation.

The teacher has the boy and girl under his or her influence in the formative, tender years, the impressionable years, when seeds are sown that bring forth the harvest. What the harvest will be, whether good or ill, depends on the home and the school.

What the children are taught in the first ten years of their school life largely forms the foundation on which they build their future. The structure can never stand unless it is built on a solid foundation. If I could have the mothers and fathers and teachers loyal to Christ for the next twenty years in English-speaking lands, we could capture the planet for the Lord Christ.

It is not enough simply to teach boys and girls to read, write, add figures and master science, art, literature and languages. They must be taught, like Timothy, the Scriptures, and learn to see God's view of men and things, and to seek first the kingdom of God and His righteousness. This is essential if boys and girls are to grow up into a generation of pure, strong, noble, clean, honest, God-fearing men and women.

Some of the biggest scoundrels I have known have been university men and women. The head may be trained and may be filled with all sorts of good things, while the heart is starved because it is estranged from God.

The truest culture is that which takes in mind, body and soul. That is the programme of Jesus Christ.

GIPSY SMITH

TRUE LOVE

Now Jesus loved Martha, and her sister, and Lazarus.
JOHN 11:5

Then He loved three souls of very different temperaments. To love all three is to love natures which are greatly contrasted in their constitutions. That is the characteristic of true love. It is comprehensive and inclusive. There is a species of love which makes a fastidious choice of its objects. It picks out a few of a particular mental colour, or of a certain moral temperament, and with rigid exclusiveness it confines its communion to these. But here is the love of the Master lavishing itself upon these very different souls, and in each of these finding joy and satisfaction. Jesus does not want all His loved ones to be of one mould and colour. He will not remove our individuality. He loves, "Martha, her sister, and Lazarus."

"Jesus loved Martha." Martha is our Biblical example of a practical woman. "Martha served." In that phrase is enshrined her character. Martha was ever eager for practical deeds, and her interpretation of "practical" was a ready ministering to the needs of the flesh.

Martha was no expert in abstract discussions. But she was great when anybody was sick and in want of immediate help, great at lifting an invalid without increasing the pain, great at sitting up through a long night without ever looking tired.

Martha is typical of a vast multitude of women who are at home in a crisis, who are calm in some terrible emergency, who are strong and self-controlled at a death bed. It is to Martha's gentle, practical hands that we must all come at last, and I am glad that she stands enrolled among the loved ones, as the chosen companions of the Lord. "Jesus loved Martha."

J.H. JOWETT

OUR LASTING LEGACY

Establish thou the work of our hands.
PSALM 90:17

My name, and my place, and my tomb all forgotten,
The brief race of time well and patiently run,
So let me pass away, peacefully, silently,
Only remembered by what I have done.

Gladly away from this toil would I hasten,
Up to the crown that for me has been won;
Unthought of by man in rewards or in praises, -
Only remembered by what I have done.

Up and away, like the odours of sunset,
That sweeten the twilight as darkness comes on;
So be my life - a thing felt but not noticed,
And I but remembered by what I have done.

Yes, like the fragrance that wanders in freshness,
When the flowers that it came from are closed up and gone -
So would I be to this world's weary dwellers,
Only remembered by what I have done.

Needs there be praise of the love-written record,
The name and the epitaph graved on the stone?
The things we have lived for - let them be our story,
We, our selves, but remembered by what we have done.

I need not be missed, if my life has been bearing,
(As its summer and autumn moved silently on)
The bloom, and the fruit, and the seed of its season;
I shall still be remembered by what I have done.

HORATIUS BONAR

SPIRITUAL BEAUTY

Moses wist not that ... his face shone.
EXODUS 34:29

Spiritual beauty is loveliest when it is unconsciously possessed. Self-conscious virtue is lean and uncrowned. Moses has been closeted with God. The glory of the Lord has been poured upon him, bathing him in unearthly brightness, so that when he returns to the mountain-base his countenance shines like the light. The same transformation is effected every day, and by the same means. Spiritual communion alters the fashion of the countenance. The supreme beauty of a face is its light, and spirituality makes "a face illumined". The power of a beautiful spirit makes many a plain face lovely. The face of Moses was transfigured by the glory of the Eternal.

But "Moses wist not that his face shone". That is the supreme height of spiritual loveliness; to be lovely, and not to know it. Surely this is a lesson we all need to learn. Virtue is so apt to become self-conscious, and so to lose its glow. Take the grace of humility. Humility is very beautiful when we see it unimpaired. It is exquisite with the loveliness of Christ. But there is a self-conscious humility which is only a very subtle species of pride. It is possible to boast of our humility. There are men and women whose only source of pride appears to be their modesty. How often we meet with men who, when requested to do some service, immediately hoist the flag of their humility, and declare that they are of the humble sort, and prefer to keep in the shade! Yes, but humility takes the lowest place, and does not know that her face shines. Pride can take the lowest place, and find her delight in the thought of her presumably shining face. Self-consciousness always tends to sour humility, and pervert it into pride. "Moses wist not that his face shone."

J.H. JOWETT

SAFE PATHS

I the Lord thy God will hold thy right hand, saying unto thee,
Fear not; I will help thee.
ISAIAH 41:13

God is not making an experiment with you. We are not pawns upon a chess board, moving which God may win or lose. Every moment is arranged. I did not know what was to come to pass today, but God was in this day before I came into it. Doing what? Choosing the place for me, making arrangements, controlling everything.

God bade me go when I would stay
('Twas cool within the wood);
I did not know the reason why.
I heard a boulder crashing by
Across the pathway where I stood.

He bade me stay when I would go;
"Thy will be done," I said.
They found one day at early dawn,
Across the way I would have gone,
A serpent with a mangled head.

No more I ask the reason why,
Although I may not see
The path ahead, His way I go;
For tho' I know not, He doth know,
And He will choose safe paths for me.

G. CAMPBELL MORGAN

COME

And the Spirit and the bride say, Come. And let him that heareth say, Come.
And let him that is athirst come.
REVELATION 22:17

There is a garden in the first chapter of the Bible, and it was lost. But you get a bigger one in the last. You get a bit of a trickle of a stream in the first book, but you have a mighty river in the last chapter. You get fruit and a tree in the first garden, but in the last you have a tree whose leaves are for the healing of the nations. There is a great deal more in the last, in Jesus Christ, than was ever lost in the first.

"And they shall see His face; and His name shall be in their foreheads."

I wonder if you carry His name in your forehead. I wonder if your face shows that you live the life of a Christian. I wonder if the people who know you say of you, "She is a Christian woman." "He is a Christian man." "She is a saint." "He is a saint." "That is a God-like man." "That is a God-like woman." They stand for the things of God and "His name shall be in their foreheads."

"I am the offspring of David, and the bright and morning star." If He had only said that, we wouldn't know how to reach Him, but He said, "I am the offspring of David."

You have seen an old tree cut down clear to the roots, and then have seen grow up from it little tender shoots. "I am the root and offspring of David." And you can approach God, the Infinite, through the root and offspring of David - Jesus. God has stooped to your need and mine by making it possible to know Him through His Son, Christ, and when Jesus saw that His disciples were overcome with the mystery of that thought, when He saw it was more than they could bear, He said, "He that hath seen Me hath seen the Father."

In coming to Jesus, you come to God. In understanding Jesus, we understand God. We only understand God through Jesus. No man can come to the Father, except through the Son.

GIPSY SMITH

SPIRITUAL CHECK-UP

Examine yourselves, whether ye be in the faith; prove your own selves.
2 CORINTHIANS 13:5

Take some time for recollection, and ask your own conscience, seriously, how matters stand between the blessed God and your soul? Whether they are as they once were, and as you could wish them to be, if you saw your life just drawing to a period, and were to pass immediately into the eternal state?

Once serious thought of eternity shames a thousand vain excuses, with which, in the forgetfulness of it, we are ready to delude our own souls. And when you feel that secret misgiving of heart, which will naturally arise on this occasion, do not endeavour to palliate the matter, and to find out slight and artful coverings for what you cannot forbear secretly condemning, but honestly fall under the conviction, and be humbled for it.

Are you walking daily by the Saviour's side?
Are you washed in the blood of the Lamb?
Do you rest each moment in the Crucified?
Are you washed in the blood of the Lamb?

PHILIP DODDRIDGE

JUST RECOMPENSE

With what measure ye mete, it shall be measured to you again.
MATTHEW 7:2

These words are usually interpreted in their application to the relationship which we sustain to others. If we are severe in our judgments, the same measure of severity shall be visited upon us. If our judgments are large in long-suffering and forbearance, the same measure of long-suffering and forbearance shall be meted to us. If our criticism of others be directed to the exposure of their faults, the same measure of searching light shall be applied to the exposure of our faults. If we are only strictly just, strict justice shall be measured out to us. If we are merciful, mercy shall flow out towards us. "With what measure ye mete, it shall be measured to you again."

Such is the common interpretation, an interpretation strictly in accordance with the whole tenor and teaching of our Master's life. But the words enshrine a principle to which our Lord gave other and varied applications; and some of these applications are perhaps too commonly ignored. Let us glance at one or two.

"Unto you that hear shall more be given." The measure of your hearing shall be the measure of your listening. The more you listen the more you shall hear. The measure of your attentions shall determine the measure of the revelation. "With what measure ye mete, it shall be measured to you again." That is a very vital and momentous application of this great principle. If you want to hear the voice of God, listen! The voice will grow clearer and clearer as your hearing becomes more earnest and intense. Listen to God's voice in conscience, and more and more pronounced and definite shall be its guidance. Do not listen much to conscience, and conscience will say less and less to you, until perhaps some day the hall where it ought to thunder shall be as silent as the tomb.

J.H. JOWETT

HAND-PICKED FRUIT

But ye shall receive power, after that the Holy Ghost is come upon you:
and ye shall be witnesses unto me.
ACTS 1:8

I wonder how much personal work you have done for Jesus Christ? I pause that you may put the question intelligently to your own heart. How many people have you tried honestly, definitely tried to bring to the Lord Jesus?

Because you know the world is not going to be saved by big preachers. It is going to be saved by personal testimony, by the power of the grace of Christ in the individual heart.

Jesus said, "Ye shall be witnesses unto me." And what God wants you to do is to be a witness bearer. If you really love Him, you won't let any one do or say anything against Him in your presence without a gentle, tender rebuke. And if you will keep it up, they will feel the smart of the insult they offer Jesus Christ.

I have been a personal worker all my life. I believe in the public declaration of religion, but I am a profound believer in personal work. Personal work results in hand-picked fruit and it fetches more in the market.

It is easier to preach a sermon to 500 or 1000 or 5000 than to get down and talk to one person about spiritual things. That is where your test comes in. That is where your real spiritual life comes out.

You know Peter was the great preacher of Pentecost. Peter and John had been through Pentecost in the morning and they were going to prayer-meeting in the evening. They saw a beggar at the gate of the Temple. They had preached to the multitude, out of which 3000 were converted. The men who are willing to sit down and help one soul, the women who are willing to help one soul, are the ones that God can trust with the multitude.

Peter and John were on their way to the Temple when they saw the beggar. They said, "Look on us, look on us." And the beggar looked on them and began to expect something. And the world is looking to you - it expects something from you. They see you going to church and coming from church, but do you ever stop and speak to them?

GIPSY SMITH

A PROMISE FOR THE SAVIOUR

I ... will hold thine hand, and will keep thee ...
ISAIAH 42:6

The figure here seems taken from a father and his little child. When a little child has to go over some very rough road, or travel in the darkness, or to wade through some deep waters, he says to his father, "I fear I shall be lost; I shall not be able to go though." "Nay, do not fear," the father answers: "I will hold thine hand; I will keep thee." Such are the words of the Father to His dear Son. I would not have dared to have imagined them, if I had not found them in the Bible.

When God called His Son to the work, it could not but be a fearful work in His eyes. Christ knew well the infinite number of men's sins; for He is the searcher of hearts and trier of reins. He knew also the infinite weight of God's anger against these sins; He saw the dark clouds of infinite vengeance that were ready to burst over the heads of sinners. He saw the infinite deluge of eternal wrath that was to drown for ever the guilty world. And, oh! how dreadful His Father's anger was in His eyes; for He had known nothing but His infinite love from all eternity. Oh! how could He bear to lie down under that wrath? How could He bear to exchange the smile of His Father's love for the dark frown of His Father's anger? How could He bear, for the sake of vile sinners to exchange the caresses of that God who is love, for the piercings and bruisings of His almighty hand? Surely the very thought would be agony. God here comforts His Son under the view: Yon sea of wrath is deep, its waves are dreadful; but "I will hold thine hand; I will keep thee."

ROBERT MURRAY McCHEYNE

YOU NEED MORE THAN MONEY

In that last day, that great day of the feast, Jesus stood and cried, saying, If any man thirst, let him come unto me, and drink.
JOHN 7:37

Jesus knew exactly how to put His finger on human needs. He knew of the need of that great multitude as they had come and gone, and were there on the last day of the feast, when probably the biggest crowd had gathered and the feast had failed to satisfy, and He knew that they were still thirsty. And He said, "If any man thirst, let him come to Me and drink."

And you know - you who are present this morning are like the multitudes at the feast, showing evidences of thirst. And the mad rush that has taken hold of the people of today, the everlasting search for something that will satisfy, shows a deep hunger.

Earthly things cannot satisfy you. The Bible and the Lord God Almighty have the things that will. Why spend money for that which is not bread?

Earthly waters are brackish. Earthly waters do not slake the thirst of the immortal soul. The Devil is a great artist and he paints beautiful pictures, but they are mirages of the desert. When you think you have them, they turn to the sand of the desert.

And you need more than money. You need more than a beautiful home. You need more than an automobile in which to ride. You need more than jewellery. You need more than real estate and a balance in the bank.

You are not a dummy to be dressed up and put in a shop window. You are built of the materials out of which God builds eternity. You are not a doll. You are a soul. You need more than food and raiment and home and a seat in the theatre. Man doesn't live by bread alone, but by every word that proceeds out of the mouth of God.

GIPSY SMITH

EXPECT AFFLICTIONS

Think it not strange concerning the fiery trial which is to try you.
1 PETER 4:12

Since "man is born unto trouble as the sparks fly upward," (Job 5:7) and Adam has entailed on all his race the sad inheritance of calamity in their way to death, it will certainly be prudent and necessary, that we should all expect to meet with trials and afflictions; and that you, reader, whoever you are, should be endeavouring to gird on your armour, and put yourself in a posture to encounter those trials which will fall to your lot as a man and a Christian.

Prepare yourself to receive your afflictions, and to endure them, in a manner agreeable to both these characters ... When at length your turn comes, as it certainly will from the first hour in which an affliction seizes you, realise to yourself the hand of God in it.

He that formed me in the womb,
He shall guide me to the tomb;
All my times shall ever be
Ordered by His own decree.

PHILIP DODDRIDGE

APRIL 30

THE QUICKENING TOUCH

As ... a ...wind
ACTS 2:2

What is the Holy Ghost? How does He come? What is the nature of His influence upon the life of man? No one can put into speech an immediate interpretation of the Spirit's work. We can search for parable and symbol. We can call in the aid of the natural to dimly shadow forth the supernatural. How does the Holy Spirit come to me? Like wind. How does the Holy Spirit influence the spirit of man? Like wind.

"Like a wind." Then He creates an atmosphere and a temperature for the soul. How susceptible we are to the influences of the wind! The north wind blows, and we are chilled with the diffused presence of ice and snow. The south wind blows, balmy, gentle, wooing, and its touch is like a soft caress. Yes, we are sensitive to the presence of the wind. It creates an atmosphere in which breathing becomes a luxury or an agony. The Holy Spirit comes like the wind. How does the atmosphere He creates affect and influence the life?

"It is the Spirit that quickeneth." Then the influence He creates is like the warm, alluring, out-calling breath of the spring. How appallingly poor even a rich garden appears in the early days of March! The riches are there, but they are buried and dormant. The garden is just a graveyard, full of buried seeds and roots, waiting for the touch of some magician's wand to people it with life and beauty. It abounds in sleeping possibilities, which will not be roused into wakeful realities until some warm breath has thawed their frozen life, and urged it in healthy and aspiring circulation. At last there comes the spring, breathing resurrection warmth into the graveyard, sending a vitalising call into the deepest tomb, and the buried powers feel the quickening touch, and clothe themselves in the beautiful garments of light.

J.H. JOWETT

MAY 1

ACCESS TO GOD

They that seek the Lord understand all things.
PROVERBS 28:5

The secret of the Lord is with them that fear Him. He deals familiarly with them. He calls them not servants only, but friends; and He treats them as friends. He affords them more than promises, for He opens to them the plan of His great designs from everlasting to everlasting, shows them the strong foundations and inviolable securities of His favour towards them, the height, and depth, and length, and breadth of His love, which passeth knowledge, and the unsearchable riches of His grace . . . The men of the world would account it a high honour and privilege to have an unrestrained liberty of access to an earthly king; but what words can express the privilege and honour of believers, who whenever they please, have audience with the King of kings.

Prayer is the simplest form of speech
That infant lips can try;
Prayer, the sublimest strains that reach
The majesty on high.

Prayer is the Christian's vital breath
The Christian's native air,
His watchword at the Gates of Death;
He enters Heaven with prayer.

JOHN NEWTON

THE COMPLETE VICTOR

We are more than conquerors through him that loved us.
ROMANS 8:37

"Ye are of God, little children, and have overcome them, because greater is He that is in you, than He that is in the world." The only man that ever conquered the world - was complete victor - was Jesus Christ. When He shouted on the cross, "It is finished!" it was the shout of a conqueror. He had overcome every enemy. He had met sin and death. He had met every foe that you and I have to meet and had come off victor. Now if I have got the Spirit of Christ, if I have got that same life in me, then it is that I have got a power that is greater than any power in the world, and with that same power I overcome the world.

Notice that everything human in this world fails. Every man, the moment he takes his eyes off God, has failed. Every man has been a failure at some period of his life. Abraham failed. Moses failed. Elijah failed. Take the men that have become so famous and that were so mighty - the moment they got their eye off God, they were weak like other men; and it is a very singular thing that those men failed on the strongest point in their character. I suppose it was because they were not on the watch.

Abraham was noted for his faith, and he failed right there - he denied his wife. Moses was noted for his meekness and humility, and he failed right there - he got angry. God kept him out of the promised land because he lost his temper. I know he was called "the servant of God" and that he was a mighty man and had power with God, but, humanly speaking, he failed and was kept out of the promised land. Elijah was noted for his power in prayer and for his courage, yet he became a coward. He was the boldest man of his day and stood before Ahab and the royal court and all the prophets of Baal; yet when he heard that Jezebel had threatened his life, he ran away to the desert and under a juniper tree prayed that he might die.

Peter was noted for his boldness, and a little maid scared him nearly out of his wits. As soon as she spoke to him, he began to tremble, and swore that he didn't know Christ. I have often said to myself that I'd like to have been there on the day of Pentecost alongside of that maid when she saw Peter preaching.

D. L. MOODY

MAY 3

FAITH AT WORK

Now faith is the substance of things hoped for,
the evidence of things not seen.
HEBREWS 11:1

*N*ow the Lord said unto Abram, Get thee out of thy country, and from thy kindred, *and from thy father's house, unto the land that I will show thee: and I will make of thee a great nation, and I will bless thee and make thy name great; and thou shalt be a blessing; and I will bless them that bless thee, and curse him that curseth thee and in thee shall all the families of the earth be blessed."* (Gen. 12:1-3) That was the call Abraham heard, a call to leave kith and kin and country, and all the conditions there, that ultimately by going from those conditions he might be a blessing to all the world.

Now obedience to that call was only possible to faith, and in the surrender to that call faith was operating. We may ask, How did he know it was God's voice speaking to him, as if he heard the voice of a friend, and not the voice of any Chaldean? I do not know, and I am not caring to know, or to find out. What I do know is that Abraham was convinced that the call had come to him to turn his back upon Ur, and that it was God's call. Of that he was perfectly sure. What process of mind and thought in Abraham may have preceded this we can only infer. We can infer that he had come to an hour of disillusionment, of bitter dissatisfaction with life as it was being lived; and the order of life which is contrary to the high, and the noble and true. Somehow he had come to a consciousness of God, had come to know God; and there in the midst of the conditions that obtained in Ur, he had known it was God speaking to him. That one thing is certain, that a man knew God had spoken. When we see that, the wonder of his action fades away. It is the kind of action one would expect; yet it was only possible to faith.

G. CAMPBELL MORGAN

DIRECTION

And the spirit bade me go .. nothing doubting
ACTS 11:12

When God called some of His followers to an out-of-the-way path, they have had to go alone in an untrodden way. Superior love necessitates a lonely walk. You shrink and say, *'That seems so hard'*. He says, "Yes I know; I wish I could make it easier, but I cannot help it because, you see, it is only they who thus love to whom the Lord tells His secrets." Then, when He gives to any soul superior light to its fellows, and that soul *follows* the light, it necessarily entails a path in advance of its fellows. Unless he can inspire and encourage them to follow, he must go on alone.

In Acts 10 when Peter saw that he had not yet explored all the ideas of the divine mind about the extension of the Kingdom, that his business was to follow his Lord's directions, and not have his own *'ifs'* and *'buts'*, but go ahead and do as the Lord bade him, then Peter went on to carry out the divine direction.

Then the Church - this new Church - which had only just itself been brought to God by a new Saviour, a new revelation, a new call, a new faith, is down upon Peter, and summons him before a council to answer for his conduct.

He tells them all about it in the truthful simplicity of a man of God, and thank God, they had sense enough, yes, and love enough, to accept his explanations, and to glorify God.

Show me Thy way, O Lord,
And make it plain;
I would obey Thy Word,
Speak yet again;
I will not take one step until I know
Which way it is that Thou would have me go.

CATHERINE BOOTH

CALVARY'S CROSS

God forbid that I should glory, save in the cross of our Lord Jesus Christ.
GALATIANS 6:14

The cross of Christ - the death of Christ on the cross to make atonement for sinners - is the central truth in the whole Bible. This is the truth we begin with when we open Genesis. The seed of the woman bruising the serpent's head is nothing else but a prophecy of Christ crucified. This is the truth that shines out, though veiled, all through the law of Moses and the history of the Jews. The daily sacrifice, the Passover lamb, the continual shedding of blood in the tabernacle and temple - all these were emblems of Christ crucified. This is the truth that we see honoured in the vision of heaven before we close the book of Revelation. "In the midst of the throne and of the four beasts," we are told, "and in the midst of the elders, stood a Lamb as it had been slain" (Revelation 5:6) Even in the midst of heavenly glory we get a view of Christ crucified.

Take away the cross of Christ, and the Bible is a dark book. It is like the Egyptian hieroglyphics without the key that interprets their meaning, curious and wonderful, but of no real use.

Reader, you may know a good deal about the Bible. You may know the outlines of the histories it contains and the dates of the events described, just as a man knows the history of England. You may know the names of the men and women mentioned in it, just as a man knows Caesar, Alexander the Great, or Napoleon. You may know the several precepts of the Bible and admire them, just as a man admires Plato, Aristotle, or Seneca. But if you have not yet found out that Christ crucified is the foundation of the whole volume, you have read your Bible hitherto to very little profit. Your religion is a heaven without a sun, an arch without a keystone, a compass without a needle, a clock without spring or weights, a lamp without oil. It will not comfort you. It will not deliver your soul from hell.

You may know a great deal about Christ by a kind of head knowledge. You may know who He was and where He was born and what He did - His miracles, His sayings, His prophecies, and His ordinances, how He lived, how He suffered, and how He died. But unless you know the power of Christ's cross by experience, unless you know and feel within that the blood shed on that cross has washed away your own particular sins, and unless you are willing to confess that your salvation depends entirely upon the work that Christ did upon the cross, Christ will profit you nothing.

J. C. RYLE

JOHN KNOX'S TEXT

Thou hast the words of eternal life.
JOHN 6:68

"Go!" said the old reformer to his wife, as he lay a-dying, and the words were his last, "Go, read where I cast my first anchor!" She needed no more eplicit instructions, for he had told her the story again and again. It is Richard Bannatyne, Knox's serving-man, who has placed the scene on record. "On November 24, 1572," he says, "John Knox departed this life to his eternal rest. Early in the afternoon he said, "Now, for the last time, I commend my spirit, soul, and body" - pointing upon his three fingers - "into Thy hands, O Lord"! Thereafter, about five o'clock, he said to his wife, "Go, read where I cast my first anchor!" She did not need to be told, and so she read the seventeenth of John's evangel." Let us listen as she reads it! *"Thou hast given him power over all flesh, that he should give eternal life to as many as thou hast given him; and this is life eternal, that they might know thee, the only true God, and Jesus Christ whom thou hast sent."*

Here was a strange and striking contrast!

"Eternal Life! Life Eternal!" says the Book.

Now listen to the laboured breathing from the bed!

The Bed speaks of Death; the Book speaks of Life Everlasting!

"Life!" the dying man starts as the great cadences fall upon his ear.

"This is Life Eternal, that they might *know Thee!"*

"Life Eternal"!

"It was *there,"* he declares with his last breath, "it was *there* that I cast my first anchor!"

We have an anchor that keeps the soul
Stedfast and sure while the billows roll;
Fastened to the Rock which cannot move,
Grounded firm and deep in the Saviour's love!

F. W. BOREHAM

MAY 7

PRE-PACKED RELIGION

Be no more children, tossed to and fro, and carried
about with every wind of doctrine.
EPHESIANS 4:14

It is not difficult to view a segment of life in our day and compare it with a correspondingly limited view of life in another day, and to become very pessimistic. One can always find a bright spot here and a black spot somewhere else, while, of course, the reverse of that is true. It is possible thus to pour contempt upon what some people call "the good old days", and to show that we live in days which are much to be preferred to the days that have gone before us. It is therefore necessary to view life as a whole, and estimate its values relatively.

While there is much in this present day of which we have reason to be proud, and for which we may well be thankful, in the material realm, I seriously question whether the world has ever known a more superficial age than this when we look at the religious aspect of things. People are accustomed nowadays to get their religion at the delicatessen store, already made up in packages, duly labelled - and they take it, asking no questions for conscience' sake! It is surprising what people can be persuaded to believe, and still more surprising what people believe without any persuasion at all.

The gospel puts no premium upon ignorance, nor does it require any man to stultify himself. We ought to exercise our God-given powers, endeavouring to prove all things, and "to hold fast that which is good."

Believe not those who say
The upward path is smooth,
Lest thou shoudst stumble in the way
And faint before the truth.

It is the only road
Unto the realms of joy;
But they who seek that blest abode
Must all their powers employ.

T. T. SHIELDS

A FULL PARDON

Blessed is he whose transgression is forgiven, whose sin is covered.
PSALM 32:1

A forgiven man is the true worker, the true lawkeeper. He can, he will, he must work for God. He has come into contact with that part of God's character that warms his cold heart. Forgiving love constrains him. He cannot but work for Him who has removed his sins from him as far as the east is from the west. Forgiveness has made him a free man and given him a new and most loving Master.

Forgiveness, received freely from the God and Father of our Lord Jesus Christ, acts as a spring, an impulse, a stimulus of divine potency. It is more irresistible than law or terror or threat. A half forgiveness, an uncertain justification, a changeable peace, may lead to careless living and more careless working; it may slacken the energy and freeze up the springs of action (for it shuts out that aspect of God's character that gladdens and quickens); but a complete and assured pardon can have no such effect. This is "the truth which is after godliness" (Titus 1:1). Its tendencies toward holiness and consistency of life are marvelous in their power and certainty.

Forgiveness gives a momentum thus to the soul, a momentum that owes its intensity to the entireness and sureness of the pardon. Some, in their ignorances of Scripture, as well as of the true deep springs of human action, doubt such forgiveness can occur for certain sins, and miss this freeing momentum. They think a pardon, doled out in crumbs or drops, requires that they be fruitful in good works. But the pardon is given at once, and given in such a way as to be sure even to the chief of sinners. This is a pardon worthy, both in its greatness and its freeness, of the boundless generosity of God.

Pardon - from an offended God!
Pardon - from sins of deepest dye!
Pardon - bestowed through Jesus' blood!
Pardon - that brings the sinner nigh!
Who is a pardoning God like Thee,
Or who has grace so rich and free?

HORATIUS BONAR

JUSTIFICATION

Being justified by faith, we have peace with God
through our Lord Jesus Christ.
ROMANS 5:1

S ome have asked "What does the word justification mean? Is faith the only means of salvation?" "To justify" in biblical usage signifies not "to make righteous" but "to reckon, declare, or show to be righteous." A person is justified before God when God reckons him righteous, that is, when God not only forgives his sins but puts all positive righteousness to his account.

There is one condition upon which people are justified before God: simple faith in Jesus Christ (Romans 3:26, 4:5; 5:1; and Acts 13:39). The atoning death of Jesus Christ on the cross in our place secures justification for us (Romans 5:9; Galatians 3:13; 2 Corinthians 5:21). His shed blood is the basis for our justification, and simple faith in Him applies that shed blood to us. We are actually justified when we believe in Him who shed His blood.

Faith is the only means of appropriating to ourselves the atoning virtue that exists in the blood of Jesus Christ. If one will not believe, there is nothing he can do that will bring him justification.

If one does believe, he is regarded as justified at the moment of belief (Acts 13:38-39). Not only are all his sins put out of God's sight, but in God's reckoning all of God's own righteousness in Jesus Christ is put into account.

The moment we believe on Him we step into His place and are just as pleasing to God as Jesus Christ Himself is.

In his gospel, the apostle John says "These things are written (that is, the things contained in the gospel of John) that ye might believe that Jesus is the Christ, the son of God, and that beleiving ye might have life through his name" (20:31). Here we see that life comes through believing that Jesus is the Christ, the Son of God.

R. A. TORREY

MAY 10

WHY SAINTS PERSEVERE

Now unto him that is able to keep you from falling, and to present you
faultless before the presence of his glory with exceeding joy.
JUDE 24

The hope that filled the heart of Paul concerning the Corinthian brethren was full of comfort to those who trembled as to their future. But why was it that he believed that the brethren would be confirmed unto the end? I want you to notice that he gives his reasons. Here they are: "God is faithful, by whom ye were called unto the fellowship of his Son, Jesus Christ" (1 Corinthians 1:9).

The apostle does noy say, "You are faithful." Alas! The faithfulness of man is a very unreliable affair; it is mere vanity. He does not say, "You have faithful ministers to lead and guide you, and therefore I trust that you will be safe." Oh, no! If we are kept by men we shall be ill kept. He puts it, "God is faithful." If we are found faithful, it will be because God is faithful. On the faithfulness of our covenant God the whole burden of our salvation must rest. On this glorious attribute of God the matter hinges.

We are variable as the wind, frail as a spiders web, weak as water. No dependence can be placed upon our natural qualities or our spiritual attainments; but God abides faithful. He is faithful in His love; He knows no variableness, neither shadow of turning. He is faithful to His purpose; He does not begin a work and then leave it undone. He is faithful to His relationships; as a Father He will not renounce His children, as a friend He will not deny His people, as a Creator He will not forsake the work of His own hands. He is faithful to His promises and will never allow one of them to fail to a single believer. He is faithful to His covenant, which He has made with us in Christ Jesus and ratified with the blood of His sacrifice. He is faithful to His Son and will not allow His precious blood to be spilt in vain. He is faithful to His people to whom He has promised eternal life and from whom He will not turn away.

The faithfulness of God is the foundation and cornerstone of our hope of final perseverance. The saints shall persevere in holiness, because God perseveres in grace. He perseveres to bless, and therefore believers persevere in being blessed. He continues to keep His people, and therefore they continue to keep His commandments.

CHARLES H. SPURGEON

MAY 11

REFLECTIONS

Remember therefore from whence thou art fallen,
and repent, and do the first works.
REVELATION 2:5

Remember from whence you have fallen. Reflect on what you once enjoyed. How was it with you in days gone by? Let me help you remember, by a few practical questions. Did you not once realise a sweet and blessed sense of your acceptance with God? And did not His Spirit witness with your spirit that you were a child of God? And did you not realise that *"there is therefore now no condemnation to them which are in Jesus Christ, who walk not after the flesh, but after the Spirit"*. How is it with you now? As you received the Lord Jesus, have you so walked in Him that your path has been like that of the just, shining brighter and brighter unto the perfect day? Or have you lost your role, and with it your peace and joy of the Lord, which once was your strength?

Again, did you not once walk in daily communication with God, your prayers being not merely petitions, but mediums of sensible intercourse with Him? What is your present experience? You once realised the power of Christ to rest upon you, so that you were more than conqueror over the world, the flesh, and the devil; sin had no more dominion over you and you could sing, *"Thanks be to God, which giveth us the victory through our Lord Jesus Christ,"* and, *"I can do all things through Christ, which strengtheneth me."*

How is it with you?

Thou know'st the way to bring me back
My fallen spirit to restore:
O for Thy truth and mercy's sake,
Forgive, and bid me sin no more;
The ruins of my soul repair,
And make my heart a House of Prayer.

CATHERINE BOOTH

MAY 12

TRUST GOD'S WISDOM

Having made known unto us the mystery of his will.
EPHESIANS 1:9

"The wisdom that is from above is first pure, then peaceable, gentle and easy to be intreated, full of mercy and good fruits, without partiality, and without hypocrisy." (James 3:17)

I can hardly recollect a single plan of mine, of which I have not since seen reason to be satisfied that, had it taken place in season and circumstances just as I proposed, it would, humanly speaking, have proved my ruin; or at least it would have deprived me of the greater good the Lord had designed for me. We judge things by their present appearance, but the Lord sees them in their consequences; if we could do so likewise, we should be perfectly of His mind; but as we cannot, it is an unspeakable mercy that He will manage for us, whether we are pleased with His management or not; and it is spoken of one of His heaviest judgements, when He gives any person or people up to the way of their own hearts, and to talk after their own counsels.

Though dark be my way, since He is my Guide,
'Tis mine to obey, 'Tis His to provide;
Though cisterns be broken, and creatures all fail,
The word He has spoken shall surely prevail.

JOHN NEWTON

MAY 13

OUT AND OUT

Seek ye first the kingdom of God, and his righteousness.
MATTHEW 6:33

There is no satisfaction for the soul except in the God of the Bible. We come back to Paul's words, and get consolation for time and eternity: "We know that an idol is nothing in the world, and that there is none other God but one. For though there be that are called gods, whether in heaven or in earth (as there be gods many, and lords many), but to us there is but one God, the Father, of whom are all things, and we in him; and one Lord Jesus Christ, by whom are all things, and we by him". (1 Corinthians 8:4-6).

My friend, can you say that sincerely? Is all your hope centred on God in Christ? Are you trusting Him alone? Are you ready to step into the scales and be weighed against this first commandment?

God will not accept a divided heart. He must be absolute monarch. There is not room in your heart for two thrones. Christ said: "No man can serve two masters; for either he will hate the one and love the other, or else he will hold to the one and despise the other. Ye cannot serve God and mammon." Mark you, He did not say - "No man *shall* serve. . .Ye *shall* not serve. . .," but "No man *can* serve. . .Ye *cannot* serve. . ." That means more than a command; it means that you cannot mix the worship of the true God with the worship of another god any more than you can mix oil and water. It cannot be done. There is not room for any other throne in the heart if Christ is there. If worldliness should come in, godliness would go out.

The road to heaven and the road to hell lead in different directions. Which master will you choose to follow? Be an out-and-out Christian. "Him only shalt thou serve." Only thus can you be well pleasing to God. The Jews were punished with seventy years of captivity because they worshiped false gods. They have suffered nearly nineteen hundred years because they rejected the Messiah. Will you incur God's displeasure by rejecting Christ too? He died to save you. Trust Him with your whole heart, for with the heart man believeth unto righteousness. I believe that when Christ has the first place in our hearts - when the kingdom of God is first in everything - we shall have power, and we shall not have power until we give Him His rightful place. If we let one false god come in and steal our love away from the God of heaven, we shall not have peace or power.

D. L. MOODY

MANY WRITERS, ONE THEME

O how I love thy law! it is my meditation all the day.
PSALM 119:97

This is an old argument, but a very satisfactory one. The Bible consists of sixty-six books, written by more than thirty different men, extending in the period of its composition over more than fifteen hundred years; written in three different languages, in many different countries, and by men on every plane of social life, from the herdman and fisherman and cheap politician up to the king upon his throne. Nevertheless, in all this wonderful conglomeration we find an absolute unity of thought.

A wonderful thing about it is that this unity does not lie on the surface. On the surface apparent contradiction often appears, and the unity only comes out after deep and protracted study.

More wonderful yet is the organic character of this unity, beginning in the first book and growing till you come to its culmination in the last book of the Bible. We have first the seed, then the plant, then the bud, then the blossom, then the ripened fruit.

Suppose a vast building were to be erected, the stones for which were brought from the quarries in Rutland, Vermont; Berea, Ohio; Kasota, Minnesota; and Middletown, Conneticut. Each stone was hewn into final shape in the quarry from which it was brought. These stones were of all varieties of shape and size, cubical, rectangular, cylindrical, etc., but when they were brought together every stone fitted into its place, and when put together there rose before you a temple absolutely perfect on every outline, with its dome, side-walls, butresses, arches, transepts - not a gap or a flaw anywhere. How would you account for it? You would say: "Back of these individual workers in the quarries was the master-mind of the architect who planned it all and gave to each individual worker his specifications for the work."

So in this marvellous temple of God's truth that we call the Bible, whose stones have been quarried at periods of time and in places so remote from one another, but where every smallest part fits each other part, we are forced to say that back of the human hands that wrought was the Master-mind that thought.

R. A. TORREY

THE ROD, THE SERPENT & HOLINESS

Thy word is a lamp unto my feet, and a light unto my path.
PSALM 119:105

He who would be like Christ must study Him. We cannot make ourselves holy by merely trying to be so, any more than we can make ourselves believe and love by simple energy and endeavour. No force can effect this. Men try to be holy, and they fail. They cannot by direct effort work themselves into holiness. They must gaze upon a holy object; and so be changed into its likeness "from glory to glory" (2 Corinthians 3:18) They must have a holy being for their bosom friend. Companionship with Jesus, like that of John, can alone make us to resemble either the disciple or the Master.

He who would be holy must steep himself in the Word, must bask in the sunshine which radiates from each page of revelation. It is through *the truth* that we are sanctified (John 17:17). Exposing our souls constantly to this light, we become more thoroughly "children of the light," and, like the stained web that whitens in the sun, grow pure by being purely shone upon.

For against evil, divine truth is quick and powerful. It acts like some chemical ingredient that precipitates all impurities and leaves the water clear. It works like a spell of disenchantment against the evil one, casting him out, and casting him down. It is "the sword of the Spirit," with whose keen edge we cut our way through hostile thousands. It is the rod of Moses, by which we divide the Red Sea, and defeat Amalek, and bring water from the desert rock. What evil, what enemy, within or without, is there that can withstand this unconquered and unconquerable Word? Satan's object at present is to undermine that Word and to disparage its perfection. Let us the more magnify it, and the more make constant use of it. It is indeed only a fragment of man's language, made up of human letters and syllables; but it is furnished with superhuman virtue.

That rod in the hand of Moses, what was it? A piece of common wood. Yet it cut the Red Sea in two. The serpent on the pole, what was it? A bit of brass. Yet it healed thousands. Why all this? Because that wood and that brass were connected with omnipotence, conductors of heavenly electricity. So let the Bible be the book of all books, for wounding, healing, quickening, strengthening, comforting, and purifying.

HORATIUS BONAR

MAY 16

ALL GOD'S DOINGS

When the fulness of the time was come, God sent forth his Son.
GALATIANS 4:4

God devised a way of salvation, and when His appointed time was come He sent forth His Son. He did not even share His glory with the angels. He did not allow the archangels to participate in His prerogative. It was the work of God; and the Son of God, one with the Father from everlasting to everlasting, came as His Messenger to execute His will, and to fulfil the provisions of His covenants. When we seek to trust God, we need no priest, no church, and no ordinances: we need nothing in order to be saved, but God. It is His prerogative to save. He provided the way of salvation, nobody else. Nobody had an infinitesimal share in it. It was His own doing - God the Son.

He "sent forth his Son, *made of a woman*" how full of wonder was Mary that she should have been chosen for that honour, to become, as Elizabeth described her, the mother of the Lord! But it was all God's doings. He asked nobody's advice. He sought counsel of no one. He commissioned an angel to make the announcement that it should be so. He sovereignly willed it. No one could prevent it.

"When the fulness of time was come" Jesus was born in Bethlehem of Judea. He chose the manner of His coming, and *He chose the place of His arrival*. It was written in the Book, but nobody understood what that writing meant until the wise men made their enquiry. The book was consulted. They read the letter of it with unseeing eyes, but never saw the Christ. Yet it was predetermined, foreordained: and Jesus came to Bethlehem just as God had planned He should come.

I am glad He was laid in a manger because there was no room for Him in the inn. He was almost the only Child for Whose advent to this world no preparation was made. His coming was a surprise to men, but it was a fulfilment of God's eternal will and purpose.

T. T. SHIELDS

WILLIAM COWPER'S TEXT

Redeemed ... with the precious blood of Christ.
I PETER 1:18-19

C owper is a patient at Dr. Cotton's private lunatic asylum. In those days such asylums usually broke the bruised reed and quenched the smoking flax. But, happily for William Cowper and the world, Dr. Cotton's is the exception. Dr. Cotton is himself a kindly gracious, and devout old man; and he treats his poor patient with sympathy and understanding. And, under this treatment, the change comes. Cowper rises one morning feeling better : he grows cheerful over his breakfast; takes up the Bible, which in his fits of madness he always threw aside, and, opening it at random, lights upon a passge that breaks upon him like a burst of glorious sunshine. Let him tell the story. "The happy period which was to shake off my fetters and afford me a clear opening of the free mercy of God in Jesus Christ was now arrived. I flung myself into a chair near the window, and, seeing a Bible there, ventured once more to apply to it for comfort and instruction. The first verses I saw were in the third of Romans: *"Being justified freely by his grace through the redemption that is in Christ Jesus, who God hath sent forth to be a propitiation, through faith in his blood, to manifest his righteousness"*: Immediately I received strength to believe, and the full beams of the Sun of Righteousness shone upon me. I saw the sufficiency of the atonement He had made, my pardon in His blood, and the fulness and completeness of His justification. In a moment I believed and received the gospel."

The long-sought mountain is found! The light has shone upon the road that leads him to the Lamb!

So shall my walk be close with God,
Calm and serene my frame;
So purer light shall mark the road
That leads me to the Lamb.

F. W. BOREHAM

CHRIST LIFTED UP

We preach Christ crucified.
1 CORINTHIANS 1:23

"Brethren," said a North American Indian after his conversion, "I have been a heathen and know how heathens think. Once a preacher came and began to explain to us that there was a God; but we told him to return to the place from whence he came. Another preacher came and told us not to lie, steal, or drink; but we did not heed him. At last another came into my hut one day and said, 'I have come to you in the name of the Lord of heaven and earth. He sends to let you know that He will make you happy and deliver you from misery. For this end He became a man, gave His life a ransom, His blood for sinners.' I could not forget his words. I told them to the other Indians, and an awakening began among us."

I say, therefore, preach the sufferings and death of Christ our Saviour if you wish your words to gain entrance amongst the heathen.

The cross is the foundation of a church's prosperity. No church will ever be honoured in which Christ crucified is not continually lifted up. Nothing whatever can make up for the want of the cross. Without it all things may be done decently and in order. Without it there may be splendid ceremonies, beautiful music, learned ministers, crowded Communion tables, and large collections for the poor; but without the cross no good will be done. Dark hearts will not be enlightened, proud hearts will not be humbled, mourning hearts will not be comforted, fainting hearts will not be cheered.

A gorgeous banqueting room and splendid gold plate on the table will never make up to a hungry man for the want of food. Christ crucified is God's grand ordinance for doing good to men. Whenever a church keeps back Christ crucified, or puts anything whatever in that foremost place which Christ crucified should always have, from that moment the church ceases to be useful.

Without Christ crucified in her pulpits, a church is little better than a cumberer of the ground, a dead carcass, a well without water, a barren fig tree, a sleeping watchman, a silent trumpet, a speechless witness, an ambassador without terms of peace, a messenger without tidings, a lighthouse without fire, a stumbling block to weak believers, a comfort to infidels, a hot-bed for formalism, a joy to the devil, and an offense to God.

J. C. RYLE

HE NEVER FAILS

All the promises of God in him are yea, and in him Amen.
2 CORINTHIANS 1:20

The experience of all believers is to much the same effect: we began our new lives of joy and peace by believing the promise-making God, and we continue to live in the same manner. A long list of fulfilled promises is present to our happy memories, awakening our gratitude and confirming our confidence. We have tested the faithfulness of our God year after year, in a great many ways, but always with the same result. We have gone to Him with promises of the common things of life, relating to daily bread and raiment and children at home; and the Lord has dealt graciously with us. We have resorted to Him concerning sickness and slander and doubt and temptation; and never has He failed us. In little things He has been mindful of us: even the hairs of our head have been numbered. When it appeared very unlikely that the promise could be kept, it has been fulfilled with remarkable exactness. We have been broken down by the falseness of man, but we have exulted and do exult in the truthfulness of God. It brings the tears into our eyes to think of the startling ways in which Jehovah, our God, has wrought to carry out His gracious promises.

"Thus far we prove that promise good,
which Jesus ratified with blood:
still He is faithful, wise and just,
and still in Him believers trust."

Let me freely speak to all who trust in the Lord. Children of God, has not your heavenly Father been true to you? Is not this your constant experience, that you are always failing, but He never fails? Well said our apostle, "Though we believe not, He abideth faithful: He cannot deny Himself. The rule of His giving is large and liberal; the promise is a great vessel, and the Lord fills it to overflowing. As the Lord in Solomon's case gave him "as He promised him", so will He in every instance, as long as the world stands. Oh reader, believe the promise and thus prove yourself to be an inheritor of it.

CHARLES H. SPURGEON

VENGEANCE BELONGS TO GOD

It is the day of the Lord's vengeance.
ISAIAH 34:8

God oftentimes simply records what others said - bad men - good men, inspired men, and uninspired men. In the Psalms we have sometimes what God said to man, and that is always true; and on the other hand we often have what men said to God, and that may or may not be true. All of the passages cited are what men said to God. They are the inspired record of men's prayers to God. To God they breathed out the agony of their hearts. And to God they cried for vengeance upon their enemies.

Judged even by Christian standards, this was far better than taking vengeance into their own hands. Indeed, this is exactly what the New Testament commands us to do regarding those who wrong us. Vengeance belongs to God, and He will repay (Romans 12:19), and instead of taking vengeance into our own hands we should put it in His hands.

There is certainly nothing wrong in asking God to break the teeth of wicked men who are using those teeth to tear the upright. This prayer is taken from a Psalm that there is every good reason to suppose is Davidic . . . But is is a well-known fact that David in his personal dealings with his enemies was most generous, for when he had his bitterest and most dangerous enemy in his hand, an enemy who persistently sought his life, he not only refused to kill him, but refused to let another kill him (1 Samuel 26: 5-9). And even when he did so small a thing to Saul as to cut off the skirt of his robe, his heart smote him even for that slight indignity offered to his bitterest and most implacable enemy (1 Samuel 24:5).

How much better we would be if instead of taking vengeance into our own hands we would breathe out the bitterness of our hearts to God and then treat our enemies in actual fact as generously as David did! While David prayed to Jehovah in Psalm 109:10: "Let his children be continually vagabonds, and beg: let them seek their bread also out of their desolate places," in point of fact, when he was in a place of power, he asked: "Is there yet any that is left of the house of Saul, that I may shew him kindness?" He found a grandson of Saul's and had him eat at the king's table as one of his own sons (2 Samuel 9:1-2, 11).

R. A. TORREY

MAY 21

THE COMMISSION

Go ye into all the world, and preach the gospel to every creature.
MARK 16:15

I have been reading of late the New Testament with special reference to the aggressive spirit of primitive Christianity, and it is wonderful what floods of light come upon you when you read the Bible with reference to any particular topic on which you are seeking for help. People say they don't see this or that; no, because they do not wish to see it; but those who are willing to obey shall have all the light they want.

It seems to me that we come infinitely short of any right and rational idea of the aggressive spirit of the New Testament saints. Satan has got Christians to accept what I call a namby-pamby, kid glove kind of system of presenting the gospel to the people. It seems to me this is utterly antagonistic and repugnant to the spirit of the early saints: *"Go ye, and preach the gospel to every creature."* And again the same idea - *"Unto whom now I send thee."* Look what is implied in these commissions.

Divesting our minds of all conventionalities and traditionalisms, what would the language? *Go ye!* To whom? To every creature: Where am I to get at them? *Where they are* "Every creature". There is the extent of your commission. Seek them out; run after them wherever you can get at them.

Men die in darkness at your side,
Without a hope to cheer the tomb:
Take up the torch, and wave it wide,
The torch that lights time's thickest gloom.

CATHERINE BOOTH

HOW DO YOU KNOW GOD

ANSWERS PRAYER?

Praying always with all prayer and supplication in the Spirit.
EPHESIANS 6:18

I know it first of all because the Bible says so, and I have conclusive proof that the Bible is the inerrant Word of God. The Bible abounds in statements that God answers prayer. For example, Jesus says in Matthew 7:11: "If ye, then being evil know how to give good gifts unto your children, how much more shall your Father which is in heaven give good things to them that ask him?" And He says again to His disciples who were united to Him by a living faith and obedient love: "Whatsoever ye shall ask in my name, that will I do, that the Father may be glorified in the Son. If ye shall ask anything in my name, I will do it." (Jn 14:13-14).

But I also know that God answers prayers because He has answered mine. Throughout the years I have asked God for things He alone could give, for things that there was no probability whatever of my getting. I even asked praying, "If you will give me this thing I will never doubt you again as long as I live," and God has given me the very thing I asked. On one occasion God gave $6,000 within two hours in answer to prayer. On another occasion, when another person and I prayed for $5,000 for the Moody Bible Institute in Chicago, word was received by telegram that $5,000 had been given for the work by a man who was almost 1,000 miles away from where the prayer was made, a man whom I had not known and never given a penny to the Moody Bible Institute before - and has never given a penny since. I could multiply instances of this sort. Now it may be said that is merely a coincidence, but the "coincidence" has occured so often and there has been such an evident connection between prayer (the cause) and the answer (the effect), that to say it is coincidence is to be unscientific.

The history of George Mueller's Orphan Homes at Bristol, England, where about 2,000 children have been housed and clothed and fed in answer to prayer through a long period of years, where no money has ever been solicited, no debt ever incurred, and no meal ever failed though often it seemed as if it might fail up to the very last moment, is to a fair-minded investigator of facts clear proof that God answers prayers. For someone to study the facts in connection with George Mueller's Orphan Homes and still doubt that God answers prayer is for that person not only to be wilfully obstinate in his unbelief but thoroughly unscientific in his treatment of demonstrated facts.

R. A. TORREY

MAY 23

THE TRIUMPH OF FAITH

Looking unto Jesus the author and finisher of our faith.
HEBREWS 12:2

In the twelfth chapter of Hebrews, at verse 16, we read: "Esau, who for one morsel of meat sold his birthright. For ye know how that afterward, when he would have inherited the blessing he was rejected: for he found no place of repentance, though he sought it carefully with tears." That does not mean that he did not repent, but that he could not make his father repent, though he sought to do so with tears. The old man, feeble, ashamed, knowing he had played the fool and had attempted to play a trick on God, which trick having been invalidated by another trick, God was vindicated; when he found that was so, he would not withdraw that blessing. He stood by it. "By faith Isaac blessed Jacob and Esau." Faith insisted upon the fulfilment of the divine purpose.

As we ponder this story, how true it is that sometimes the deepest faith a man has in God is seen in his attitude towards his own wrong-doing. That was the deepest fact in Isaac; that faith in the God of his father Abraham, that faith that had been the inspiration of his quiet, passive life, and that faith that prevailed after all. He attempted to change the divine purpose as declared to him, but faith nevertheless was the greatest thing in his personality. We see it plainly in his attitude resulting from his failure, when he stood rebuked in the presence of the purpose of God, and the God of purpose. This is often so. It was so in the case of David. It was never more completely revealed than in the attitude he took up, after his outstanding sin. It was so in the case of Peter. He cursed and swore that he did not know Jesus. But watch him, see the breaking heart, and watch all that followed after. Out of absolute failure, resulting from a failure of faith, at last faith burned brightly and triumphed.

G. CAMPBELL MORGAN

MAY 24

HEAVEN RULES

Thou art great, and doest wondrous things: thou art God alone.
PSALM 86:10

As Nebuchadnezzar walked on the terrace in the palace of Babylon, and looked over the great city, he exclaimed, "Is not this great Babylon, that I have built for the house of the kingdom by the might of my power, and for the honour of my majesty." What a great man he was! He was a magnificent little Jack Horner! The world is full of little Jack Horners, sitting in corners, eating their Christmas pie. They stick in a thumb, and pull out a plum, and say - if not, What a good boy, then, "What a great boy am I!"

Nebuchadnezzar thought he was great until he was made to eat grass like oxen, and his nails grew like birds' claws, and his hair like eagles' feathers. Then by and by, his understanding returned to him, and when it did, he said, "I blessed the most High, and I praised and honoured Him that liveth for ever."

No man's understanding returns to him until in his thinking he gets God in the right place, or, rather, gets himself in right relation to God.

What did Nebuchadnezzar discover? That the inhabitants of the earth before the most High were reputed as nothing, and that "He (God) doeth accordingly to His will in the army of heaven, and among the inhabitants of the earth: and none can stay His hand, or say unto Him, What doeth Thou?" He is sovereignly independent of every one and every thing, of all conditions, of every sort of circumstance; He dwells apart and alone in splendid isolation in unique and solitary grandeur. He is God, and "beside Him there is none else."

Unchangeable, all-perfect Lord,
Essential life's unbounded sea,
What lives and moves, lives by Thy word;
It lives, and moves, and is from Thee.

Greatness unspeakable is Thine,
Greatness, whose undiminished ray,
When short-lived words are lost, shall shine
When earth and heaven are fled away.

T. T. SHIELDS

POWER IN THE BLOOD

Made nigh by the blood of Christ.
EPHESIANS 2:13

The blood of Jesus has an intimate connection with remission of sins. The Bible says, "This is my blood of the new testament (covenant), which is shed for many for the remission of sins" (Matthew 26:28). Jesus, suffering, bleeding, dying, has produced for sinners the forgiveness of their sins.

Of what sins?

Of all the sins of every sort and kind, however heinous, aggravated, and multiplied. The blood of the covenant takes every sin away, be what it may. There was never a sin believingly confessed and taken to Christ that ever baffled His power to cleanse it. This fountain has never been tried in vain. Murderers, thieves, liars, and adulterers have come to Jesus by penitence and faith, and through the merit of His sacrifice their sins have been put away.

Of what nature is the remission?

It is pardon freely given, acting immediately and abiding forever, so that there is no fear of the guilt ever again being laid to the charge of the forgiven one. Through the precious blood our sins are blotted out, cast into the depths of the sea, and removed as far from us as the east is from the west. Our sins cease to be. They are made an end of. They cannot be found against us anymore forever. Yes, hear it, hear it, oh wide earth! Let the glad news startle your darkest dens of infamy; there is absolute remission of sins! The precious blood of Christ cleanses from all sin; yes, turns the scarlet into a whiteness that can never be tarnished. Washed by Jesus, the blackest sinners shall appear before the judgement seat of the all-seeing Judge without spot.

How is it that the blood of Jesus effects this?

The secret lies in the vicarious, substitutionary character of our Lord's suffering and death. Because He stood in our place, the justice of God is vindicated, and the threatening of the law is fulfilled. It is now just for God to pardon sin. Christ's bearing the penalty of human sin instead of man has made the moral government of God perfect in justice, has laid a basis for peace of conscience, and has rendered sin immeasurably hateful, though its punishment does not fall upon the believer.

That is the great secret, this is the heavenly news, the gospel of salvation, that through the blood of Jesus, sin is justly put away.

CHARLES H. SPURGEON

HUMILITY

He forgetteth not the cry of the humble.
PSALM 9:12

Have we been decreasing of late? Do we think less of ourselves and of our position than we did a year ago? Are we seeking to obtain the same position of dignity? Are we wanting to hold onto some title, and are we offended because we are not treated with the courtesy that we think is due us?

Some time ago I heard a man in the pulpit say that he should take offense if he was not addressed by his title. My dear friend, are you going to take the position that you must have a title and that you must have every letter addressed with that title or you will be offended? John the Baptist did not want any title, and, when we are right with God, we shall not be caring about titles. In one of his early epistles Paul calls himself "the least of all the apostles.' Later on he claims to be "less than least of all saints," and again, just before his death, he humbly declares that he is the "chief of sinners." Notice how he seems to have grown smaller and smaller in his own estimation. So it was with John. And I do hope and pray that as the days go by we may feel like hiding ourselves and let God have all the honour and glory.

"When I look back upon my own religious experience," says Andrew Murray, "or round upon the Church of Christ in the world, I stand amazed at the thought of how little humility is sought after as the distinguishing feature of the discipleship of Jesus. In preaching and living, in the daily activities of the home and social life, in the more special fellowship with Christians, in the direction and performance of work for Christ - alas, how much proof there is that humility is not esteemed the cardinal virtue, the only root from which the graces can grow, the one indispensable condition of true fellowship with Jesus."

See what Christ says about John. "He was a burning and shining light." Christ gave him the honour that belonged to him. If you take a humble position, Christ will see it. If you want God to help you, then take a low position.

I am afraid that if we had been in John's place, many of us would have said, "What did Christ say about me? I am a burning and shining light!" Then we would have had the recommendation put in the newspapers and would have sent them to our friends, with that part marked in blue pencil.

D. L. MOODY

DAVID LIVINGSTONE'S TEXT

For ever, O Lord, thy word is settled in heaven.
PSALM 119:89

"*It is the word of a gentleman of the most strict and sacred honour, so there's an end of it!*" says Livingstone to himself as he places his finger for the thousandth time on the text on which he stakes his life. He is surrounded by hostile and infuriated savages. During the sixteen years that he spent in Africa, he has never before seemed in such imminent peril. Death stares him in the face. He thinks sadly of his life-work scarcely begun. For the first time in his experience he is tempted to steal away under cover of the darkness and to seek safety in flight. He prays! "Leave me not, forsake me not!" he cries. But let me quote from his own journal: it will give us the rest of the story.

"*January 14, 1856. Evening.* Felt much turmoil of spirit in prospect of having all my plans for the welfare of this great region and this teeming population knocked on the head by savages to-morrow. But I read that Jesus said : "All power is given unto Me in heaven and in earth. Go ye therefore, and teach all nations, and lo, *I am with you alway, even unto the end of the world.*" It is the word of a gentleman of the most strict and sacred honour, so there's an end of it! I will not cross furtively to-night as I intended. Should such a man as I flee? Nay, verily, I shall take observations for latitude and longitude to-night, though they may be last. I feel quite calm now, thank God!'

Lord, Thy Word abideth,
And our footsteps guideth,
Who it's truth believeth
Light and joy receiveth.

F. W. BOREHAM

THE HOLY FIGHT

The Lord our God delivered all unto us.
DEUTERONOMY 2:36

He that would be holy must fight. He must "war a good warfare" (1 Timothy 1:18), "fight the good fight of faith" (1 Timothy 6:12) though not with "carnal weapons" (2 Corinthians 10:4). He must fight upon his knees, "being sober, and watching unto prayer" (1 Peter 4:7). He must wrestle with principilities and powers, being strong in the Lord and in the power of His might, having put on the whole armour of God, girdle, breastplate, shield, helmet, and sword (Ephesians 6:13-17). This "battle is not to the strong" (Ecclesiastes 9:11), but to the weak; it is fought in weakness, and the victory is to those who have "no might"; for in this conflict "time and chance" do not happen to all. Instead, we count upon victory from the first onset, being made more than conquerors through Him who loved us, and are cheered with the anticipation of the sevenfold reward "to him that overcometh" (Revelation 2:7). And though, in this our earthly course and combat, we have the hostility of devils, we have the ministry of angels in aid (Hebrews 1:4), as well as the power of the Holy Spirit (Ephesians 1:13).

He that would be holy must watch. "Watch thou in all things" (2 Timothy 4:5); "watch ye, stand fast in the faith, quit you like men, be strong" (1 Corinthians 16:13). Let the sons of night sleep or stumble in the darkness, but let us, who are of the day, be sober, lest temptation overtake us, and we be ensnared in the wiles of the devil or the seductions of this wanton world. "Blessed is he that watcheth". (Revelation 16:15). In watching, too, let us "witness a good confession" (1 Timothy 6:13), not ashamed of Him whose badge we bear; let us run a swift and patient race, all the while having our eye upon the coming and the kingdom of our Lord Jesus.

He that would be holy must feel his responsibility for being so, both as a member of Christ's body and a partaker of the Holy Spirit. The thought that perfection is not to be reached here ought not to weaken that sense of responsibility nor to lead us to give way to anything that would "grieve the Holy Spirit of God whereby we are sealed unto the day of redemption. "Let us hold to the sevenfold fullness of the risen Christ (Revelation 2:1) and the sevenfold fullness of the Holy Ghost (5:6), for these are the church's birthright.

HORATIUS BONAR

EQUIPPED

And take the helmet of salvation, and the sword of the Spirit,
which is the word of God.
EPHESIANS 6:17

We need men and women who are trained for the fight; not only people who have experienced a change of heart, but who are drilled in the use of the weapons of the Spirit - knowing how to handle God's truth. You would think if you heard some people's presentation of the truth of God that it was all honey and soap; you would not think there was any cut in it, any dividing asunder. A great deal of the truth preached nowadays would not cut the wings off a fly, much less pierce asunder soul and spirit.

Tell a man the truth about himself then the truth about God, then tell the truth about his obligations to others. That is, if you believe the things I have been saying are true. If you do not believe them, then do not go to chapel, do not have the Bible.

And those of us who have so far acted upon the truth as to give up the greater portion of our lives to the service of God, what will be our regret when we come to face eternity and look back on the past? That we have done so much? Oh, no; that we have done so little, that we have not made God and eternity the all absorbing theme of our lives, that we have wasted any energy, time, or strength on less important things.

I would the precious time redeem,
And longer live for this alone,
To spend, and to be spent, for them
Who have not yet my Saviour known;
Fully on these my mission prove,
And only breathe, to breathe Thy love.

CATHERINE BOOTH

MAY 30

GREATER RICHES

Who through faith subdued kingdoms.
HEBREWS 11:33

I hope there never creeps into your thought or accent pity for Moses, that he had to give up the splendour of the court and spend forty years as a nomad, taking care of sheep under the shadow of the mountains and in the wilderness. I hope you do not pity him. It was a great life. It was a life of discipline and meditation. It was a life of training, all unknown to him, a method of preparation for what in the economy and purpose of God lay before him. No, do not pity him. Believe me, there is far more splendour and majesty under the mountains of God, and in the wilderness, which speaks of His power, than in all the courts of kings.

And then the surprising morning, when about his ordinary calling he saw a bush burning, flaming, blazing, and drew near; and wonder of wonders, the bush burned with fire but it was not being destroyed. The lambent flames around it played, and it flourished unconsumed in fire. The call came to him, the call of God, to become the leader of the people, still oppressed, and more cruelly oppressed then ever in the land of Egypt, to be the one who should lead them out. I thank God for all these stories. The hesitation of Moses is fear, "Who am I?" and the answer of God, full of gentle satire, "Who made thy mouth?" The words I speak thou shalt speak - and so that communion with God.

After the hesitations had all ended as the result of that communion, he went down, and again you know the story. I need not tell it. He gathered the people. He led them out. He forsook Egypt, taking with him all those oppressed people into the wilderness. What was the secret?" "He endured, as seeing Him Who is invisible."

G. CAMPBELL MORGAN

THE LORD, OUR SHEPHERD

The Lord is faithful, who shall stablish you, and keep you from evil.
2 THESSALONIANS 3:3

Surely in a world like this, where everything is uncertain, where we are exposed to trials on every hand, and know not but a single hour may bring forth something painful, yea dreadful, to our natural sensations, there can be no blessedness but so far as we are thus enabled to entrust and resign all to the direction and faithfulness of the Lord our Shepherd. For want of more of this spirit multitudes of professing Christians perplex and wound themselves and dishonour their high calling by continuing anxieties, alarms, and complaints ... But blessed is the man who trusteth in the Lord and whose hope the Lord is.

Shepherd of the chosen number,
They are safe whom Thou dost keep;
Other shepherds faint and slumber,
And forget to watch the sheep;
Watchful Shepherd!
Thou dost wake while others sleep.

When the lion came, depending
On his strength to seize his prey,
Thou wert there, Thy sheep defending,
Thou didst then Thy power display;
Mighty Shepherd!
Thou didst turn the foe away.

JOHN NEWTON

JUNE 1

WHOLLY FOR GOD

Whom have I in heaven but thee? and there is
none upon earth that I desire beside thee.
PSALM 73:25

*A*lone with God - this is a word of the deepest importance. May we seek grace from God to reach its depths. Then shall we learn that there is another word of equally deep significance - *Wholly for God.*

As we find that it is not easy to persevere in this being *"Alone with God,"* we begin to realise that it is because the other is lacking: we are not *"Wholly for God."* Because He is the Only God and He alone the Adorable One, God has a right to demand *that He should have us wholly for Himself.* Without this surrender He cannot make His power known. We read in the Old Testament that His servants, Abraham, Moses, Elijah and David, gave themselves wholly and unreservedly to God so that He could work out His plans through them. It is only the fully surrendered heart that can fully trust God for all He has promised.

Nature teaches us that if anyone desires to do a great work, he must give wholly to it. This law is especially true of the love of a mother for her child. She gives herself wholly to the little one whom she loves. And shall we not think it reasonable that the great God of Love should have us wholly for Himself? And shall we not take the watchword, "Wholly for God" as the keynote for our devotions every morning as we rise? *As wholly as God gives Himself to us, so wholly He desires that we give ourselves to Him.*

Let us in the inner chamber meditate on these things alone with God and with earnest desire ask Him by His almighty power to work in us all that is pleasing in His sight.

Wholly for God! What a privilege. What wonderful grace to fit us for it. Wholly for God! What separation from people and work and all that might draw us away. Wholly for God! What ineffable blessedness as the soul learns what it means and what God gives with it.

"Thou shalt love the Lord thy God with all thine heart, and with all thy soul and with all thy mind" (Deut 6:5; Matt 22:37).

"They ... sought Him with their whole desire; and He was found of them" (2 Chron 15:15).

ANDREW MURRAY

JUNE 2

HE SEES US THROUGH AND THROUGH

I know thy works.
REVELATION 2:19

What knowledge of man's heart our Lord Jesus possesses! We see Him exposing the false motives of those who followed Him for the sake of the loaves and fishes. They had followed Him across the Lake of Galilee. They seemed at first sight ready to believe in Him and do Him honour. But He knew the inward springs of their conduct and was not deceived. "Ye seek me," he said, "not because ye saw the miracles, but because ye did eat of the loaves and were filled."

The Lord Jesus, we should never forget, is still the same. He never changes. He reads the secret motives of all who profess and call themselves Christians. He knows exactly why they do all they do in their religion.

Let us be real, true and sincere in our religion, whatever else we are. The sinfulness of hypocrisy is very great, but its folly is greater still. It is not hard to deceive ministers, relatives and friends. A little decent outward profession will often go a long way. But it is impossible to deceive Christ. "His eyes are as a flame of fire" (Rev 1:14). He sees us through and through. Happy are those who can say, "Thou, Lord who knowest all things, knowest that we love thee" (John 21:17).

Our Lord told the crowds who followed Him so diligently for the loaves and fishes, "not to labour for the meat that perisheth".

What our Lord did mean to rebuke was that excessive attention to labour for the body, while the soul is neglected which prevails everywhere in the world. What He reproved was the common habit of labouring only for the things of time and letting alone the things of eternity, of minding only the life that now is and disregarding the life to come. Against this habit he delivers a solemn warning. Happy are those who learn the respective value of soul and body and give the first and best place in their thoughts to salvation.

J. C. RYLE

DOUBT IS THE DEVIL'S TOOL

In whom ye also trusted, after that ye heard the word of truth,
the gospel of your salvation.
EPHESIANS 1:13

Therefore mark how the devil works, for he attacks nothing but faith. Pagans, the unbelieving, the non-Christians he does not tempt. They cling to him like scales to fish. But when he sees those who have the Word of God, faith, and the Holy Ghost, he cannot get at them. He well knows that he can never win the victory over them, though they may stumble. He well perceives that even if one falls into gross sin, he is not lost thereby, for he can always rise again. Therefore he realises that he must try a different method and take away their greatest good. If he can prevail upon the soul and make her doubt whether it is the Word of God, the game is won. For God can work all things for good, however often we may stumble, only if we abide by the pure, true Word of God.

When storms arise
And dark'ning skies
About me threat'ning lower,
To Thee, O Lord, I raise my eyes
To Thee my tortured spirit flies
For solace in that hour.

Upon Thy breast
Secure I rest
From sorrow and vexation;
No more by sinful cares oppressed,
But in Thy presence ever blest,
O God of my salvation.

MARTIN LUTHER

JUNE 4

THE UNHAPPY BACKSLIDER

Our backslidings are many; we have sinned against thee.
JEREMIAH 14:7

Peter speaks of some who through waywardness have gotten so far out of fellowship with God that they have forgotten that they were purged from their old sins. This is a sad state to be in. It is what is commonly called in the Old Testament "backsliding". "The backslider in heart shall be filled with his own ways" (Proverbs 14:14). An old preacher I knew as a boy used to say, "Backsliding always begins in the knee". And this is very true indeed. Neglect of prayer will soon dull the keen edge of one's spiritual sensibilities and make it easy for a believer to drift into worldliness and carnalities, as a result of which his soul's eyesight will become dimmed and he will lose the heavenly vision.

The backslider is short-sighted. He sees the things of this poor world very vividly, but he cannot see afar off, as he could in the days of his former, happy state. To such comes the exhortation, "Anoint thine eyes with eyesalve, that thou mayest see." Get back to your Bible and back to you knees. Let the Holy Spirit reveal to your penitent heart the point of departure where you left your first love, and judge it definitely before God. Acknowledge the sins and failures that have caused eternal things to lose their preciousness. Cry with David, as you confess your wanderings, "Restore unto me the joy of thy salvation". And He who is married to the backslider will give you again to know the blessedness of fellowship with Himself, and once more your peace will flow as a river and the full assurance of hope be yours.

As you walk with God your faith will grow exceedingly, your love unto all saints will be greatly enlarged, and the hope laid up for you in heaven will fill the vision of your opened eyes, as your heart is occupied with the Lord Himself who has restored your soul.

For it is well to remember that He Himself is our hope. He has gone back to the Father's house to prepare a place for us, and He has promised to come again and receive us unto Himself, that where He is we may be also.

HARRY IRONSIDE

A WORLDWIDE BODY

Now ye are the body of Christ, and members in particular.
1 CORINTHIANS 12:27

Stating it in the most simple terms, the Christian Church, called to be the Body of Christ on earth, is the assembly of redeemed saints.

We meet in local congregations and assemblies, yet we know that we are not an end in ourselves. If we are going to be what we ought to be in the local church, we must come to think of ourselves as part of something more expansive, something larger that God is doing throughout the world.

There is an important sense here in which we find that we "belong" - belonging to something that is worthy and valuable, and something that is going to last forever!

These are considerations concerning the whole Church, the Body of Christ, and the fact that in our local congregation we have the joyful sense of belonging to an amazing fellowship throughout the world. Every believing church has a part with us and we a part with them.

Brethren, the Church must have the enabling and the power of the Holy Spirit and the glow of the Shekinah glory - God within us. For then, even lacking everything else, you still have a true church!

Unshaken as eternal hills,
Immovable she stands,
A mountain that shall fill the earth,
A house not made with hands.

A. W. TOZER

JUNE 6

WEIGHED AND WANTING

Doth not he see my ways, and count all my steps?
JOB 31:4

Let us look once again at the Sermon on the Mount, that men think so much of, and see what Christ had to say: "Ye have heard that it has been said by them of old time, Thou shalt not kill; and whosoever shall kill shall be in danger of the judgment: but I say unto you, that whosoever is angry with his brother without a cause shall be in danger of the judgment: and whosoever shall say to his brother, Raca [an expression of contempt], shall be in danger of the council: but whosoever shall say, Thou fool [an expression of condemnation], shall be in danger of hell fire."

As someone has said, Jesus described "three degrees of murderous guilt, all of which can be manifested without a blow being struck: secret anger, the spiteful jeer, [and] the open, unrestrained outburst of violent abusive speech".

Again, what does John say? "Whosoever hateth his brother is a murderer; and ye know that no murderer hath eternal life abiding in him."

Did you ever in your heart wish a man dead? That was murder. Did you ever get so angry that you wished any one harm? Then you are guilty. I may be addressing someone who is cultivating an unforgiving spirit. That is the spirit of the murderer, and it needs to be rooted out of your heart.

We can only read men's acts - what they have done. God looks down into the heart. That is the birthplace and home of the evil desires and intentions that lead to the transgression of all God's laws.

Listen once more to the words of Jesus: "From within, out of the heart of men, proceed *evil thoughts, adulteries, fornications, murders, thefts, covetousness, wickedness, deceit, lasciviousness, an evil eye, blasphemy, pride, foolishness ...*"

May God purge our hearts of these evil things, if we are harbouring them! Ah, if many of us were weighed now, we should find Belshazzar's doom written against us: *"Tekel"* - wanting!

D. L. MOODY

WOUNDED FOR ME

We love him, because he first loved us.
1 JOHN 4:19

Could you and I pass this day through these heavens, and see what is now going on in the sanctuary above ... could you see the Lord with the scars of His five deep wounds in the very midst of the throne ... all singing, "Worthy is the Lamb that was slain," and were one of these angels to tell you, "This is He that undertook the cause of lost sinners: He undertook to be the second Adam - the man in their stead; and lo! there He is upon the throne of heaven; consider Him - look long and earnestly upon His wounds - upon His glory, and tell me, do you think it would be safe to trust Him? Do you think His sufferings and obedience will have been enough? Yes, yes, every soul exclaims, Lord it is enough!

Jesus sought me when a stranger,
Wandering from the fold of God;
He to rescue me from danger,
Interposed with precious blood.

Oh, to grace how great a debtor;
Daily I'm constrained to be!
Let that grace now, like a fetter,
Bind my wandering heart to Thee.

ROBERT MURRAY McCHEYNE

JUNE 8

ALL SHALL RISE

There shall be a resurrection of the dead, both of the just and unjust.
ACTS 24:15

The doctrine of the resurrection teaches that all men will rise again - not a certain portion of the race, not a few thousand persons, but all men. It might be easier to believe in an Elijah, who should raise a dead man occasionally, or in a Christ, who should call back to life a young man at the gates of Nain or raise a Lazarus or say, "Talitha cumi" to a little deceased girl. But hard for reason is the doctrine that **all** shall rise - the myriads before the Flood, the multitudes of Nineveh and Babylon, the hosts of Persia and of Media, the millions that followed at the feet of Xerxes, the hosts that marched with Alexander, and all he innumerable millions that fell beneath the Roman sword.

Think of the myriads who have passed away in countries like China, swarming with men, and conceive of these throughout six thousand years fattening the soil. Remember those who have perished by shipwreck, plague, earthquake, and worst of all, by bloodshed and war; and remember that all these will rise without exception; not one of woman born shall sleep on forever, but all the bodies that ever breathed and walked this earth shall live again. "O, monstrous miracle," says one. "It wears the aspect of a thing incredible." Well, we shall not dispute the statement but will give even yet more reason for it.

The wonder increases when we remember in what strange places many of these bodies now may be. For the bodies of some have been left in deep mines where thy will never be reached again; they have been carried by the wash and swell of tides into deep caverns of the ancient main; there they lie, far away on the pathless desert where only the vulture's eye can see them, or buried beneath mountains of fallen rock. In fact, where are not man's remains? Who shall point out a spot of earth where the crumbling dust of Adam's sons is not? Blows there a single summer wind down our streets without whirling along particles of what once was man? Is there a single wave that breaks upon any shore that holds not in solution some relic of what was once human? They lie beneath the meadow grass; yet surely from anywhere, from everywhere, the scattered bodies shall return, like Israel from captivity.

As certainly as God is God, our dead shall live, and stand upon their feet, an exceeding great army.

CHARLES H. SPURGEON

JUNE 9

HEAVENLY MEDITATION

I remember thee upon my bed, and meditate on thee in the night watches.
PSALM 63:6

Concerning the fittest place for heavenly meditation it is sufficient to say that the most convenient is some private retirement ... Withdraw thyself from all society, even the society of godly men, that thou mayest awhile enjoy the society of the Lord ... Christ had His accustomed place, and consequently accustomed duty, and so much we ... Only there is a wide difference in the object: Christ meditates on the sufferings that our sins had deserved, so that the wrath of His Father passed through all His soul; but we are to meditate on the glory He hath purchased, that the love of the Father, and the joy of the Spirit, may enter at our thoughts, revive our affections, and overflow our souls.

Talk with us, Lord, Thyself reveal,
While here o'er earth we move;
Speak to our hearts, and let us feel
The kindling of Thy love.

With Thee conversing, we forget
All time, and toil, and care;
Labour is rest, and pain is sweet,
If Thou my God, art here.

RICHARD BAXTER

RECKON ON GOD'S FAITHFULNESS

O thou that hearest prayer, unto thee shall all flesh come.
PSALM 65:2

Reckon, or depend, on God for answers to prayer. Once you have handed the matter over to God, thoughtfully and deliberately, you must dare to believe that He has taken it in hand and that, though He may keep you waiting, He will not be at rest until He has finished it. The Lord will perfect that which concerneth me: His mercy endureth forever: He will not forsake the work of His own hands.

Prayer is co-operation of the human spirit with the divine. As a slight noise will sometimes dislodge an avalanche, so the prayer of faith sets in motion the power of the ascended Christ. Believing prayer supplies the fulcrum on which God rests the lever of His omnipotence. In prayer there is union between the divine and the human so that, as the human body of our Lord provided the channels along which the divine life-power was able to reach us, the prayer of faith opens a wide channel by which God's grace and providence may come to man.

Effective prayer has two characteristics. First, we must allow the Holy Spirit to winnow away what is inconsistent with God's will. We cannot impose our will on God, but must wait for the solution of our life problems, which He will most certainly grant, sometimes by a flash, at other times by the slow unfolding of His will. When we cannot solve our problem in our own way, we must trust Him to deal with it in a better way; and He cannot fail. Second, we must cease to worry. However long the interval, however strong the combination of adverse circumstances, we may still our hearts, in the patience of unwavering faith, sure that our Lord will not rest until He has finished the matter in hand, which we have entrusted to Him.

Never forget to reckon on God's faithfulness! That anchorage will never fail to hold.

F. B. MEYER

JUNE 11

THE SONG OF THE LAMB

*Thou wast slain, and hast redeemed us to God by thy
blood out of every kindred, and tongue, and people and nation.*
REVELATION 5:9

The Song of the Lamb tells us that the redeemed shall come from all the different tribes and nations of the whole earth. The many languages into which the Bible has been translated and the still greater number into which the New Testament or portions of the Bible have been translated gives us some idea of how strenuous work by missionaries in many lands is making known Christ and His Gospel.

Think for a little while of the extent of blessed work done by missionaries all over the earth! Christ came as a propitiation not for our sins alone, but for the sins of the whole world and to complete the great work of the redemption of mankind. When He had accomplished His share of the work, He entrusted the rest of the work to His people, trusting them to take the message of redemption to all parts of the world. As holy and divine as was Christ's part as an indispensable beginning, so equally holy is the second part of the work - to bring souls everywhere to know of and accept this great salvation.

In the Song of the Lamb we find this twofold truth - the Lamb upon the Throne has brought salvation to all the nations and tribes of the earth, and to the Church of the Lamb has been entrusted the distribution of the salvation by the power of the Holy Spirit. Unspeakably glorious is the task of the Missionary!

We shall only be able to understand this aright when we have seen the great multitude which no man can number, out of every nation of all tribes and peoples and tongues, standing before the Throne and before the Lamb, arrayed in white robes with palms in their hands; and they cry, saying: "Salvation unto our God which sitteth upon the Throne and unto the Lamb."

May the Holy Spirit imprint deeply in our hearts the wonder of missionary work! Just as the Lamb of God gave Himself to die that He might send the glad tidings to all, let us offer ourselves wholly and without reserve to live and to die that souls may be led to join in the Song of the Lamb before the Throne of God.

ANDREW MURRAY

JUNE 12

NO CAUSE FOR FEAR

There is no fear in love; but perfect love casteth out fear.
1 JOHN 4:18

I ... call upon you to learn the true and proper definition of Christ out of these words of Paul, "which gave Himself for our sins." If He gave Himself to death for our sins, then undoubtedly He is no tyrant or judge which will condemn us for our sins. He is no caster-down of the afflicted, but a raiser-up of those that are fallen, a merciful reliever and comforter of the heavy and broken-hearted ... Here is then no fear, but altogether sweetness, joy, peace of conscience ... We teach no new thing, but we repeat and establish old things, which the apostles and all godly teachers have taught us. And would to God we could so teach and establish them that we might not only have them in our mouth, but also well grounded in the bottom of our heart.

My heart is fixed, my mind is made,
I shall not ever be afraid,
Love conquers fear, our God will do
What He has promised me and you.

My heart is fixed, I trust His Name,
Forever and a day the same,
His Holy Spirit from above
Will fill my soul with perfect love.

MARTIN LUTHER

NO CONDEMNATION

He that believeth on me hath everlasting life.
JOHN 6:47

C hrist's lowly condition, when He was upon earth, is a stumbling-block to the natural man. We read that "The Jews murmured, because Jesus said, I am the bread that came down from heaven. And they said, Is not this Jesus, the son of Joseph, whose father and mother we know? How is it then that He saith, I came down from heaven?" Had our Lord come as a conquering king, with wealth and honours to bestow on his followers and mighty armies in his train, they would have been willing enough to receive Him. But a poor and lowly and suffering Messiah was an offence to them. Their pride refused to believe that such a one was sent from God.

There is nothing that need surprise us in this. It is human nature showing itself in its true colours. We see the same thing in the says of the apostles. Christ crucified was "to the Jews a stumbling-block, and to the Greeks foolishness" (1 Cor 1:23). The cross was an offence to many wherever the gospel was preached.

The salvation of a believer is a present thing. Our Lord Jesus Christ says, "Verily, verily, I say unto you, he that believeth on me hath everlasting life." How many seem to think that forgiveness and acceptance with God are things which we cannot attain in this life, that they are things which are to be earned by a long course of repentance and faith and holiness - things which we may receive at the bar of God at last, but must never pretend to touch while we are in this world! It is a complete mistake to think so. The very moment a sinner believes on Christ he is justified and accepted. There is no condemnation for him. He has peace with God and that immediately and without delay. His name is in the book of life, however little he may be aware of it. He has a title to heaven, which death and hell and Satan cannot overthrow. Happy are they that know this truth! It is an essential part of the good news of the gospel.

J. C. RYLE

MORE THAN A PARDON

For godly sorrow worketh repentance to salvation not to be repented of.
2 CORINTHIANS 7:10

It is a fact that the New Testament message of good news, "Christ died for our sins according to the scriptures," embraces a great deal more than an offer of free pardon.

Surely it is a message of pardon - and for that may God be praised - but it is also a message of repentance!

It is a message of atonement - but it is also a message of temperance and righteousness and godliness in this present world!

It tells us that we must accept a Saviour - but it tells us also that we must deny ungodliness and worldly lusts!

The gospel message includes the idea of amendment - of separation from the world, of cross-carrying and loyalty to the kingdom of God even unto death!

These are all corollaries of the gospel and not the gospel itself; but they are part and parcel of the total message which we are commissioned to declare. No man has authority to divide the truth and preach only a part of it. To do so is to weaken it and render it without effect!

Faithful and just art Thou,
Forgiving all;
Loving and kind art Thou,
When poor ones call:
Lord, let the cleansing blood,
Blood of the Lamb of God,
Pass o'er my soul.

A. W. TOZER

JUNE 15

FULL ASSURANCE OF FAITH

By one offering he hath perfected for ever them that are sanctified.
HEBREWS 10:14

The feeblest faith in Christ is saving faith. The strongest faith in self, or any thing else but Christ, is but a delusion and a snare, and will leave the soul at last unsaved and forever forlorn.

And so when we are bidden to draw near to God with true hearts in full assurance of faith, the meaning is that we are to rest implicitly on what God has revealed concerning His Son and His glorious work for our redemption. This is set forth admirably in Hebrews 10. There we have set out in vivid contrast the difference between many sacrifices offered under the legal dispensation and the one perfect, all-sufficient oblation of our Lord Jesus Christ. Note some of the outstanding differences:

1. They were many and often repeated. His is but one, and no other will ever be required.
2. They did not have the necessary value to settle the sin question. His is of such infinite value, it has settled that problem for evermore.
3. They could not purge the consciences of those who brought them. His purges all who believe, giving a perfect conscience because all sin has been put away from under the eye of God.
4. They could not open the way into the Holiest. His has rent the veil and inaugurated the new and living way into the very presence of God.
5. They could not perfect the one who offered them. His one sacrifice has perfected forever those who are sanctified.
6. In them there was a remembrance again of sins from year to year. His has enabled God to say, "Their sins and iniquities will I remember no more."
7. It was not possible that the blood of bulls and of goats should put away sin. But Christ has accomplished that very thing by the sacrifice of Himself.

Here then is where faith rests, on the finished work of Christ. It will help us greatly to understand this if we glance at what is revealed concerning the sin offering of the old dispensation.

HARRY IRONSIDE

JUNE 16

OUR EXPECTATION

Our conversation is in heaven; from whence also we look for the Saviour.
PHILIPPIANS 3:20

I would desire, if I might have my way, to be drawn to my grave by white horses or to be carried on the shoulders of men who would express joy as well as sorrow in their dress, for why should we sorrow over those who have gone to glory and inherited immortality? Sound the gladsome trumpet! The conqueror has won the battle; the king has climbed to his throne.

"Rejoice," say our brethren from above, "rejoice with us, for we have entered into our rest." "Blessed are the dead which die in the Lord from henceforth. Yea, saith the Spirit, that they may rest from their labours, and their works do follow them." Bless God evermore that over the pious dead we sing His living promises! There is a place where you shall sleep, perhaps in a lone grave in a foreign land, or perhaps in a niche where your bones shall lie side by side with those of your ancestors; but to the dust return you must. Well, let us not repine. It is but for a little, a rest on the way to immortality. Let us meet death not only with equanimity but with expectation, since it is to resurrection that we aspire.

Then again, if we are expecting a blessed resurrection, let us respect our bodies. Let not our members become instruments of evil. Be pure. In your baptism, your bodies were washed with pure water to teach you that henceforth you must be clean from all defilement. Put away from you every evil thing.

Lastly, the ungodly are to rise again, but it will be to a resurrection of woe. Their bodies sinned, and their bodies will be punished. "Fear him," says Christ, "who is able to destroy both soul and body in hell." He will cast both of them into a suffering that shall cause perpetually enduring destruction to them. This is terrible indeed. To slumber in the grave would be infinitely preferable to such a resurrection - "the resurrection of damnation," as the Scripture calls it.

A certain Acilius Aviola was seized with an apoplexy, and, his friends conceiving him to be dead, carried him to his funeral pyre. But when the heat had warmed his body, he awoke to find himself hopelessly encircled with funeral flames. In vain he called for deliverance; he could not be rescued, but passed from torpor into intolerable torment. Such will be the dreadful awakening of every sinful body when it shall be aroused from its slumber in the grave. May we believe in Jesus Christ now, and obtain a resurrection to life eternal.

CHARLES H. SPURGEON

GOD SPEAKS

Thy testimonies are wonderful: therefore doth my soul keep them.
PSALM 119:129

I f it were known that God Himself was going to speak once again to man, what eagerness and excitement there would be. For nearly nineteen hundred years He has been silent. No inspired message has been added to the Bible for nearly nineteen hundred years. How eagerly all men would listen if God should speak once more. Yet men forget that the Bible is God's own Word, and that it is as truly His message today as when it was delivered of old. The law that was given at Sinai has lost none of its solemnity. Time cannot wear out its authority or the fact of its authorship.

I can imagine someone saying, "I won't be weighed by that law, I don't believe in it."

Now men may dispute as much as they like about other parts of the Bible, but I have never met an honest man who found fault with the Ten Commandments. Infidels may mock the Lawgiver and reject Him who has delivered us from the curse of the law, but they can't help admitting that the commandments are right. Renan said that they are for all nations and will remain the commandments of God during all the centuries.

If God created this world, He must make some laws to govern it. In order to make life safe we must have good laws; there is not a country the sun shines upon that does not possess laws. Now this is God's law. It has come from on high, and infidels and skeptics have to admit that it is pure. Legislatures nearly all over the world adopt it as the foundation of their legal systems.

"The law of the Lord is perfect, converting the soul: the testimony of the Lord is pure, making wise the simple: the statutes of the Lord are right, rejoicing the heart: the commandment of the Lord is pure, enlightening the eyes."

Now the question for you and me is - are we keeping these commandments? If God made us, as we know He did, He had a right to make that law; and if we don't use it rightly it would have been better for us if we had never had it, for it will condemn us. We are found wanting. And being found condemned, we have only one hope for deliverance - Jesus Christ the righteous.

D. L. MOODY

JUNE 18

LEAVE YOUR FEARS BEHIND

What man is he that feareth the Lord? him shall he teach
in the way that he shall choose.
PSALM 25:12

The infinite heart of the infinite God flows out in love towards our Lord Jesus Christ. And there is no fear in the bosom of Christ. All His fears are past. Once He said, "While I suffer thy terrors I am distressed"; but now He is in perfect love, and perfect love casteth our fear. Hearken, trembling souls! Here you may find rest to your soul. You do not need to live another hour under your tormenting fears. Jesus Christ has borne the wrath of which you are afraid. He now stands a refuge for the oppressed - a refuge in the time of trouble. Look to Christ, and you will find rest. Call upon the name of the Lord, and you will be delivered.

I heard the voice of Jesus say,
"Come unto Me and rest;
Lay down, thou weary one, lay down
Thy heard upon by breast."

I came to Jesus as I was,
Weary, and worn, and sad;
I found in Him a resting place,
And He has made me glad.

ROBERT MURRAY McCHEYNE

THE CHRIST-LIFE FOR THE SELF-LIFE

If our heart condemn us not, then have we confidence toward God.
1 JOHN 3:21

We must begin at the bottom; we must begin at the root of our self-confidence. The prime cause of all failure in private life as well as in public ministry is the assertion of self. As long as men and women think it is all right with them, nothing can be done for them. It is only when there is excited within them a fear that, after all, things may not be quite so well as they seem, a dread that, after all, they may have made a mistake and be self-deceived - only then, in the secret of their own chambers, they begin to ask God: "Am I just what I expected?" It is then that the heart is laid open, and they are brought to understand how a man may be almost a castaway and yet be taken back to the bosom of Christ as Peter was; for within six weeks the man who was nearly cast away became the Apostle of Pentecost.

Paul said, "Lest ... I myself should be a castaway." He knew he had a perfect right to go to an idol temple, but chose not to go for fear that other men seeing him might follow him, and that what might be innocent to him might be death to them. He knew he had rights as a Christian, but chose to abstain rather than possibly ruining a man's soul by going. He may well have thought, *I have a perfect right, if I choose, to take a wife; but I shall not do it. I will live a bachelor life, and toil with my hands, because by being lonesome myself I may touch some other man who is lonesome too, and by working with my own hands I shall stay upon the bench beside others who will be drawn to me by sympathy. There are many things this body of mine may have in innocence, but I shall not take them because I wish to keep my body under, lest it should master me and cause me to be a castaway.*

Christ waits - the sweet, strong, pure Son of God, His heart yearning over men and yearning to pour itself through us to save them. But many of us have choked Him, resisted Him, thwarted Him. One feels like asking the whole audience to fall before Him in confession and to ask that this holy day may not pass until He has restored us to fellowship with Himself.

F. B. MEYER

JUNE 20

SET YOUR HEART ON GOD

I have set the Lord always before me: because he is at my
right hand, I shall not be moved.
PSALM 16:8

It is but right that our hearts should be on God, when the heart of God is so much on us. If the Lord of glory can stoop so low as to set His heart on sinful dust, methinks we should easily be persuaded to set our hearts on Christ ... and ascend to Him, in our daily affections ... Christian, dost thou not perceive that the heart of God is set upon thee, and that He is still minding thee with tender love? ... But when He speaks of our regards to Him, the case is otherwise: "Can a maid forget her ornaments, or a bride her attire? Yet My people have forgotten Me days without number." Let us not give God cause thus to expostulate with us. Rather let our souls get up to God, and visit Him every morning, and our hearts be toward Him every moment.

Come ye that love the Saviour's name.
And joy to make it known;
The sovereign of your heart proclaim,
And bow before His throne.

Lo, He on David's ancient throne,
His power and grace displays;
While Salem with its echoing hills,
Sends forth the voice of praise.

Sing, ye redeemed! Before the throne,
Ye white-robed myriads fall;
Sing, for the Lord of glory reigns,
The Christ, the heir of all.

RICHARD BAXTER

JUNE 21

SPIRITUAL OR CARNAL?

And I, brethren, could not speak unto you as unto spiritual, but as unto carnal, even as unto babes in Chirst.
1 CORINTHIANS 3:1

The Apostle here uses three words describing the spiritual condition of each person. There is *the natural man* in his unconverted state - one who cannot "receive the things of the Spirit of God" (I Cor 2:14). There is *"the spiritual man*, who can discern spiritual things" (1 Cor 2:13, 14). And between the two there is *the carnal man*, who is called "a babe in Christ," and who lives in jealousy and strife (1 Cor 3:3).

It is important for us to know whether we are carnal Christians, giving way to sin and the lusts of the flesh. With the thought that things cannot be otherwise, we are apt to be content to allow much that is sinful and wrong in our lives. God calls us and the Spirit draws us to be spiritual men and women - that is to say, people who pray each day to be led and guided each day into a truly spiritual life.

When the Lord Jesus promised the Spirit to His disciples, it was in the full expectation that they *would yield themselves wholly to the leading and power of the Spirit.* And it is in the same expectation that the Spirit will be granted anew each day, if we yield ourselves unreservedly to be sanctified in all our walk and conversation. Oh, that our eyes were open to see how right and how blessed this is!

Many Christians pray for the Holy Spirit but always with a certain reservation, for they intend in many things still to do their own will. Oh, Christian, when you pray, entrust yourself fully to the guidance of the Holy Spirit for the whole day. If there is true willingness on your part, then the Holy Spirit will take full possession of you and will preserve and sanctify your life. Do not serve God half-heartedly.

God has His best thing for the few,
That dare to stand the test;
God has His second choice for those,
Who will not have His best.

I want in this short life of mine,
As much as can be pressed;
Of serving true for God and man:
Make me to be Thy best.

ANDREW MURRAY

SEPARATION FROM THE WORLD

What communion hath light with darkness?
2 CORINTHIANS 6:14

Therefore come out from among them, and be ye separate, saith the Lord, and touch not the unclean thing; and I will receive you. And I will be a Father unto you, and ye shall be my sons and daughters, saith the Lord Almighty" (2 Corinthians 6: 17-18).

I do not believe that there is any doctrine more needed today in the Christian church than the doctrine of separation. We have lost power because the line between the church and the world has been almost obliterated. A good many people profess Christianity, but their profession does not mean much; the result is that the world does not know what Christians really believe. For every unconverted man that reads the Bible, a hundred read you and me; and if they see us hand-in-glove with the ungodly they are not going to have any confidence in our professions.

"Be not unequally yoked together with unbelievers." How is it with matrimony? How many ministers would marry a godly woman to an ungodly man? Why not take a stand and say you will not be a party to it? The courts are filled with divorce cases because Christian men and women have been yoked with unbelievers. Look at the mothers whose children have been unequally yoked with infidels and men of the world! My friends, if we want the power of God we must obey God's Word, cost us what it may.

How is it with your life? Are you hand-in-glove with the world? If you are, how can you expect God to fill you with the Holy Spirit? I believe that the cause of Christ is suffering more from this one thing than any other ten things put together. God cannot give us power because we are allied with the ungodly. The mirth that satisfies the world will not satisfy the true child of God, and yet how many of us are just looking to the world for our pleasure.

If we walk with God, we will not be asking, "What is the harm of this and that?" The question will be, "What is the good?" If a thing does not help us we will give it up for something better.

D. L. MOODY

JUNE 23

WHAT ABOUT WORSHIP?

Not a novice, lest being lifted up with pride he fall into the
condemnation of the devil.
1 TIMOTHY 3:6

Strange things are happening all around us in Christian circles because we are not truly worshippers.

For instance, any untrained, unprepared, unspiritual empty rattletrap of a person can start something "religious" and find plenty of followers who will listen and promote it! Beyond that, it may become very evident that he or she had never heard from God in the first place.

All of the examples we have in the Bible illustrate that glad and devoted and reverent worship is the normal employment of human beings. Every glimpse that is given us of heaven and of God's created beings is always a glimpse of worship and rejoicing and praise - because God is who He is!

Because we are not truly worshippers, we spend a lot of time in the churches just spinning our wheels; making a noise but not getting anywhere.

What are we going to do about this awesome, beautiful worship that God calls for? I would rather worship God than do any other thing I know of in all of this wide world!

Thou has given so much to me,
Give one thing more - a grateful heart:
Not thankful when it pleaseth me,
As if Thy blessings had spare days,
But such a heart whose Pulse may be Thy Praise.

A. W. TOZER

THE ONLY SAFE GROUND

Without the sheeding of blood is no remission.
HEBREWS 9:22

There is an apparently authentic story told of the great Queen Victoria, so long ruler of Britain's vast empire. When she occupied her castle at Balmoral, Scotland, she was in the habit of calling, in a friendly way, upon certain cottagers living in the neighbourhood. One aged Highland woman, who felt greatly honoured by these visits and who knew the Lord, was anxious about the soul of the Queen. As the season came to a close one year, Her Majesty was making her last visit to the humble home of this dear child of God. After the goodbyes were said, the old cottager timidly inquired, "May I ask Your Gracious Majesty a question?"

"Yes," replied the Queen, "as many as you like."

"Will Your Majesty meet me in heaven?"

Instantly the royal visitor replied, "I will, through the all-availing blood of Jesus."

That is the only safe ground for assurance. The blood shed on Calvary avails for all classes alike.

When Israel of old was about to leave Egypt, and the last awful plague was to fall on that land and its people, God Himself provided a way of escape for His own. They were to slay a lamb, sprinkle its blood on the doorposts and lintel of their houses, go inside, and shut the door. When the destroying angel passed through that night, he would not be permitted to enter any blood-sprinkled door, for Jehovah had said, "When I see the blood, I will pass over you." Inside the house, some might have been trembling and some rejoicing, but all were safe. Their security depended, not on their frames of mind or feelings, but on the fact that the eye of God beheld the blood of the lamb and they were sheltered behind it. As they recalled the word that He had given concerning it and truly believed it, they would have much assurance.

So it is today! We cannot see the blood shed so long ago for our redemption on Calvary, but there is a sense in which it is ever before the eyes of God. The moment a repentant sinner puts his trust in Christ, he is viewed by God as sheltered behind the blood-sprinkled lintel.

HARRY IRONSIDE

OUR FAITHFUL FRIEND

For the Lord is good; his mercy is everlasting; and his truth
endureth to all generations.
PSALM 100:5

I expect more goodness from Kate my wife, from Philip Melanchthon, and from others ... than from my sweet and blessed Saviour Jesus Christ; and yet I know for certain that neither she nor any other person on earth will or can suffer that for me which He has suffered. Why then should I be afraid of Him? This my foolish weakness grieves me very much. We plainly see in the Gospel how mild and gentle He showed Himself towards His disciples; how kindly He passed over their weakness, their presumption, yea, their foolishness ... Fie on our unbelieving hearts that we should be afraid of this Man who is more loving, friendly, gentle, and compassionate towards us than are our own kindred, our brothers and sisters - yea, than parents towards their own children.

What'er my God ordains is right;
My light, my life is He,
Who cannot will me aught but good;
I trust Him utterly;
For well I know,
In joy or woe,
We soon shall see, as sunlight clear,
How faithful was our guardian here.

What'er my God ordains is right;
Here will I take my stand,
Tho' sorrow, need, or death make earth
For me a desert land,
My Father's care
Is round me there,
He holds me that I shall not fall;
And so to Him I leave it all.

MARTIN LUTHER

JUNE 26

SEEN OF ALL

They shall see his face.
REVELATION 22:4

Handle me, and see; for a spirit hath not flesh and bones, as ye see me have." This same Jesus, with a material body, is to come in the clouds of heaven. In the same manner as He went up, He shall come down. He shall be literally seen. The words cannot be honestly read in any other way: "Every eye shall see Him."

Yes, I do literally expect to see my Lord Jesus with these eyes of mine, even as that saint expected who long ago fell asleep, believing that though the worms devour his body, yet in his flesh should see God, whom his eyes should see for himself, and not another. There will be a real resurrection of the body, though the moderns doubt it; such a resurrection that we shall see Jesus with our own eyes. We shall not find ourselves in a shadowy, dreamy land of floating fictions, where we may perceive but cannot see. We shall not be airy nothings, mysterious, vague, impalpable; but we shall literally see our glorious Lord, whose appearing will be no phantom show or shadow dance. Never day more real than the day of judgment; never sight more true than the Son of Man upon the throne of His glory.

We are getting too far away from facts nowadays and too much into the realm of myths and notions. However, "every eye shall see Him"; in this there shall be no delusion.

Note well that He is to be seen of all kinds of living men; every eye shall see Him; the king and the peasant, the most learned and the most ignorant. Those that were blind before shall see when He appears. I remember a man born blind who loved our Lord most intensely, and he was wont to glory in this - that his eyes had been reserved for his Lord. He said, "The first whom I shall ever see will be the Lord Jesus Christ. The first sight that greets my newly-opened eyes will be the Son of Man in His glory."

CHARLES H. SPURGEON

THE DIVINTY OF CHRIST

My Lord and my God.
JOHN 20:28

Christ was addressed by a disciple as "God", without prohibition or rebuke on his part. The noble exclamation which burst from the lips of Thomas, when convinced that his Lord had risen indeed - the noble exclamation, "My Lord and my God" - admits of only one meaning. It was a distinct testimony to our blessed Lord's divinity. It was a clear, unmistakable declaration that Thomas believed him, whom he saw and touched that day, to be not only man, but God. Above all, it was a testimony which our Lord received and did not prohibit and a declaration which he did not say one word to rebuke. When Cornelius fell down at the feet of Peter and would have worshipped him, the apostle refused such honour at once: "Stand up; I myself also am a man" (Acts 10: 26). When the people of Lystra would have done sacrifice to Paul and Barnabas, "they rent their clothes and ran in among the people ... saying, Sirs, why do ye these things? We also are men of like passions with you" (Acts 14: 14, 15). But when Thomas says to Jesus, "My Lord and my God," the words do not elicit a syllable of reproof from our holy and truth-loving Master. Can we doubt that these things were written for our learning?

Let us settle it firmly in our minds that the divinity of Christ is one of the grand foundation truths of Christianity and let us be willing to go to the stake rather than let it go. Unless our Lord Jesus is very God of very God, there is an end of His mediation, His atonement, His advocacy, His priesthood, His whole work of redemption. These glorious doctrines are useless blasphemies, unless Christ is divine. For ever let us bless God that the divinity of our Lord is taught everywhere in the Scriptures and stands on evidence that can never be overthrown.

He is God and therefore is "able to save to the uttermost all who come unto God by Him".

J. C. RYLE

SPIRITUAL WORSHIP

Worthy is the Lamb that was slain.
REVELATION 5:12

Our Saviour tells us that the Father "seeketh" such to worship Him; and the grave question for us all is whether He ever bends over us, as we kneel, receiving as grateful incense the ascriptions of our worshipping love. He hears us babble in petitions, which we may have uttered for years! He hears our intercessions for others, which are the expression of human affection! But does He often hear the outburst of worship and praise from hearts that have obeyed the psalmist's injunction to join the universal chant arising from the unfallen universe? To this the psalmist calls us when he says: "O come, let us sing unto the Lord; let us make a joyful noise to the Rock of our salvation. O come, let us worship and bow down; let us kneel before the Lord our Maker."

Let us kindle our hearts to praise by listening, as Isaiah did to the chant of the seraphim - "Holy, holy, holy, is the Lord of hosts, the whole earth is full of his glory"; or by listening to the song of the virgin-mother: "My soul doth magnify the Lord, and my spirit hath rejoiced in God my Saviour"; or by listening as John did to the out-circling song of heaven, beginning with the inner circle of the redeemed, and reaching out to every created thing, which is in the heaven, and on the earth, and on the sea! "Unto Him that sitteth on the throne, and unto the Lamb, be the blessing and the honour, and the glory, and the dominion, for ever and ever. And the four living creatures said, Amen! And the elders fell down and worshipped"

In order to incite our sluggish souls to worship, we may recite aloud the Psalms, or the *Te Deum*, or any of the great hymns of the church. But, best of all, it is for the soul to pour out its adoring gratitude and love in its own glad words. "We give Thee thanks for our creation, preservation, and for all the good things in our lives, but above all for the redemption of our world by our Lord Jesus Christ and for our own adoption into eternal union with Thyself."

F. B. MEYER

JUNE 29

FULL POSSESSION

So run, that ye may obtain.
1 CORINTHIANS 9:24

Heaven is above thee, and dost thou think to travel this steep ascent without labour and resolution? Canst thou get that earthly heart to heaven and bring that backward mind to God, while thou liest still and takest thine ease? If lying down at the foot of a hill and looking toward the top and wishing we were there would serve the turn, then we should have daily travellers for heaven. But the "kingdom of heaven suffereth violence, and violent men take it by force." There must be violence used to get these firstfruits, as well as to get the full possession. Dost thou not feel it is, though I should not tell thee? Will thy heart get upwards, except thou drive it?

Teach me, O Lord, Thy love to know,
With all my powers of mind and thought;
The utmost consecration show,
Of all this being Thou hast brought.

To do Thy will, most Merciful,
I seek Thy guidance day by day;
To bear the trials that befall,
I would for constant courage pray.

RICHARD BAXTER

THE GREAT QUESTION

Believe ye that I am able to do this? They said unto him, Yea, Lord.
MATTHEW 9:28

I f thou canst believe, all things are possible to him that believeth. And straightway the father of the child said with tears: "Lord, I believe, help Thou mine unbelief" (Mark 9: 23-24). "Jesus said, He that believeth in Me, though he were dead, yet shall he live. Believest thou this? She saith unto Him, Yea, Lord, I believe" (John 11: 25-27).

To what we have seen and heard of Christ Jesus, our heart is ready to say with Martha in answer to Christ's question: "Yea, Lord, I have believed that Thou art the Christ, the Son of God." But when it comes to the point of believing that what Christ promises to us of the power of the resurrection life, of His abiding presence every day and all the day, we do not find it so easy to say, "I do believe that this omnipotent, omnipresent, unchangeable Christ, our Redeemer God will in very deed walk with me all the day and give me the unceasing consciousness of His holy presence" - it almost looks too much to venture. And yet it is just this faith that Christ asks and is waiting to work within us.

It is well that we understand clearly what the conditions are on which Christ offers to reveal to us in experience the secret of His abiding presence. God cannot force His blessings on us against our will. He seeks in every possible way to stir our desire and to help us to realise that He is able and most willing to make His promises true. The resurrection of Christ from the dead is His great plea, His all-prevailing argument. If He could raise that dead Christ who had died under the burden of all our sin and curse, surely He can, now that Christ has conquered death and is to us the Resurrection and the Life, fulfil in our hearts His promise that Christ can be so with us and so in us that He Himself should be our life all the day.

And now the great question comes, whether in view of what we have said and seen about Christ as our Lord, as our redeeming God, whether we are willing to take His word in all simplicity in its divine fullness of meaning and to rest in the promise: "Lo, I am with you all the day." Christ's question comes to us: "Believe thou this?" Let us not rest until we have bowed before Him and said: "Yea, Lord, I do believe."

ANDREW MURRAY

HOW TO READ GOD'S WORD

His delight is in the law of the Lord.
PSALM 1:2

Here are some simple rules for Bible reading. *Read God's Word with great reverence.* Meditate a moment in silence on the thought that the words come from God Himself. Bow in deep reverence. Be silent unto God. Let Him reveal His Word in your heart.

Read with careful attention. If you read the words carelessly, thinking that you can grasp their meaning with your human understanding, you will use the words superficially and not enter into their depths. When someone tries to explain anything wonderful or beautiful to us, we give our entire attention to try to understand what is said. How much higher and deeper are God's thoughts than our thoughts. "As the heaven is higher than the earth, so are My thoughts higher than your thoughts." We need to give our undivided attention to understand even the superficial meaning of the words. How much harder to grasp the spiritual meaning!

Read with the expectation of the guidance of God's Spirit. It is God's Spirit alone that can make the Word a living power in our hearts and lives. Read Psalm 119. Notice how earnestly David prays that God will teach him and open his eyes and give him understanding and incline his heart to God's ways. As you read, remember that God's Word and God's Spirit are inseparable.

Read with the firm purpose of keeping the Word day and night in your heart and in your life. The whole heart and the whole life must come under the influence of the Word. David said, "O how I love Thy law, it is my meditation all the day.' And so in the midst of his daily work, the believer can cherish God's Word in his heart and meditate on it. Read Psalm 119 again, until you accept God's Word with all your heart.

ANDREW MURRAY

PRAYER BORN OF COMPASSION

When he saw the multitudes,
he was moved with compassion on them.
MATTHEW 9:36

We are speaking here particularly about spiritual compassion, that which is born in a renewed heart and which finds hospitality there. This compassion has in it the quality of mercy, is of the nature of pity, and moves the soul with tenderness of feeling for others. Compassion is moved at the sight of sin, sorrow and suffering. It stands at the other extreme to indifference of spirit to the wants and woes of others. It is far removed from insensibility and hardness of heart in the midst of want and trouble and wretchedness. Compassion stands beside sympathy for others, is interested in them, and is concerned about them.

That which excites and develops compassion and puts it to work is the sight of multitudes in want and distress, helpless to relieve themselves. Helplessness especially appeals to compassion. Compassion is silent but does not remain secluded. It reaches out at the sight of trouble, sin and need. First of all compassion flows out in earnest prayer for those for whom it feels and has a sympathy for them. Prayer for others is born of a sympathetic heart. Prayer is natural and almost spontaneous when compassion is begotten in the heart. Prayer belongs to the compassionate man.

Soften my heart, Lord, soften my heart,
From all indifference set me apart,
To feel Your compassion, to weep with Your tears,
Come soften my heart, O Lord, soften my heart.

E. M. BOUNDS

JULY 3

CHRISTIAN COMMUNION

There is one body, and one Spirit,
even as ye are called in one hope of your calling.
EPHESIANS 4:4

We need one another; are dependent on one another - not as fountains, but as channels of blessing. When mutual intercession takes the place of mutual accusation, then will the differences and difficulties of brethren be overcome. (Job 42:8-10).

The infirmities of our brethren are fair occasions for our patience and long-suffering: let us have grace for each opportunity.

The hearts of true believers crave a fellowship which will last - a fellowship in the Spirit with each other, because of common fellowship with the Father and with His Son Jesus Christ.

Humility is the secret of fellowship, and pride the secret of division.

If Christ be not the bond of friendship and of communion, and if His blood be not the life of love, how quickly may indifference take the place of warm affections and how easily may close friends turn to stubborn adversaries, through the clashings of self-seeking and thwarted pride, of man's native fickleness!

In John 17 and in Ephesians 1 we see what the Church is in the sight of God in Christ - what it ought to be in its ways; and would be, did we not grieve the Holy Ghost, which is given to us to lead us into all truth, and to glorify Christ in us. But the Church has not been true to her heavenly calling; she has forgotten her dignity; she has lost her strength; the grey hairs are here and there upon her, and she knoweth it not. (Hosea 7:9).

The fellowship of believers ought to be like the fellowship of the Father and the Son: any differences of judgment, therefore, which arise between two members of Christ about the truth of God should be a cause of humiliation, but not of strife and separation. God would soon make His children of one mind, did they steadfastly set their faces toward the Mercy-seat, seeking unity according to 1 Corinthians 1 and Ephesians 4:5.

ROBERT CLEAVER CHAPMAN

JULY 4

CHRIST'S CREDENTIALS

Whereas I was blind, now I see.
JOHN 9:25

Think of the gracious revelation of God's purpose and power in the healing of the man born blind (John 9). Think of his case, and in many another that might be named. Away back in the councils of eternity God determined to redeem the human race, putting the iniquity of us all upon the Person of His own Son, our Saviour Jesus Christ. It was necessary that the Son should take upon Himself our human nature; that He should come to earth; and that He should be known and identified when He came, by the works He should do, that men might believe on Him.

And so, for your redemption, and mine, and that of the whole world, God caused this child to be born blind. The impairment brought sorrow to his parents and to himself. Day after day, week after week, month after month, year after year he sat there. All Jerusalem knew him; thousands of people from Judea and Galilee knew him and knew he had been born blind.

And now the reason for it all! The Son of Man has left the glory He had with the Father before the world was; He has come down to earth to suffer and die; and He is about to be identified as the Son of God and the Saviour of the world. On this memorable day He is passing by the temple gate and, seeing this man, speaks to him the word of power that gives him the sight he never had. The man returns to his home, and it is known there - and in all Jerusalem and in all Judea and in all the world - that God did it to certify to the well-beloved One, whose blood cleanseth us from all sin.

Was it not worth the while of that man to have been born blind and to have suffered so? Was it not worth while for his parents to have suffered? Does God ever put suffering upon His faithful witnesses when reward does not follow it? It was well worth his while, not only for his own sake, but for that of millions of redeemed souls who have been won to God through Jesus Christ. They are in His presence now, because of the testimony he bore to Him by sitting at the temple gate until He restored his sight.

JAMES M. GRAY

OLD THINGS PASS AWAY

If any man be in Christ ... old things are passed away;
behold, all things are become new.
2 CORINTHIANS 5:17

The New Testament is, among other things, a record of the struggle of twice-born men and women to live in a world run by the once-born! That should indicate that we are not being as helpful as we ought to be when we fail to instruct the new Christian, that one who is "a babe in Christ," that our Lord told His earliest disciples, "In this world you will have tribulation."

The Apostle Paul knew what he was talking about when he told Christian believers, "All that will live godly in Christ Jesus will suffer persecution."

Take the example of a person recently converted to Christ. His inner witness is clear and up to the light he has, he is beginning to live as he believes a Christian should. But this new world is altogether different from the one he has just left. Standards, values, objectives, methods - all are different. Many solid pillars upon which he had previously leaned without question are now seen to be made of chalk and ready to crumble.

There will be tears but there will be joy and peace with the continuing discovery that in Christ, indeed, "old things pass away and all things become new."

Thy nature, gracious Lord, impart;
Come quickly from above,
Write Thy new name upon my heart,
Thy new, best name of love.

A. W. TOZER

JULY 6

TRUE FOREVER

... senses exercised to discern both good and evil.
HEBREWS 5:14

Our spiritual constitution must be braced, not only that we may be strong for work or fight, but that we may be proof against the infection of the times, against the poison which the god of this world, "the prince of the power of the air," has impregnated our atmosphere. For this we need not only the "strong meat" recommended by the apostle (Hebrews 5:12-14) but the keen, fresh mountain air of trial, vicissitude, and hardship - by means of which we shall be made hardy in constitution and robust in frame, impervious to the contagion around, whether that come from ecclesiastical pictorialism or religious liberalism; impregnable against the assaults of Satan the Pharisee or Satan the Sadducee.

They who have slid into creed (they know not how) or been swept into it by the crowd; they to whom the finding of a creed has been a matter of reading, education, or emotion - they possess not the true power of resistance; they carry no disinfecting virtue, no error-repelling power about with them. The epidemics of the age tell sorely upon them, and, even though they may have taken hold of the truth, it becomes evident that the truth has not taken hold of them. In a time of uncertainty, skepticisim, speculation, false progress, we need to recognise the full meaning of the apostolic "we know" (1 John 5:19-20), "we believe" (2 Corinthians 4:13), "we are confident" (2 Corinthians 5:6), "we are persuaded" (2 Timothy 1:12). For that which is divine must be true; and that which is revealed must be certain; and that which is thus divinely true and certain must be immortal. Like the results of the exact sciences, it is fixed, not varying with men and ages. That which was true is true and shall be true forever.

It is the more needful to recognise all this, because the ground underneath us has been thoroughly mined and is very largely hollow; a process of skeptical decomposition and disintegration has been going on, the extent of which will soon be manifest when the treacherous crust gives way.

HORATIUS BONAR

GRATITUDE AND THANKSGIVING

Present your bodies a living sacrifice, holy, acceptable unto God,
which is your reasonable service.
ROMANS 12:1

Consideration of God's mercies not only begets gratitude, but induces a large consecration to God of all we have and are. Thus, prayer, thanksgiving and consecration are all inseparably linked together. Gratitude and thanksgiving always look back at the past though they may also take in the present. But prayer always looks to the future. Thanksgiving deals with things already received. Prayer deals with things desired, asked for and expected. Prayer turns to gratitude and praise when the things asked for have been granted by God. As prayer brings things to us which beget gratitude and thanksgiving, so praise and gratitude promote prayer and induce more praying and better praying.

Gratitude and thanksgiving forever stand opposed to all murmuring at God's dealings with us, and all complaining at our lot. Gratitude and murmuring never abide in the same heart at the same time. An unappreciative spirit has no standing beside gratitude and praise. True prayer corrects complaining and promotes gratitude and thanksgiving. Dissatisfaction at one's lot, and a disposition to be discontented with things which come to us in the providence of God, are foes to gratitude and enemies to thanksgiving.

All my life, Lord, to You I want to give;
This is my worship, please show me how to live,
Take every part of me, make it Your own,
Me on the cross, Lord, You on the Throne.

E. M. BOUNDS

JULY 8

BY LOVE COMPELLED

Love your enemies, bless them that curse you, do good to them that hate you,
and pray for them which despitefully use you, and persecute you.
MATTHEW 5:44

True charity holds out, in spite of ingratitude, opposition and persecution. Its possessor takes the good of all men, not because he ought merely, but because he cannot help it. His heart is on the side of God and truth. He loves righteousness and, therefore, cannot desist from seeking to bring all beings to love it, too, although they hate and despise him for so long. Jesus held out in this glorious love even in the agonies of the crucifixion. "Father, forgive them; they know not what they do". His heart was set on bringing men back to God and He went through with it. His soul did not draw back and His divine love constrained Him even unto death.

Paul followed his Master in this respect; and though the more he loved some of his converts, the less he was loved, he went on, seeking their highest good, not being hindered for a moment by their ingratitude. He loved them - not their good opinion or applause. A spurious charity soon tires when the objects of it prove unworthy. Its possessor says, "I have had enough of this; the kinder I am, the worse people treat me. I shall button up my pocket and take my ease, till I am better appreciated."

Self-glory is the very life of spurious charity: it dies right out under ingratitude and contempt.

CATHERINE BOOTH

THE KING IS COMING

Even so, come, Lord Jesus.
REVELATION 22:20

You remember the story of David, King of Israel, when his ungrateful son, Absalom, whom he loved best, rebelled against him and drove him from his throne. The rebellion was soon quashed and Absalom himself slain, but David was in exile beyond the Jordan still. And one day the men of Judah, David's tribe, came together and began to talk about it. Their consciences were smiting them, and they said to one another, "Why say ye never a word about bringing back the king?" And when they began to think and talk about it they began to act, and they crossed the Jordan and brought him back.

I ask you,

Why say ye not a word of bringing back the King?
Why speak ye not of Jesus and His reign?
Whey tell ye of His glory and of His praises sing,
But not a word about His coming back again?

How many in our churches today are testifying to the second coming of Christ? What are we doing to hasten His return? When we become conscience-smitten upon this matter and begin to talk about it, we will begin to act, and to live and witness for Him in such a way that the day shall be hastened. God give us the grace to do it, and the love and the power!

That dear old Scottish saint Andrew Bonar visited this country once - sad for us he could not have visited it oftener. On that occasion, as he was about returning home, New York friends gave him a farewell meeting. One of them, in closing the address, applied the words of Paul to Timothy to him, saying: "There is a crown of righteousness laid up for him which the Lord, the righteous judge, shall give him in that day." But Mr. Bonar, coming forward and holding up his hand for silence, concluded the quotation, adding: "And not to me only, but also to all them that love His appearing."

Ah! there is no respect of persons with God! Do you love His appearing? Are you longing for His coming? Are you ready should He come today?

JAMES M. GRAY

JULY 10

PRAYER, PRAISE AND THANKSGIVING

The Lord hath done great things for us, whereof we are glad.
PSALM 126:3

Prayer, praise and thanksgiving all go in company. A close relationship exists between them praise and thanksgiving are so nearly alike that it is not easy to distinguish between them or define them separately. The Scriptures join these three things together. Many are the causes for thanksgiving and praise. The Psalms are filled with many songs of praise and hymns of thanksgiving, all pointing back to the results of prayer.

Thanksgiving includes gratitude. In fact, thanksgiving is but the expression of an inward conscious gratitude to God for mercies received. Gratitude is an inward emotion of the soul, involuntarily arising therein, while thanksgiving is the voluntary expression of gratitude.

Thanksgiving is oral, positive, active. It is the giving out of something to God. Thanksgiving comes out into the open. Gratitude is secret, silent, negative, passive, not showing its being till expressed in praise and thanksgiving. Gratitude is felt in the heart. Thanksgiving is the expression of that inward feeling.

There's a psalm of praise filling all my days,
Since to Jesus my heart did bow;
O what a melody! Glorious harmony!
Life is wonderful now.

E. M. BOUNDS

GOOD DEEDS AND GOOD WILL

Trust in the Lord, and do good; so shalt thou dwell in the land,
and verily thou shalt be fed.
PSALM 37:3

The saintly children of God do their good deeds out of sheer good will, seeking no reward but alone God's honour and will, and are ready and eager to do good, and would be even if there were neither heaven nor hell. And this is proved fully by the words of Christ, when he says, "Come ye blessed of my Father, inherit the kingdom prepared for you from the foundation of the world." Now, could they merit, as reward of their deeds, that Kingdom, which is prepared for them before they are created? The Kingdom is not being prepared, for it is   prepared already, but the children are being prepared for the Kingdom ... The Kingdom wins the children and not the children the Kingdom.

Let me but do my work from day to day
In field or forest, at desk or loom,
In roaring market place or tranquil room;
Let me but find it in my heart to say,
When vagrant wishes beckon me astray,
"This is my work; my blessing, not my doom;
Of all who live, I am the one by whom
This work can best be done in the right way."

Then shall I see it not too great, nor small,
To suit my spirit and to prove my powers;
Then shall I cheerful greet the labouring hours,
And cheerful turn, when the long shadows fall
At eventide, to play and love and rest,
Because I know for me my work is best.

MARTIN LUTHER

GOD KNOWS MY PRAYER

Blessed are the dead which die in the Lord ...
that they may rest from their labours.
REVELATION 14:13

We modern Christians seem to be a strange breed in many of our ways. We are so completely satisfied with earthly things and we enjoy our creature comforts so much that we would just rather stay on here for a long, long time!

Probably most of us do not tell God about that kind of desire when we pray. But for years I have made a practice of writing many of my earnest prayers to God in a little book - a book now well worn. I remind God often of what my prayers have been.

One prayer in the book - and God knows it well by this time - is an honest supplication:

"Oh, God,

Let me die rather than go on day by day living wrong. I do not want to become a careless, fleshly old man.

I want to be right so that I can die right! Lord, I do not want my life to be extended if it would mean that I should cease to live right and fail in my mission to glorify You all of my days!

I would rather go home right now than to live on - if living on was to be a waste of God's time and my own!"

A. W. TOZER

JULY 13

ONE GREAT LESSON

This is the word of the Lord unto Zerubbabel ... Not by might, nor by power,
but by my spirit, saith the Lord of hosts.
ZECHARIAH 4:6

It was not until the primitive Christians began to admit worldly principles of action, and to substitute the material for the spiritual, that their influence began to wane, and their testimony to lose its power. It was the gradual substitution of the human for the divine, the material for the spiritual, that overspread Christendom for ages with papal darkness and death.

During the long night of error and suffering, however, God raised up many witnesses to the sufficiency of the Holy Ghost to attract and convert men - many making long pilgrimages and suffering great privations, in order to visit and converse which those endued with this divine gift.

And when at length the light of the Reformation broke over the nations, this one great lesson was again engraven on the hearts of God's chosen instruments: "It is not by might, nor by power, but by my spirit, saith the Lord of hosts." Thus, after the lapse of ages, we find the gospel, when preached with the old power, the same mighty instrumentality, both for attracting the multitudes and converting the soul.

CATHERINE BOOTH

JULY 14

TOKENS

Show me a token for good.
PSALM 86:17

I t seems a natural thing for a man who seeks God's face to offer reasons why God should hear him. The Pharisee may suggest that his virtues merit God's attention: the Publican can only beg God's merciful interest in his case. Through various reasons of poverty and necessity he mounts to ask for some token of good.

The desire for some outward support of inward trust has been cherished in every generation. "Show me a token for good," was the prayer of the man who in his own time and for his own task desired some confirming evidence from God; not something to gratify his curiosity, but something to show in support of his faith; he wanted it for his own sake and for the sake of others that they too might believe.

Our Lord encountered repeated petitions for some sign or token of Himself. His miracles were intended to make faith easy, but in the ultimate He was Himself His own best token, "He that hath seen me hath seen the Father." He urged that the people had Moses and the prophets; if they did not believe them, neither would they believe though one rose from the dead. The Scriptures were to Christ's mind a reasonable and perpetual support of faith.

The supreme answer to the petition was given in the Upper Room, "He showed them His hands and His side; then were the disciples glad when they saw the Lord." When our sense of sin, our bitter regrets and our oppressive glooms disturb our hope, there is always His token, the mark of His wounds, the sign of His cross, to give us confidence and peace.

Hath He marks to lead me to Him,
If He be my Guide?
In His feet and hands are wound-prints,
And His side.

JOHN MACBEATH

GOD SEEKS INTERCESSORS

He saw that there was no man, and wondered
that there was no intercessor.
ISAIAH 59:16

From of old God had among His people intercessors to whose voice He had listened and given deliverance. Here we read of a time of trouble when He sought for an intercessor, but in vain. And He wondered! Think of what that means - the amazement of God that there should be none who loved the people enough or who had sufficient faith in His power to deliver, to intercede, on their behalf. If there had been an intercessor, He would have given deliverance; without an intercessor, His judgments came down (see Isaiah 64:7; Ezek. 22:30-31).

Of what infinite importance is the place the intercessor holds in the Kingdom of God! Is it not indeed a matter of wonder that God should give men such power and yet that there are so few who know what it is to take hold of His strength and pray down His blessing on the world?

Let us try to realise the position. When God had in His Son wrought out the new creation and Christ had taken His place on the Throne, the work of the extension of His Kingdom was given into the hands of men. He ever liveth to pray; prayer is the highest exercise of His royal prerogative as Priest-King upon the throne. All that Christ was to do in heaven was to be in fellowship with His people on earth. In His divine condescension God has willed that the working of His Spirit shall follow the prayer of His people. He waits for their intercession, showing the preparation of heart - where and how much of His Spirit they are ready to receive.

God rules the world and His Church through the prayers of His people. "That God should have made the extension of His Kingdom to such a large extent dependent on the faithfulness of His people in prayer is a stupendous mystery and yet an absolute certainty." God calls for intercessors; in His grace He has made His work dependent on them; He waits for them.

ANDREW MURRAY

JULY 16

LISTEN TO JESUS

Take the helmet of salvation, and the sword of
the Spirit, which is the word of God.
EPHESIANS 6:17

This is the Father's will that we should listen to what the man Jesus says and give ear to His Word. You are not to try to be clever in connection with His Word, to master it or to argue about it, but simply to hear it. Then the Holy Spirit will come and dispose your heart so that you will believe and say from the bottom of your heart concerning the preaching of the divine Word: "That is God's Word and is the pure truth" and you will risk your life upon it. But if you yourself want to be heard, and to obliterate the Word of Christ with your own reason, if you attempt to subject the Word to your own ideas ... if you ponder it as though you were in doubt about it, wanting to judge it according to your own mind, that is not listening to it, or being a disciple.

Within this ample volume lies
The mystery of mysteries.
Happiest they of human race
To whom their God has given grace
To read, to fear, to hope, to pray,
To lift the latch, to force the way;
But better had they ne'er been born
That read to doubt, or read to scorn.

MARTIN LUTHER

JULY 17

COUNSELS AND WARNINGS

Let your light so shine ...
MATTHEW 5:16

If sin be but a common scar or wrinkle, to be erased from the soul's surface by a few simple touches; if pardon be a mere figure of speech, meaning God's wide benevolence or good-natured indifference to evil, why tell of wrath, and fire, and judgment? Does God love to torment His creatures by harsh words or fill their imaginations with images of woe that He does not intend to realise? Or why did the Son of God suffer, weep and grieve? If error be but a trifle, a foible, a freak at worst; or if it be a display of honest purpose and the inevitable result of free thought, why is the "strong delusion" (literally, "the energy of error") spoken of so awfully: "that they all might be damned who believed not the truth" (2 Thessalonians 2:12). Even the Lord Himself has said concerning false doctrine that it is that "thing I hate".

As the strongest yet calmest thing in the world is light, so should a Christian life be the strongest and greatest as well as the calmest and brightest. As the only perfectly straight line is a ray of light, and as the only pure substance is sunshine, so ought our course to be, and so should we seek to shine as lights in the world; reflections of Him who is its light, the one straight, pure thing on earth.

Let us then shine. Stars indeed, not suns; but still stars, not candles or meteors. Let us shine! Giving perhaps slender light, but that light certain and pure; enough to say to men, "It is night" lest they mistake. Our light should be enough to guide the seeking or the erring in the true direction, though it is not enough to illuminate the world. The sun alone can do that. It is the sun that shows us the landscape; stars show but themselves. Let us then show ourselves beyond mistake. The day when all things shall be seen in full warm light is the day of the great sun-rising.

"The night is far spent, the day is at hand". We shall not set nor be clouded; we shall simply lose ourselves in light. And we need not grudge thus losing ourselves, when we call to mind that the splendour in which our light is to be absorbed is that of the everlasting Sun.

HORATIUS BONAR

THE MOTHERHOOD OF ZION

This and that man was born in her.
PSALM 87:5

The choice of Zion as the early centre of worship in Israel was God's own selection. The temple of Zion was built and wrecked, and built and wrecked again, but the significance was not so much in the place as in the faith that was proclaimed there. Zion was the habitation of the Presence, the seat of divine government, the shrine of divine worship. "Begin at Jerusalem" said our Lord, making Zion the originating centre of the gospel.

The attractiveness of Zion explains its reputation: "Glorious things are spoken of thee, O city of God."

> *Glorious things of thee are spoken,*
> *Zion city of our God;*
> *He whose word cannot be broken*
> *Formed thee for His own abode.*
> *On the Rock of Ages founded,*
> *What can shake thy sure repose?*
> *With salvation's walls surrounded*
> *Thou may'st smile at all thy foes.*

The faith that emanated from Zion was to go out to gather to itself the former enemies of Israel and make them friends; the pagan peoples were to become citizens enjoying equal rights with Israel. The faith of Christ is not the exclusive privilege of any people, it is the redeeming possession of all the world.

The record of Zion is kept by God Himself; He does not give the keeping of the citizen roll to any official of church or state. He keeps His own book of remembrance; in His book of life He writes the names with His own hand, and He counts His people as a shepherd counts his sheep. Saints, apostles, prophets, martyrs, the humble and true of every age are written in the book of God. The record of Zion is the roll-book of heaven. "To be mentioned in a book is part of immortality," wrote George Matheson. To be mentioned in the Book of Life is immortality itself.

JOHN MACBEATH

THE NATURE OF GROWTH

If ye do these things, ye shall never fall.
2 PETER 1:10

The Holy Spirit is a great teacher, who when He begins a subject completes it. That is the reason we should always study a text in the light of its context in order to learn the mind of the Spirit.

For example, in 2 Peter 1 He not only tells us the basis and the means of Christian growth, but also describes its nature. In the simplest terms He reveals how we may know whether it is being accomplished in us or not:

"And beside this, giving all diligence, add to your faith virtue; and to virtue, knowledge; and to knowledge, temperance; and to temperance, patience; and to patience, godliness; and to godliness, brotherly kindness; and to brotherly kindness, charity" (verses 5-7).

Here is a superstructure of seven stories we are to erect upon the great, broad, deep foundation of our faith.

So let our lips and lives express
The Holy Gospel we profess,
So let our words and virtues shine
To prove the doctrine all Divine.

JAMES M. GRAY

GROWING ACQUAINTANCE
WITH CHRIST

That the life also of Jesus might be made manifest in our body.
2 CORINTHIANS 4:10

Christ twice passed the angels by. He sank far below them in His humiliation; He rose far above them in His exaltation. If Christ be the life and beauty of our days of sunshine, so is He the brother born for our adversity; and His love shall gild and strike through the darkest cloud. Having been once a sufferer, He communes with His suffering members, and instructs us to put our trials into a just balance; to call our affliction light and momentary. (2 Cor 4:17-18).

Resting wholly on Christ! ceasing wholly from the works of the flesh - is the secret of abiding in Him.

Growing acquaintance with Christ makes Him more and more precious to our souls. If Christ were anything less than unsearchable, He could not satisfy us - could neither fill the heart, nor give peace to the conscience.

The strength of love is shown in great things; the tenderness of love in little things. Christ showed the strength of His love on the cross by dying and bearing the curse for us; the tenderness of His love when He said, "Behold thy mother!" "Children, have ye any meat?" "Woman, why weepest thou?"

There was an immeasurable difference between the state of Christ on the Cross when He said, under the terrors of the Judge: "My God, My God, why hast Thou forsaken Me?" and when He said: "Father, into Thy hands I commend My Spirit."

"Let this mind be in you, which was also in Christ Jesus" (Phil 2:5). He could not sink lower than His Cross: we can no more fathom the depths of His humiliation than comprehend the glory of His Godhead. His exaltation answers to His Cross. He cannot rise higher than the right hand of God, nor find sweeter resting place from His sufferings and His toil than the bosom of the Father.

ROBERT CLEAVER CHAPMAN

RECONCILED

God was in Christ, reconciling the world unto himself,
not imputing their trespasses unto them.
2 CORINTHIANS 5:19

Account for it how you will, there is a fear in the human conscience that, somehow or other, it is not safe for God to pardon offenders. Conscience cannot feel that he may do it consistently, with his relation as God, and we have to get conscience to comprehend that the Son has paid the ransom before the soul will venture on it. Then we can see the absolute necessity for an atonement. Who, with any due estimate of his guilt, dare presume on the pardon of God without?

Conscience must have the assurance that God can be just and yet the justifier of the ungodly. This necessity lies deep down in our own nature; even the heathen feel it, on whom revelation has never dawned, hence they offer the fruit of their body for the sin of their soul, and inflict on themselves unheard of tortures and cruelties. They feel they are transgressors, and that they need something wherewith to appease justice, and so they try to make atonement for themselves.

Sinner, the sacrifice of Christ meets your deepest need. God has looked the subject all around, and met the whole case by letting His Son, the eternal Word, offer a sacrifice which heaven, earth and hell pronounce enough! Now you can safely venture your guilty soul on the virtue of that blood.

A mind at perfect peace with God,
Oh! what a word is this!
A sinner reconciled through blood;
This, this indeed is peace!

CATHERINE BOOTH

THE GOSPEL, A SOLACE AND COMFORT

The entrance of thy words giveth light.
PSALM 119:130

The gospel is like a fresh, mild, and cool air in the extreme heat of summer, a solace and comfort in the anguish of the conscience. But as this heat proceeds from the rays of the sun, so likewise the terrifying of the conscience must proceed from the preaching of the law, to the end that we may know we have offended against the laws of God. Now, when the mind is refreshed and quickened again by the cool air of the gospel, we must not then be idle, or lie down and sleep. That is, when our consciences are settled in peace, quieted and comforted through God's Spirit, we must prove our faith by such good works as God has commanded.

Lord, keep us steadfast in Thy Word;
Curb those who fain by craft or sword
Would wrest the Kingdom from Thy Son;
And set at naught all He hath done.
Lord Jesus Christ, Thy power make known,
For Thou art Lord of lords alone;
Defend thy Christendom, that we
May evermore sing praise to Thee.

O Comforter of priceless worth,
Send peace and unity on earth;
Support us in our final strife,
And lead us out of death to life.

MARTIN LUTHER

RECOVERY OF THE REPROBATE

There is none that doeth good.
PSALM 14:1

The reprobate state of a people is the long sorrow of God. It is not a reprobate heart but a reprobate generation that is under review. The writer's judgment upon his time is that it is so corrupt that "no one is doing good". Widespread evil is the disease of his time; society is so deluged with wrong that there is neither ark nor righteous man to deliver or to be delivered from its darksome flood. The root of its evil is its practical denial of God.

The research of God Himself is quoted to verify the condition of society: "Jehovah looked from heaven upon the sons of men to see if there were any seeking after God - there is not even one." The divine heart yearned to find hearts that were turned toward itself and the result was sore disappointment. What God wanted to see was very different from what He did see. There was none looking in His direction. "To make an order understood" wrote Lord Charles Beresford, "the men must be looking at the officer who gives it. Silence and attention are the first necessities for discipline." But God Himself was not given this measure of courtesy and devotion.

The recovery of the people is the set purpose of God. The writer foresaw the interventions of God, he foresaw the power of God frustrating evil and he anticipated the deliverance that was sure to come, "when Jehovah brings back the captivity of His people". From the captivity of misfortune, sorrow, sin, prejudice, fear or care, He sets His people free. There is no captivity He cannot break, nor captive He cannot free. Of all service His alone is perfect freedom.

Make me a captive, Lord,
And then I shall be free;
Force me to render up my sword,
And I shall conqueror be.

JOHN MACBEATH

LET US MOVE FORWARD

That ye might be filled with all the fulness of God..
EPHESIANS 3:19

The Apostle Paul's greatest desire was to always move forward in the knowledge and blessing of God. But some modern Bible teachers now call that kind of hunger and thirsting fanaticism, instead of desire for spiritual maturity.

These teachers assure the new Christian: "You are now complete in Christ. Just relax and be glad that there is nothing more you will ever need."

With great desire, Paul wrote: "That I may win Christ" - and yet he already had Christ! With obvious longing he said: "That I may be found in Him" - and yet he was already in Him!

Paul humbly and intensely breathed his great desire: "That I may know Him" - even though he already knew Him!

Because he did not want to stand still, Paul testified: "I follow after; I press toward the mark. I am striving to lay hold of that for which Christ laid hold on me!"

It is very plain that the apostle had no other desire than to be completely available to God. Many of us refuse to follow his example!

Walk thou with Him; that way is light,
All other pathways end in night:
Walk thou with Him; that way is rest;
All other pathways are unblest.

A. W. TOZER

PRAYER AND THE ENTIRE MAN

I pray God your whole spirit and soul and body be preserved blameless
unto the coming of our Lord Jesus Christ.
1 THESSALONIANS 5:23

P rayer has to do with the entire man. Prayer takes in man in his whole being
- mind, soul and body. It takes the whole man to pray, and prayer affects the
entire man in its gracious results. As the whole nature of man enters into
prayer, so also all that belongs to man is the beneficiary of prayer. All of man
receives benefits in prayer. The whole man must be given to God in praying.

The largest results in praying come to him who gives himself - all of himself, all
that belongs to himself - to God. This is the secret of full consecration, a condition
of successful praying, and the sort of praying which brings the largest fruits.

The men of olden times who were very successful in prayer, who brought the
largest things to pass, who moved God to do great things, were those who were
entirely given over to God in their praying. God wants, and must have, all that
there is in man in answering his prayers. He must have wholehearted men through
whom to work out His purposes and plans concerning men. God must have men
in their entirety. No double-minded man need apply. No vacillating man can be
used. No man with a divided allegiance to God, the world and self, can do the
praying that is needed.

Holiness is wholeness, and so God wants holy men, men wholehearted and
true, for His service and for the work of praying.

E. M. BOUNDS

REDEEMING THE TIME

The time is short.
1 CORINTHIANS 7:29

If we would aim at a holy and useful life, let us learn to redeem time. "I am large about redeeming time," says Richard Baxter in the preface to his Christian Directory, "because therein the sum of a holy, obedient life is included." Yes; "let us redeem the time, because the days are evil" (Ephesians 5:16; Colossians 4:5). A wasted life is the result of unredeemed time. Desultory working, impulsive giving, fitful planning, irregular reading, ill-assorted hours, perfunctory or unpunctual execution of business, hurry and bustle, loitering and unreadiness - these, and such like, are the things that take the power from life, hinder holiness, and eat like a canker into our moral being. Misuse of time makes success and progress an impossibility, either in things temporal or spiritual.

There needs not to be routine, but there must be regularity; there ought not to be mechanical stiffness, but there must be order; there may not be haste, but there must be no trifling with our own time or that of others; "Whatsoever thy hand findeth to do, do it with thy might" (Ecclesiastes 9:10). If the thing is worth doing at all, it is worth doing well; and, in little things as well as great, we must show that we are in earnest. There must be no idling, but a girding up of the loins; a running the race with patience; the warring of a good warfare. The call is to be "steadfast and ... always abounding in the work of the Lord."

The flowers are constant in their growing, the stars are constant in their courses; the rivers are constant in the flowing - they lose not time. So must our life be, not one of fits, or starts, or random impulses, not one of levity or inconstancy, or fickle scheming, but steady and resolute. We must be resolute men and women, those who know their earthly mission and have their eye upon the heavenly goal.

HORATIUS BONAR

JESUS THE CRUCIFIED

*God hath made that same Jesus, whom ye have
crucified, both Lord and Christ.*
ACTS 2:36

We have spoken of Christ as King in more than one respect. But there is one word more that may not be lacking. This King is none other than the crucified Jesus. All that we have to say of Him, His divine power, His abiding presence, His wonderful love does not teach us to know Him aright unless we maintain the deep consciousness: This our King is the crucified Jesus. God has placed Him in the midst of His throne as a Lamb, as it had been slain, and it is thus that the hosts of heaven adore Him. It is thus that we worship Him as a King.

Christ's cross is His highest glory. It is through this that He has conquered every enemy and gained His place on the throne of God. And it is this that He will impart to us too if we are to know fully what the victory over sin is to mean. When Paul wrote: "I have been crucified with Christ, Christ liveth in me," he taught us that it was as the crucified One that Christ ruled on the throne of His heart and that the spirit of the cross would triumph over us as it did in Him.

This was true of the disciples. This was their deepest preparation for receiving the Holy Spirit. They had with their Lord been crucified to the world. The old man had been crucified; in Him they were dead to sin and their life was hid with Christ in God. Each one of us needs to experience this fellowship with Christ in His cross if the Spirit of Pentecost is really to take possession of us. It was through the Eternal Spirit that Christ gave Himself as a sacrifice and became the King on the throne of God. It is as we become "comformable to His death" in the entire surrender of our will in the entire self-denial of our old nature, in the entire separation from the spirit of this world, that we can become the worthy servants of a crucified King, and our hearts the worthy temples of His glory.

ANDREW MURRAY

THE DEVIL

Now the serpent was more subtil ...
GENESIS 3:1

Do you believe in a personal devil? Most assuredly I do. I could not believe in the Bible without believing in a personal devil. I have conclusive proof that the Bible is the Word of God, therefore I believe what it teaches about the existence of a personal devil.

In the account of the temptation of our Lord recorded in the gospels of Matthew and Luke, we are distinctly told that the devil (and the whole account evidently means a personal devil) was the author of the temptations that came to our Lord (see Matthew 4:1-11; Luke 4:1-13). These accounts have no meaning if we try to make the devil of the passage a mere figure of speech.

Furthermore, our Lord in the parable of the sower (in Matthew 13:1-23) distinctly teaches that there is a personal devil. The devil does not appear in the parable, where it might be explained as being figurative, but in the interpretation of the parable: "Then cometh the wicked one ... " Now in parables we have figures, and in the interpretation of parables we have the literal facts for which the figures stand, so we have a literal devil in the interpretation of this parable. It is only one of the numerous instances in which Jesus teaches the existence of a personal devil.

Paul teaches the same, "Put on the whole armour of God, that ye may be able to stand against the wiles of the devil. For our wrestling is not against flesh and blood but against the principalities, against the powers, against the world rulers of this darkness, against the spiritual hosts of wickedness in the heavenly places."

No rational interpretation of the Bible can interpret the devil out of it. Any system of interpretation that does away with the devil would do away with any doctrine a man does not wish to believe.

But I also believe that there is a personal devil because my own experience and observation teach me the existence of an unseen, very subtle, very cunning spirit of evil, who has domination over men throughout human society wherever found. The more I come into contact with men, the more I study history, and the more men open their hearts to me, the more firmly convinced I become that there is such a devil as the Bible teaches that there is.

R. A. TORREY

JULY 29

DEALING WITH THE FAULTS

OF OTHERS

*Thou shalt not hate thy brother in thine heart: thou shalt in any wise rebuke
thy neighbour, and not suffer sin upon him.*
LEVITICUS 19:17

If we would wisely reprove the flesh in our brethren, we must first, after the
Lord's example, remember and commend the grace in them. Those who are
much acquainted with the cross of Christ, and with their own hearts, will be
slow to take the reprover's office: if they do reprove, they will make it a solemn
matter, knowing how much evil comes of the unwise handling of a fault.

Let us begin by searching ourselves, if we would be profitable reprovers of
others.

Much self-judgment makes a man slow to judge others; and the very gentleness
of such a one gives a keen edge to his rebukes.

In reproving sin in others, we should remember the ways of the Holy Spirit of
God towards us. He comes as the Spirit of Love; and whatever His rebukes, He
wins the heart by mercy and forgiveness through Christ.

To forgive without upbraiding, even by manner or look, is a high exercise of
grace - it is imitation of Christ.

If I have been injured by another, let me bethink myself - How much better to be
the sufferer than the wrongdoer!

The flesh would punish to prevent a repetition of wrongs; but grace teaches us
to defend ourselves without weapons. The man who "seventy times seven"
forgives injuries, is he who best knows how to protect himself.

If one do me a wrong, let me with the bowels of Christ seek after him, and
entreat God to move him to repentance.

We partake in the guilt of an offending member of Christ, until we have
confessed his sins as our own (Dan 9), mourned over it, prayed for its forgiveness
and sought in the spirit of love, the restoration of the erring one.

ROBERT CLEAVER CHAPMAN

THE DYING OF THE
LORD JESUS

Always bearing about in the body of the dying of the Lord Jesus.
2 CORINTHIANS 4:10

Paul here is very bold in speaking of the intimate union that there was between Christ living in him and the life he lived in the flesh with all its suffering. He had spoken (Gal 2:20) of his being crucified with Christ and Christ living in him. Here he tells how he was always bearing about in the body the dying of Jesus; it was through that that the life also of Jesus was manifested in his body. And he says that it was because the death of Christ was thus working in and through him, that Christ's life could work in them.

We often speak of our abiding in Christ. But we forget that that means the abiding in a crucified Christ. Many believers appear to think that when once they have claimed Christ's death in the fellowship of the cross and have counted themselves as crucified with Him, that they may now consider it as past and done with. They do not understand that it is in the crucified Christ and in the fellowship of His death that they are to abide daily and unceasingly. The fellowship of the cross is to be the life of a daily experience, the self-emptying of our Lord, His taking the form of a servant, His humbling Himself and becoming obedient unto death, even the death of the cross - this mind that was in Christ is to be the disposition that marks our daily life.

"Always bearing about in the body the dying of Jesus". This is what we are called to as much as Paul. If we are indeed to live for the welfare of others around us, if we are to sacrifice our ease and pleasure to win souls for our Lord, it will be true of us as of Paul, that we are able to say: "Death worked in us, but life in those for whom we pray and labour." It is in the fellowship of the sufferings of Christ that the crucified Lord can live out and work out His life in us and through us.

ANDREW MURRAY

THE UNRIGHTEOUS STEWARD

He that is faithful in that which is least is faithful also in much.
LUKE 16:10

A very puzzling passage in the Bible to many is the story of the unrighteous steward recorded in Luke 16:1-14. Why did Jesus "hold this dishonest scoundrel up for our imitaiton"? The answer is found in the text itself. Jesus did not hold him up for imitation. He held him up, first of all, as a warning of what would overtake unfaithful stewards, how they would be called to give account of their stewardship, and their stewardship be taken from them.

Having taught this solemn and salutary lesson, one that is much needed today, Jesus went on to show how "the sons of this world are for their own generation wiser than the sons of the light" (verse 8). They are wiser because they use their utmost ingenuity and put forth their utmost effort to make present opportunities count for the hour of future need. "The sons of light" often do not do that. Indeed, how many twentieth century sons of light, who profess to believe that eternity is all and time is nothing in comparison, are suing their utmost ingenuity and efforts to make the opportunity of the present count most for the needs of the great eternity that is to follow?

The average professed Christian today uses the utmost ingenuity and puts forth his utmost effort to bring things to pass in business and other affairs of this brief present world, but when it comes to matters that affect eternity he is content with the exercise of the least possible amount of ingenuity and with putting forth of the smallest effort that will satisfy his conscience.

Jesus did not point to the steward's dishonesty to stir our emulation - He plainly rebuked his dishonesty, but he did point to his common sense in using the opportunity of the present to provide for the necessities of the future and would have us learn to use the opportunities of the present to provide for the necessities of the future, the eternal future. Even in pointing out his common sense, Jesus carefully guarded His statement by saying that the unjust steward was wiser in his own generation. He knew only the life that now is, and from that narrow and imperfect standpoint he was wiser than "the sons of light" from his broad and true standpoint of knowing eternity, but an eternity for which he is not wise enough to live wholly.

R. A. TORREY

AUGUST 1

A FAITHFUL GOD

Through faith also Sara received strength to conceive seed, and was delivered
of a child when she was past age, because she judged him
faithful who had promised.
HEBREWS 11:11

All God's giants have been weak men, who did great things for God because they reckoned on God being with them. See the cases of David, of Jonathan, and his armour-bearer, of Asa, Jehoshaphat, and many others. Oh! beloved friends, if there is a living God, faithful and true, let us hold His faithfulness. Holding His faithfulness, we may face, with calm and sober but confident assurance of victory, every difficulty and danger. We may count on grace for the work, on pecuniary aid, on needful facilities, and on ultimate success. Let us not give Him a partial trust, but daily, hourly, serve Him, "holding God's faithfulness."

O God of the impossible!
Since all things are to Thee
But soil in which omnipotence
Can work Almightily

Each trial may to us become
The means that will display
How o'er what seems impossible
Our God hath precious sway!

O God of the impossible,
When we no hope can see,
Grant us the faith that still believes,
All possible to Thee!

J. HUDSON TAYLOR

AUGUST 2

ACTIONS SPEAK LOUDER

If ye know these things, happy are ye if ye do them.
JOHN 13:17

We read, "If ye know these things, happy are ye if ye do them." It sounds as if our Lord would warn His disciples that they would never be really happy in His service if they were content with a barren head-knowledge of duty and did not live according to their knowledge.

Nothing is more common than to hear people saying of doctrine or duty, "We know it, we know it," while they sit still in unbelief or disobedience. They actually seem to flatter themselves that there is something creditable and redeeming in knowledge, even when it bears no fruit in heart, character, or life. Yet the truth is precisely the other way. To know what we ought to be, believe and do, and yet to be unaffected by our knowledge, only adds to our guilt in the sight of God. To know that Christians should be humble and loving, while we continue proud and selfish, will only sink us deeper in the pit unless we awake and repent. Practice, in short, is the very life of religion. "To him that knoweth to do good, and doeth it not, to him it is sin" (James 4:17).

Of course, we must never despise knowledge. It is in one sense the beginning of Christianity in the soul. So long as we know nothing of sin, or God, or Christ, or grace, or repentance, or faith, or conscience, we are, of course, nothing better than heathens. But we must not overrate knowledge. It is perfectly valueless unless it produces results in our conduct and influences our lives and moves our wills. In fact knowledge without practice does not raise us above the level of the devil.

Satan knows truth, but has no will to obey it and is miserable. He that would be happy in Christ's service must not only know, but do.

J.C. RYLE

OUR COMMISSION

Wilt thou not revive us again: that thy people may rejoice in thee?
PSALM 85:6

I am disturbed by the attitude of the Church in general toward aggressive evangelism or revival. By evangelism I do not mean just an effort to get people back into the Church; this effort, while commendable, does not get us very far. What I mean is something much more; it is the getting of men and women into vital, saving and covenant relationship with Jesus Christ, and so supernaturally altered that holiness will characterise their whole being: body, souls and spirit. It seems to me that the time has surely come when we must, with open mind and true heart, face ourselves with unqualified honesty and ask the question: "Am I alive to my responsibility as a labourer in God's vineyard?" I, personally, have constantly to remind myself that I can be a very busy man, and yet a very idle minister. How easy it is to live more or less in the enjoyment of God's free grace, and yet not realise that we are called to fulfil a divinely-appointed purpose. Our commission is to declare the whole counsel of God in the midst of men: "to open their eyes, and to turn them from darkness to light, and from the power of Satan unto God" - that, brethren, is our privilege and our task. And yet we must confess that too often the great things of God have not been the predominating things: the lesser things of life have been allowed to absorb our interest, and the lure of the lesser loyalty has blurred our vision and robbed us of our passion to win souls for Jesus Christ.

DUNCAN CAMPBELL

PRINCIPLES FOR PRAYER

We know not what we should pray for as we ought.
ROMANS 8:26

I often say my prayers,
but do I ever pray?
And do the wishes of my heart
Go with the words I say?
I may as well kneel down
And worship gods of stone,
As offer to the living God
A prayer of words alone.

It is many years since the writer was taught these lines by his mother - now "present with the Lord" - but their searching message still comes home with force to him. The Christian can no more pray without the direct enabling of the Holy Spirit than he can create a world. This must be so, for real prayer is a felt need awakened within us by the Spirit so that we ask God, in the name of Christ, for that which is in accord with His holy will. "If we ask any thing according to his will, he heareth us" (I John 5:14). But to ask something which is not according to God's will is not praying, but presuming. True, God's revealed will is made known in His Word, yet not in such a way as a cookery book contains recipes and directions for preparing various dishes. The Scriptures frequently enumerate principles which call for continuous exercise of heart and divine help to show us their application to different cases and circumstances. Thus we are being profited from the Scriptures when we are taught our deep need of crying "Lord, teach us to pray" (Luke 11:1), and are actually constrained to beg Him for the spirit of prayer.

A. W. PINK

AUGUST 5

SEARCHING OUT THE PROMISE

Having therefore these promises.
2 CORINTHIANS 7:1

You pray, but have not the liberty in prayer that you desire. A definite promise is what you want. You try one and another of the inspired words, but they do not fit. The troubled heart sees reasons to suspect that they are not strictly applicable to the case in hand, and so they are left in the old Book for use another day; for they are not available in the present emergency. You try again, and in due season a promise presents itself which seems to have been made for the occasion; it fits as exactly as a well-made key fits the wards of the lock for which it was originally prepared. Having found the identical word of the living God, you hasten to plead it at the throne of grace, saying, "Oh, my Lord, you have promised this good thing unto Thy servant; be pleased to grant it!" The matter is ended; sorrow is turned to joy; prayer is heard.

Frequently the Holy Spirit brings to our remembrance with life and power the words of the Lord that otherwise we might have forgotten. He also sheds a new light upon well-remembered passages and so reveals a fullness in them that we had little suspected. In cases known to me, the texts have been singular, and for a while the person upon whose mind they were impressed could hardly see their bearing.

For years one heart was comforted with the words "His soul shall dwell at ease; and his seed shall inherit the earth." This passage was seldom out of his mind; indeed, it seemed to him to be perpetually whispered in his ear. The special relation of the promise to his experience was made known by the event. A child of God who mourned his years of barrenness was lifted at once into joy and peace by that seldom-quoted word "I will restore to you the years that the locust hath eaten." The bitter experiences of David as to slander and malice led to the utterance of consoling promises, which have been a thousand times appropriated by obscure and broken-hearted Christians when afflicted with "trials of cruel mockings."

CHARLES H. SPURGEON

AUGUST 6

BLOOD AND FIRE

Lo, this hath touched thy lips; and thine iniquity is taken away.
ISAIAH 6:7

We read in Isaiah 6 when Isaiah cried, one of the seraphim immediately went for the live coal. Now, mark this: the angel was not told to go, but he knew just what to do. The fact is, the angels have gone so often for the live coal that whenever they hear a sinner crying that he is undone, they go for it; they do not need to be told. It is as if a druggist's boy were so in the habit of getting the same medicine for the same symptoms that when the patient comes to the door, he knows just what medicine to seek without going to the doctor to get advice.

The seraph took the live coal from off the altar, and that stood for blood and fire, the two things we want today. We want blood and fire.

Blood! Can you not hear the hiss of the blood of the Lamb as it flows gurgling around that coal? As he takes it up with his tongs of gold and bears it to the prophet's lips, it takes the atoning blood with it. We want that first. I call upon all of you to claim that first - the blood. Nothing else will do. "This is he that came by water and blood; not by water only, but by water and blood." You and I need blood first. Let us then betake ourselves to our compassionate Lord and seek from Him that forgiveness which He purchased on the cross. Do you want it? Are you quite satisfied? Do you look upon your past with perfect complacency? Is there nothing to regret? Are there no sins to put away?

It is natural to respond that you are undone. Then let us begin by opening our whole nature to Christ and believe that His blood now cleanses from all sin. Let us dare to believe that as soon as we turn to that blood, and claim the forgiveness that is based on it, the whole of our past sin is gone, blotted out, lost to view; and if we remind God about it, He will say: "My child, you need not tell me about it. I have forgotten it. It is as though it had never been."

Next we need the fire, the live coal. God grant that the live coal, which has never lost its glow since the day of Pentecost, may come to every heart, to every mouth, to every life; and that this day a fire shall begin to burn in every mission, in every Sunday school, in every church.

F. B. MEYER

AUGUST 7

READY FOR SERVICE

In all things shewing thyself a pattern of good works.
TITUS 2:7

We read that the fruit of the Spirit is love. God is love, Christ is love, and we should not be surprised to read about the love of the Spirit. What a blessed attribute is this. May I call it the dome of the temple of the graces. Better still, it is the crown of crowns worn by the Triune God. Human love is a natural emotion that flows forth toward the object of our affections. But divine love is as high above human love as the heaven is above the earth. The natural man is of the earth, earthy and however pure his love may be, it is weak and imperfect at best. But the love of God is perfect and entire, wanting nothing. It is as a mighty ocean in its greatness, dwelling with and flowing from the eternal Spirit.

In Romans 5:5 we read: "And hope maketh not ashamed, because the love of God is shed abroad in our hearts by the Holy Ghost which is given to us." Now if we are co-workers with God, there is one thing we must possess and that is love. A man may be a very successful lawyer and have no love for his clients, and yet get on very well. A man may be a very successful physician and have no love for his patients, and yet be a very good physician; a man may be a very successful merchant and have no love for his customers, and yet he may do a good business and succeed; but no man can be a co-worker with God without love. If our service is mere profession on our part, the quicker we renounce it, the better. If a man takes up God's work as he would take up any profession, the sooner he gets out of it, the better.

We cannot work for God without love. It is the only tree that can produce fruit on this sin-cursed earth, that is acceptable to God. If I have no love for God nor for my fellow man, then I cannot work acceptably. I am like sounding brass and a tinkling cymbal. We are told that "the love of God is shed abroad in our hearts by the Holy Ghost." Now if we have had that love shed abroad in our hearts, we are ready for God's service; if we have not, we are not ready.

It is so easy to reach a man when you love him; all barriers are broken down and swept away. Paul, when writing to Titus (2:2), tells him to be sound in faith, in charity, and in patience.

D. L. MOODY

STUDY YOUR PLANS

This kind can come forth by nothing, but by prayer and fasting.
MARK 9:29

Study the New Testament with special reference to working for God and you will be surprised how every page of it will give you increased light. You will see that God holds you absolutely responsible for every iota of capacity and influence He has given you, that He expects you to improve every moment of your time, every faculty of your being, every particle of your influence, and every penny of your money *for Him*. When once you get *this* light, it will be a marvellous guide in all other particulars and ramifications of your life. Men in earthly warfare study plans of stratagem, and adopt measures in order that they may take the enemy by surprise! But how little care and attention God's people give to taking souls; and yet it is *far harder work to take souls than it is to take cities*.

I say those who want to be successful in winning souls require to watch not only days but nights. They (need) much of the Holy Ghost, for it is true still *"this kind can come forth by nothing, but by prayer and fasting."* We have grown wiser than our Lord nowadays; but I tell you, it is the same old-fashioned way, and if you want to pour out living waters upon souls you will have to drink largely at the fountain yourself. May God rouse us up.

Take my life, and let it be
Consecrated, Lord to Thee;
Take my moments and my days,
Let them flow in ceaseless praise.

Take my silver and my gold,
Not a mite would I withhold;
Take my intellect, and use
Every power as Thou shalt choose.

Take my love; my Lord I pour
At Thy feet its treasure-store;
Take myself, and I will be
Ever, only all for Thee.

CATHERINE BOOTH

WHAT HEAVEN IS

A city which hath foundations, whose builder and maker is God
HEBREWS 11:10

The Word teaches that Heaven is:
(1) *A Kingdom.* It is a region where the unrivalled supremacy of the King of kings is acknowledged. It is, therefore, perfect in its constitution, just and merciful in its laws, and immaculate in its administrations. What a contrast to the corruption of earthly politics!

(2) *An Abiding city.* It is unshakable in its foundations, and never hoary with the years. It is glorious in its architecture and its construction. It is the City of the Loving God. Its glories having "Jesus for its King, angels for its guards, and saints for its citizens." Its walls are Salvation and its gates Praise.

(3) *A Reserved Inheritance.* As such it is retained inviolate for all who are "meet to be partakers". Unlike an earthly heritage, it can never be forfeited or withdrawn.

(4) *The Believer's Home.* What tender, beautiful memories cluster around the word "home". It cannot be described in terms of material things. The word "house" and "mansion" leave the heart cold, but the mention of home quickens the pulse and warms the spirit. Heaven is a glorious climax, a goal of desire, the consummate joy and rest of the pilgrim.

The Fullness of Heaven is Jesus Himself.
The Duration of Heaven is the Eternity of Jesus.
The Light of Heaven is the Face of Jesus.
The Joy of Heaven is the Presence of Jesus.
The Melody of Heaven is the Name of Jesus.
The Harmony of Heaven is the Praise of Jesus.
The Theme of Heaven is the Work of Jesus.
The Employment of Heaven is the Service of Jesus.

REGINALD WALLIS

GOD'S STANDARD

Enoch ... had this testimony, that he pleased God.
HEBREWS 11:5

I believe the greatest contribution we can make to the cause of Christ is in the impact of our unconscious influence. Today we are inclined to think a great deal of cleverness, and even of smartness, but the day is coming when there will be startling reversal. Goodness will be first and greatness last. Here I would recall the testimony of one Christian worker concerning another: "She is all she professes to be and much more". The writer of the following verses puts this very aptly:

"I'd rather see a sermon than hear one any day,
I'd rather one would walk with me than merely show the way;
The eye's a better pupil, more willing than the ear,
Fine counsel is confusing, but example's always clear;
The best of all the preachers are the men who live their creeds,
For to see good put in action is what everybody needs;
I soon can learn to do it if you'll let me see it done,
I can watch your hands in action, but your tongue too fast may run;
The lectures you deliver may be very wise and true,
But I'd rather get my lessons by observing what you do;
I may not understand the high advice that you may give,
But there's no misunderstanding how you act and how you live."

The late Dr Stuart Holden, speaking of the early disciples, said: "Here were men who were with Him long enough to capture His spirit, and so were made competent to go forth to reproduce Him in the world". The success or failure of our work as a church or mission depends, in the last resort, largely, not in the number of preachers we put into the field, nor on the size of our congregations, but rather on the character of Christianity we and our work produce.

DUNCAN CAMPBELL

AUGUST 11

THE BLESSING

In thee shall all families of the earth be blessed.
GENESIS 12:3

O ur Heavenly Father is love. The proof is the gift of His Son. Jesus is love.
The proof is the gift of Himself. The Spirit is love. The proof is, He brings
Jesus into the heart of faith.

Hence, the Scripture is framed by the hand of love, as a chart to show the
glories of the Lord to the children of men. Each page adds new tints to the glowing
picture. Almost each person is a herald preceding Jesus with a clearer note. Thus
Abraham appears from the shades of idolatry, and instantly the gospel is preached,
Gal 3:8. The tidings sound aloud, - "In thee shall all families of the earth be blessed."
Faith hears and cries, this must be a prophecy of Jesus. Who but He is the blessing
of the world?

When the Patriarch was raised to the pinnacle of truth, what prospects, as floods
of light were spread before him! He gazed on countless masses of immortals, blessed
through countless ages. "Your father, Abraham rejoiced to see my day, and he saw
it, and was glad." John 8:56.

Reader, would you behold like wonders, and share like joys? Would you be
blessed while you live, and when you die, and throughout eternity? Would you
bask each day in the smiles of God's favour, and repose each night under the
shelter of his wings, and go down to the grave leaning on His arm, and passing
through the gate of death into the new Jerusalem? - There is all this blessedness in
Christ.

Would you at each moment lift up a tranquil heart, and say - "The great Creator
is my Father: - Jesus is my redeeming kinsman; - the Spirit is my indwelling teacher
and sanctifier and comforter; - the saints in light are my brethren; - the angels are
my guardian-attendants; - Heaven is my home; - a throne of glory is my seat; - a
weight of glory is my crown?" Would you realise, that the wheels of Providence
revolve for your welfare - and that the world, with all its intricate perplexities of
machinery, is a scaffold to build up the fabric of your best interests? There is all this
blessedness in Christ.

HENRY LAW

GOD'S WORD OUR DELIGHT

I will not forget thy word.
PSALM 119:16

If a cluster of heavenly fruit hangs within reach, gather it. If a promise lies upon the page as a blank cheque, cash it. If a prayer is recorded, appropriate it, and launch it as a feathered arrow from the bow of your desire. If an example of holiness gleams before you, ask God to do as much for you. If a truth is revealed in all its intrinsic splendour, entreat that its brilliance may ever irradiate the hemisphere of your life like a star. Entwine the climbing creepers of holy desire about the latticework of Scripture. So shall you come to say with the psalmist, "Oh, how I love Thy law! It is my meditation all the day."

It is sometimes well to read over, on our knees, Psalm 119, so full of devout love for the Bible. And if any should chide us for spending so much time upon the Old Testament or the New, let us remind them of the words of Christ, "Man shall not live by bread alone, but by every word that proceedeth out of the mouth of God". The Old Testament must be worth our study since it was our Saviour's Bible, deeply pondered and often quoted. And the New demands it, since it is so full of what He said and did, not only in His earthly life but through the medium of His holy apostles and prophets.

The advantages of a deep knowledge of the Bible are more than can be numbered here. It is the Storehouse of the Promises. It is the Sword of the Spirit, before which temptation flees. It is the all-sufficient Equipment of Christian usefulness, It is the believer's guidebook and directory in all possible circumstances. Words fail to tell how glad, how strong, how useful shall be the daily life of those who can say with the prophet: "Thy words were found, and I did eat them; and thy word was unto me the joy and rejoicing of mine heart."

But there is one thing, which may be said last, because it is most important and should linger in the memory and heart, though all the other exhortations of this chapter should pass away as a summer brook. It is this. It is useless to dream of making headway in the knowledge of Scripture unless we are prepared to practice each new and clearly-defined duty which looms out before our view.

F. B. MEYER

A TEMPTATION AND A SNARE

The love of money is the root of all evil.
1 TIMOTHY 6:10

Think of Balaam. He is generally regarded as a false prophet, but I do not find that any of his prophecies that are recorded are not true, they have been literally fulfilled. Up to a certain point his character shone magnificently, but the devil finally overcame him by the bait of covetousness. He stepped over a heavenly crown for the riches and honours that Balak promised him. He went to perdition backwards. His face was set toward God, but he backed into hell. He wanted to die the death of the righteous, but he did not live the life of the righteous. It is sad to see so many who know God miss everything for riches.

Then consider the case of Gehazi. There is another man who was drowned in destruction and perdition by covetousness. He got more out of Naaman than he asked for, but he also got Naaman's leprosy. Think how he forfeited the friendship of his master, Elisha, the man of God! So today lifelong friends are separated by this accursed desire. Homes are broken up. Men are willing to sell out peace and happiness for the sake of a few dollars.

Didn't David fall into foolish and hurtful lusts? He saw Bathsheba, Uriah's wife, who was "very beautiful to look upon," and David became a murderer and an adulterer. The guilty longing hurled him into the deepest pit of sin. He had to reap bitterly as he had sowed.

I heard of a wealthy German out west who owned a lumber mill. He was worth nearly two million dollars, but his covetousness was so great that he once worked as a common labourer carrying railroad ties all day. It was the cause of his death.

Achan was no different. "Indeed I have sinned against the Lord God of Israel, and thus and thus have I done: When I saw among the spoils a goodly Babylonish garment, and two hundred shekels of silver, and a wedge of gold of fifty shekels weight, then I coveted them, and took them; and, behold, they are hid in the earth in the midst of my tent, and the silver under it" (Joshua 7:20-21).

He saw, he coveted, he took, and he hid! The covetous eye was what led Achan up to the wicked deed that brought sorrow and defeat upon the camp of Israel.

D. L. MOODY

AUGUST 14

ALL IN GOD'S HAND

The Lord gave, and the Lord hath taken away; blessed be the name of the Lord.
JOB 1:21

Was not Job mistaken? Should he not have said: "The Lord gave, and Satan hath taken away"? No, there was no mistake. He was enabled to discern the hand of God in all these calamities. Satan himself did not presume to ask God to be allowed himself to afflict. He says to God: "Put forth thine hand now, and touch his flesh and bone, and he will curse thee to thy face" … Oftentimes shall we be helped and blessed if we bear this in mind - that Satan is servant and not master, and that he, and wicked men incited by him, are only permitted to do that which God by his determined counsel and foreknowledge had before determined should be done. Come joy or come sorrow, we may always take it from the hand of God.

Lord of the years that are left me,
I give them to Thy hand:
Take me and break me, mould me to
The pattern Thou hast planned.

J. HUDSON TAYLOR

A MIDNIGHT CRY

Looking for and hasting unto the coming of the day of God.
2 PETER 3:12

*A*t midnight there was a cry made. "Behold, the Bridegroom cometh!" This phrase is the startling climax in one of the prophecies that the Lord Jesus Himself made concerning His Second Coming. Yes, the Lord Jesus Christ is certainly coming again. His second advent will be just as actual, literal, personal, staggering and unexpected as His first coming. All those Old Testament prophecies which marvellously foretold the details of His birth, life, death and resurrection were precisely fulfilled. The Word of God is still more abundantly emphatic upon this other great basic truth of the gospel that He will again appear the second time. Yet there are scoffers who disclaim and ridicule this blessed truth. That only affords greater evidence however, that His return is really drawing nigh.

The prominence given to this subject in the Word of God is both striking and convincing in itself. Here is a final negative to the suggestion that advent truth is merely a "side-line" or a pet theme for prophetic fanatics and whimsical scare-mongers. Over 1,500 times in the Old Testament, and more than 300 times in the New Testament, this tremendous truth is affirmed and reaffirmed with no un-certain sound. Indeed, it is essentially fundamental. Eliminate this truth and the whole structure of faith collapses. It is imperative to the realisation of God's eternal purpose. In the very nature of the case He must come, or the divine programme for the age cannot be consummated. He alone can solve the world problems of today. "Vain is the help of man." Christ Himself is the only solution. His Gospel is the sole panacea for the ills of a devil-usurped universe. Centuries of human government have sadly demonstrated this fact. History declares the utter impotence of man and the tragedy of rejecting the God-Man.

Lo, He comes! with clouds descending,
Once for favoured sinners slain;
Thousand thousand saints attending
Swell the triumph of His train;
Hallelujah!
Jesus comes and comes to reign!

REGINALD WALLIS

THE SHIELD

Fear not, Abram: I am thy shield.
GENESIS 15:1

Abraham had heard the terrible clang of war. He had been in perils of fight. Thus he knew, that without the safeguard of a Shield, the warrior must go forth to overthrow and death.

The sword was scarcely sheathed, when the Lord, remembering His mercy, visits His faithful servant. Seasonable are His words of comfort. "Fear not, Abram, I am thy shield." Here was assurance, that all foes were as chaff: for the patriarch was encompassed with God, as with a buckler.

In Abraham warring, and Abraham shielded, every soldier of the blessed Jesus sees himself. The service of the Lord, soothed as it is with heaven's own peace, is still a storm of assaults from earth and hell. The repose of faith excludes not the fight of faith. Rest in trouble is not rest from trouble. Hostile bands must meet us in hostile land. Satan is yet at large, and is full of wrath. The flesh is still the flesh, and lusts against the spirit. The world is still the world; and, though worn out by centuries of sin, is vigorous to hate, apt to wound, powerful to captivate, strong to enchain. Hence a ceaseless tide of battle rolls. But it is vain, for Jesus ever lives, and ever loves, and still cheers every believer, saying, "Fear not, I am thy shield."

But what is a shield? It is armour framed for defence. Borne on the arm of the combatant, by rapid movement, it baffles the assailant's aim. Whatever be the attack, its broad surface intervenes, and all behind is safe. Just so in the fierce battle-field of faith, Jesus is a widespread covering. Hence every foe hurls every dart, as an innocuous reed.

Therefore, ye servants of the living God, bless His holy name. He always causes you to triumph in Christ. Go on with the shield of faith, and under the covering of your Lord. Soon will the conflict end: and in Salvation's kingdom you will sing the glories of Salvation's Shield.

HENRY LAW

AUGUST 17

ALTOGETHER LOVELY

Behold, thou art fair, my beloved.
SONG OF SOLOMON 1:16

Our Beloved is most handsome from every point of view. Our various experiences are given to us by our heavenly Father to furnish us with fresh views of the loveliness of Jesus. How pleasant are our trials when they give us a clearer view of Jesus.

We have seen Him from the top of Amana, from the top of Shenir and Hermon (Song of Solomon 4:8). He has shone on us as the sun at noon. But we have also seen Him "from the lion's den and from the mountains of the leopards" (Song of Solomon 4:8) and He has lost none of His loveliness.

From the languishing sick bed or even from the edge of the grave, we have turned our eyes to our soul's spouse, and He has never been anything but handsome.

Many of His saints have looked on Him from the gloom of the dungeons and through the red flames of the stake. Yet they never uttered a bad word about Him but died extolling His surpassing charms. What a noble and pleasant occupation, to gaze forever on our sweet Lord Jesus.

It is an unspeakable delight to see the Saviour in all His offices and discover Him matchless in each, to shift the kaleidoscope, as it were, and find fresh combinations of matchless grace.

In the manger and in eternity, on the cross and on His throne, in the garden and in His kingdom, among thieves or in the midst of cherubim, He is altogether lovely. Carefully examine every little act of His life and every trait of His character and you will find Him as lovely in the minute as in the majestic.

Judge Him as you will, you cannot criticise Him. Weigh Him as you please, you will find a full measure. Eternity will not discover the shadow of a spot in our Beloved. Rather as ages revolve, His glories will shine with inconceivable splendour, and His unutterable loveliness will more and more ravish all celestial minds.

CHARLES H. SPURGEON

FITTED FOR HEAVEN, STILL HERE ON EARTH

Ye are complete in him.
COLOSSIANS 2:10

By leaving His people here for a season opportunity is given for:
1. God to manifest His keeping power: not only in a hostile world, but sin still indwelling believers.

2. To demonstrate the sufficiency of His grace: supporting them in their weakness.

3. To maintain a witness for Himself in a scene which lieth in the Wicked One.

4. To exhibit His faithfulness in supplying all their need in the wilderness before they reach Canaan.

5. To display His manifold wisdom unto angels (1 Corinthians 4:9; Ephesians 3:10).

6. To act as "salt" in preserving the race from moral suicide: by the purifying and restraining influence they exert.

7. To make evident the reality of their faith: trusting Him in sharpest trials and darkest dispensations.

8. To give them an occasion to glorify Him in the place where they dishonoured Him.

9. To preach the gospel to those of His elect yet in unbelief.

10. To afford proof that they will serve Him amid the most disadvantageous circumstances.

11. To deepen their appreciation of what He has prepared for them.

12. To have fellowship with Christ who endured the cross before He was crowned with glory and honour.

A .W. PINK

AUGUST 19

STEADFASTNESS IN CONVICTION

My son, fear thou the Lord and the king: and meddle not with
them that are given to change.
PROVERBS 24:21

How true are the words of Oswald Chambers: "You can never give another person that which you have found, but you can make him homesick for what you have", and surely this is what was in the mind of the apostle when he wrote to the Philippians: "Only let your conversation be as it becometh the gospel of Christ: that whether I come and see you, or else be absent, I may hear of your affairs, that ye stand fast in one spirit, with one mind striving together for the faith of the gospel" (Phil 1:27). In that passage of Scripture Paul pleads for reality, consistency and STEADFASTNESS. Your "manner of life" (2 Tim 3:10) is how he puts it - a "manner of life" such as will cry aloud that this is "the work of God" (John 6:29). The Apostle Paul also wrote: "If we live in the Spirit, let us also walk in the Spirit" (Gal 5:25). So, in its final analysis, the secret of such a life is in the fullness of the Holy Ghost.

I read some time ago of a pair of scales, so exquisitely poised and balanced, that if you wrote your name on a sheet of paper and put it on the scale, and at the same time put the companion sheet on the other side of the scale, the paper with the signature would tilt down the scale, and the other would go up. On ordinary scales the signature would make no difference, but on the exquisitely balanced scale, it made all the difference. It is the signature of the Holy Ghost upon our work and witness that makes all the difference.

DUNCAN CAMPBELL

AUGUST 20

BORN AGAIN

You hath be quickened, who were dead in trespasses and sins.
EPHESIANS 2:1

What a mighty change our Lord declares to be needful to salvation, and what a remarkable expression He uses in describing it! He speaks of a new birth. He says to Nicodemus, "Except a man be born again, he cannot see the kingdom of God." He announced the same truth in other words, in order to make it more plain to His hearer's mind: "Except a man be born of water and of the Spirit, he cannot enter into the kingdom of God." By this expression He meant Nicodemus to understand that no one could become His disciple, unless his inward man was as thoroughly cleansed and renewed by the Spirit as the outward man is cleaned by water. To possess the privileges of Judaism a man only needed to be born of the seed of Abraham after the flesh. To possess the privileges of Christ's kingdom a man must be born again of the Holy Ghost.

The change which our Lord here declares needful to salvation is evidently no slight or superficial one. It is not merely reformation, or amendment, or moral change, or outward alteration of life. It is a thorough change of heart, will and character. It is a resurrection. It is a new creation. It is a passing from death to life. It is the implanting in our dead hearts of a new principle from above. It is the calling into existence of a new creature, with a new nature, new habits of life, new tastes, new desires, new appetites, new judgments, new opinions, new hopes and new fears. All this, and nothing less than this, is implied when our Lord declares that we all need a "new birth".

Would we know what the marks of the new birth are? The man born of God "believes that Jesus is the Christ," "doth not commit sin", "doeth righteousness", "loves the brethren", "overcomes the world", "keepeth himself from the wicked one". This is the man born of the Spirit!

J.C. RYLE

AUGUST 21

BEHOLD THE MAN

Then came Jesus forth, wearing the crown of thorns, and the purple robe.
JOHN 19:5

If there is one place where our Lord Jesus most fully became the joy and comfort of His people it is where He plunged deepest into the depths of woe.

Come, gracious souls, behold the Man in the garden of Gethsemane. Behold His heart so brimming with love that he cannot hold it in, yet so full of sorrow that it must be vented. Behold the bloody sweat as it distils from every pore of His body and falls to the ground.

Behold the Man as soldiers drive nails into His hands and feet. Look up, repenting sinners, and see the sorrowful image of your suffering Lord. Mark Him, as ruby drops glisten on His crown of thorns and adorn it with priceless gems.

Behold the Man when all His bones are out of joint, and He is poured out like water and brought to the dust of death. God has forsaken Him; hell surrounds Him.

Behold, and see. Was there ever sorrow like His sorrow? You who pass by, stop and draw near. Look on this spectacle of grief. It is unique and unparalleled, a wonder to men and angels, and a prodigy unmatched.

Behold the King of Misery, the Emperor of Woe, the one who had no equal or rival in agonies! Gaze on Him, all you who mourn. If there is no consolation in a crucified Christ, there is no joy in earth or heaven. If in the ransom price of His blood there is no hope, then there is no pleasure at the right hand of God.

We have only to sit at the foot of the cross to be less troubled about our doubts and woes. We have only to see His sorrows to be ashamed to mention our sorrows. We have only to look at His wounds to heal our own.

If we are to live holy lives, it must be by the contemplation of is death. If we would rise to dignity, it must be by considering His humiliation and His sorrow.

CHARLES H. SPURGEON

PEACE THROUGH THE BLOOD

While we were yet sinners, Christ died for us.
ROMANS 5:8

One gaze at Him will be enough to reward us for all we have had to bear. Yes, there is peace for the past, grace for the present, and glory for the future. These are three things that every child of God ought to have. When the angels came bringing the gospel, they proclaimed, "Glory to God, peace on earth, and good will towards men." That is what the blood brings - sin covered and taken away, peace for the past, grace for the present, and glory for the future.

Would you now turn to John 19:34: "But one of the soldiers with a spear pierced his side, and forthwith came there out blood and water."

You know that in Zechariah it was foretold that there should be opened in the house of David a fountain for sin and for uncleanness. Now we have it opened. The Son of God has been pierced by that Roman soldier's spear. It seems to me that that was the crowning act of earth and hell - the crowning act of sin. Look at that Roman soldier as he pushed his spear into the very heart of the God-Man. What a hellish deed! But what took place? Blood covered the spear! Oh, thank God, the blood covers sin.

A usurper has got this world now, but Christ will have it soon. The time of our redemption draws near. A little more suffering, and He returns to set up His kingdom and reign upon the earth. He will rend the heavens, and His voice will be heard again. He will descend from heaven with a shout. He will sway His sceptre from the river to the ends of the earth. The thorn and the briar shall be swept away, and the wilderness shall rejoice. Let us rejoice also. We shall see better days. The dreary darkness and sin that sweep along our earth shall be done away with, the dark waves of death and hell shall be beaten back. Oh, let us pray to the Lord to hasten His coming!

Let us remember Romans 3:24: "Being justified freely by his grace, through the redemption that is in Christ Jesus."

What God does He does freely, because He loves to do it. Mark these words, "through the redemption that is in Christ Jesus." Then in the fifth chapter, ninth verse, we read, "Much more then, being now justified by his blood, we shall be saved from wrath through him." The sinner is justified with God by His matchless grace through the blood of His Son.

D. L. MOODY

NOT WHAT WE GET, BUT WHAT WE GIVE

A sacrifice acceptable, wellpleasing to God.
PHILIPPIANS 4:18

Jesus knew He would tread the winepress alone. He knew that though He loved the race and desired to save every individual, the majority would repudiate Him.

He knew that He would stand before unfallen worlds and ranks of beings, as identified with the world's sin. He knew His Father's face would be hidden, as by an eclipse. He knew that the conflict would break His heart and force the sweat of blood out of His forehead. He knew that the Serpent of hell would bruise His heel and that He would appear as a Lamb that had been slain. He knew that those whom He had chosen out of the world would deny Him and flee.

Yet He slackened not His pace, but laying aside the insignia of His glory, He became obedient unto death, event he death of the cross!

Looking at this stupendous act, shall we not catch the infection of His self-giving? Shall we not follow Him so far as we can? "Christ," says the apostle, "has left us an example that we should follow His steps." It is not what we get but what we give; not our own pleasure, but the uplifting of the fallen and the extrication of those who are slipping into the pit; not ridding ourselves of burdens but bearing the burden of others. This is the path of true blessedness, the path trodden by all saints, the path that led Christ to Gethsemane and Calvary, but has ended in the throne. Follow that path, and life will become transcendently useful and blessed!

But there is an infinite chasm between our highest attainments and the Divine self-giving of our Saviour to redeem and save us. He trod that winepress alone, and of all the people there were none with Him. So far as we know, Gethsemane and Calvary have no equivalents throughout God's universe. They are the wonder into which angels desire to look, and the theme of the untiring song of the redeemed.

F. B. MEYER

AUGUST 24

STEADFASTNESS IN CONFLICT

Go out, fight with Amalek.
EXODUS 17:9

The story is often told of Luther burning the "Pope's Bull". Standing in the presence of the crowd, with the flaming paper in his hand, he said: "See, here, this is the 'Pope's Bull'!". Spurgeon, referring to the incident, says: "What cared he for all the Popes that were ever in, or out of hell!" He was God's instrument and the human agent in revival.

One thinks of the great revival of New England, and of Jonathan Edwards' great address to the people around him, on the subject of, "Sinners in the hands of an angry God." God's instrument in this revival was so mightily used by God that, on this occasion, trembling sinners were heard to cry: "Edwards, Edwards, be merciful!" When this awakening swept that part of New England, another chosen instrument was preaching to the Red Indians, and thousands were brought to a saving knowledge of Jesus Christ. David Brainerd was God's instrument. By day and by night he gave himself to prayer. It is said of him that whole nights were spent in agonising prayer until his clothes were drenched in the sweat of his travail.

Coming nearer our own day we have Evan Roberts. Was he not God's man for Wales for his day and generation? It is estimated that in a very short period thousands were added to the Church.

Faith, mighty faith, the promise sees,
And looks to that alone;
Laughs at impossibilities,
And cries "it shall be done!"

DUNCAN CAMPBELL

STEWARDSHIP

Moreover it is required in stewards, that a man be found faithful.
1 CORINTHIANS 4:2

The very idea of service means the remuneration of the will of the servant for the will of the master; the giving up of the personal freedom of the servant to the master; the consecrating of the servant's time and energy and interests to the promotion, not of his own, but of the master's interests.

Look at the servants of the Lord Jesus Christ. Is this the idea of the service which God Almighty demands from his servants? Can it be imagined that he requires less than a man requires from his fellows? Is this service less comprehensive? Does it embrace less abandonment of self and less consecration to the interests of God?

If there was one truth that Jesus Christ laboured more persistently to inculcate into the minds of His disciples more than another it was this - that they were not, in any sense, their own; that they absolutely belonged to Him, body, soul and spirit. If they were stewards they were to hold their stewardship for Him; if they were husbandmen they were to cultivate their ground for Him. If they possessed talents they were to improve their talents for Him. If they possessed money they were to use it for His interests and not their own. This is assumed in every single parable and is implied in every bit of His teaching.

CATHERINE BOOTH

AUGUST 26

GOOD CHEER

Son, be of good cheer; thy sins be forgiven thee.
MATTHEW 9:2

A sick man is brought into the Saviour's presence by four friends. Looking down in compassion upon him, His piercing eye penetrates that broken physical frame. Underneath, he discerns a heart that is paralysed with sin. Listen to His words, "Son, thy sins -" *thy sins*! Ah, the Lord has touched the vital spot here. Sin is the greatest joy-destroyer in the universe. Sin produces every antagonist to true happiness. Where sin enters, spiritual gladness makes it exit. At first hearing, it savours of a paradox to speak of "good cheer" and "sin" in the same breath. The Lord knew what He was doing. The root cause must be exposed. Facing the fact of personal sin is the first step towards the attainment of our goal. Evade sin; deny sin; prevaricate about sin; flirt with sin; roll it around your tongue like a sweet morsel; and your search after a chorus in the heart will be as futile as chasing the wind. *Thy sins, first.* Face the issue. "But, Lord, I did not come to hear about sin: I came to get my body healed." "Son, thy sins." Yes, sin must be faced. There is no other way. "All have sinned." This is the bitterest pill that most of us have to swallow. To acknowledge the verdict, however, is healing medicine. Notice the words that follow: "Son, be of good cheer; thy sins be forgiven thee." Yes, He wounds to heal. He turns sadness into gladness. You who are searching for a carol in your heart, have you heard the first "good cheer"? Have you been to the place called Calvary? Can you sing from the depths of a redeemed heart?

"I know a Fount where sins are washed away.
I know a place where night is turned to day;
Burdens are lifted, blind eyes made to see;
There's a wonder-working power in the blood of Calvary."

REGINALD WALLIS

SUPERNATURAL POWER

Ye are of God, little children, and have overcome them: because greater
is he that is in you, than he that is in the world.
1 JOHN 4:4

God's power is available power. We are supernatural people, born again by a supernatural birth, kept by a supernatural power, sustained on supernatural food, taught by a supernatural Teacher from a supernatural Book. We are led by a supernatural Captain in right paths to assured victories. The risen Saviour, ere He ascended on high said, "All power is given unto Me. Go ye therefore." Again He said to His disciples: "Ye shall receive power when the Holy Spirit is come upon you." ... The power given is not a gift from the Holy Spirit. He himself is the power. Today, He is as truly available and as mighty in power as He was on the day of Pentecost ... We have given too much attention to method, and to machinery, and to resources, and too little to the source of power.

Be strong!
We are not here to play, to dream, to drift.
We have hard work to do, and loads to lift.
Shun not the struggle - face it; 'tis God's gift.

Be strong!
Say not the days are evil. Who's to blame?
And fold the hand and acquiesce - oh, shame!
Stand up, speak out, and bravely, in God's name
Be strong!

J. HUDSON TAYLOR

OUR TITLE TO GLORY

Having therefore, brethren, boldness to enter into the holiest
by the blood of Jesus.
HEBREWS 10:19

The perfect and indefeasible title of every believer is in the merits of Christ. His vicarious fulfilling of the law, whereby He magnified and made it honourable, secured for all in whose stead He acted the full reward of the law. It is on the all-sufficient ground of Christ's perfect obedience being reckoned to His account that the believer is justified by God and assured that He shall "reign in life" (Romans 5:17). If He had lived on earth another hundred years and served God perfectly it would add nothing to His title. Heaven is the "purchased possession" (Ephesians 1:14), purchased for His people by the whole redemptive work of Christ. His precious blood gives every believing sinner the legal right to "enter the holiest" (Hebrews 10:19). Our title to glory is found alone in Christ. Of the redeemed now in heaven it is said, they have "washed their robes and made them white in the blood of the Lamb: therefore are they before the throne of God and serve Him day and night in His temple" (Revelation 7: 14, 15).

The holiest now we enter,
In perfect peace with God;
Regaining our lost centre
Through Christ's atoning blood:
Though great may be our dullness
In thought, and word, and deed,
We glory in the fullness
Of Him Who meets our need.

A. W. PINK

THE MARTYRS

Who through faith subdued kingdoms ... (of whom the world was not worthy.)
HEBREWS 11:33,38

As the greatest manifestation of God to the world was by suffering, so the most influential revelations of His people to the world has been by suffering. They are seen to be the best advantage in the furnace. The blood of the martyrs has ever been the seed of the Church. The patience, meekness, firmness and happiness of God's people in circumstances of suffering, persecution and death, have paved the way for the gospel in almost all lands and ages. A baptism of blood has prepared the hard and sterile soil of humanity for the good seed of the Kingdom, and made it double fruitful. The exhibition of the meek and loving spirit of Christianity under suffering has doubtless won thousands of hearts to its divine author, and tamed and awed many a savage persecutor, besides Saul of Tarsus.

When men see their fellow men enduring with patience and meekness what they know would fill them with hatred, anger and revenge, they naturally conclude that there must be a different spirit in them. When they see Christians suffering the loss of things, and cheerfully resigning themselves to bonds, imprisonment and death, they cannot help feeling that they have sources of strength and springs of consolation all unknown to themselves.

CATHERINE BOOTH

SALVATION

I have waited for Thy salvation, O Lord.
GENESIS 49:18

Salvation! Blessed be God, that our fallen earth has heard the joyful sound! It is unheard in hell. Reader, blessed be the grace which brought it to your ears! Multitudes of man's family are strangers to it. But thrice-blessed be the Spirit's love, if it is the sweetest melody which charms you - the loudest note, by day and by night, of your unwearied praise! To multitudes, it is a tuneless cymbal.

Salvation! It peoples the many mansions of the heavenly kingdom. It is the bliss of the ever-blissful. It is the joy of the ever-joyful. It is the happiness of the ever-happy. It is the song of the ever-singing. It is the peace of the ever-peaceful. It is the rest of the ever-resting. It is the glory of the ever-glorified. O my soul! See to it, that you are saved.

Salvation! It is a roll written by Jehovah's pen. It is the decree of Divine councils: the fruit of omniscient mind: the first-born of unmeasured love: the perfection of eternal thought: the strength of omnipotence. It is the fabric, which every attribute of God erected, with concurring hand; in which every stone is brought by mercy, and shaped by wisdom, and laid by grace; in which there is no defect - no blemish - no decay. It is the soul-built temple, which will rise and shine in growing splendour through all ages. O my soul! See to it, that you are saved.

Salvation! It is the work for which Jesus was born in Bethlehem, and lived on earth, and died at Calvary, and descended into the grave, and burst the bonds of death, and mounted to heaven, and sits on the right hand of God. For this He trod the lowest vale of shame and grief. For this He drank the deepest cup of wrath and torment. For this He grappled with the powers of darkness. For this He reigns and prays on high.

HENRY LAW

YOU CAN'T TAKE IT WITH YOU

Lay up for yourselves treasures in heaven.
MATTHEW 6:20

A couple of friends of mine in the war called upon one of our great Illinois farmers, to get him to give some money for the soldiers, and during their stay he took them up to the cupola of his house and told them to look over yonder, just as far as their eyes could reach, over that beautiful rolling prairie, and they said: "That is very nice." Yes, and it was all his. Then he took them up to another cupola, and said: "Look at that farm, and that, and that:" these were farms stocked, improved, fenced; and they said, "Those are very nice;" and then he showed them horses, cattle, and sheep-yards, and said, "They are all mine."

He showed them the town where he lived, which had been named after him, a great hall, and building lots, and those were all his; and, said he, "I came out West a poor boy, without a farthing, and I am worth all this;" but when he got through, my friend said, "How much have you got up yonder?" and the old man's countenance fell, for he knew very well what that meant. "What have you got up there - in the other world?" "Well," he says, "I have not got anything there." "Why," says my friend, "what a mistake! A man of your intelligence, and forethought, and judgment, to amass all this wealth; and now that you are drawing to your grave, you will have to leave it all.

"You cannot take a farthing with you, but you must die a beggar and a pauper," and the tears rolled down his cheeks as he said, "It does look foolish."

Only a few months after he died, as he had lived, and his property passed to others.

D. L. MOODY

SEPTEMBER 1

DAILY EXPERIENCE

If we live in the Spirit, let us also walk in the Spirit.
GALATIANS 5:25

The Holy Spirit is in the heart of every believer (Romans 8:9); but alas, too often He is shut up in some mere attic in the back of the house, while the world fills the rest. As long as it is so, there is one long weary story of defeat and unrest. But He is not content. The Spirit, which God has made to dwell in us, yearns even with a jealous envy (see James 4:5). Happy are they who yield to Him. Then He will fill them, as the tide fills the harbour and lifts the barges off the banks of mud. He will dwell in them, shedding abroad the perfume of the love of Jesus, and He will reveal the deep things of God.

We can always tell when we are wrong with the Spirit of God; our conscience darkens in a moment when we have grieved Him. If we are aware of such a darkness, we do well never to rest until, beneath His electric light, we have discovered the cause and confessed it and put it away. Besides this, if we live and walk in the Spirit, we shall find that He will work against the risings of our old nature, counteracting them as disinfecting power counteracts the germs of disease floating in an infected house, so that we may do the things that we would (see Galatians 5:17). This is one of the most precious words in the New Testament. If you have never tried it, I entreat you to begin to test it in daily experience. "Walk in the Spirit," hour by hour, by watchful obedience to His slightest promptings, and you will find that "you will not fulfil the lust of the flesh."

As soon as you are aware of temptation, look instantly to Jesus. Flee to Him quicker than a chicken runs beneath the shelter of its mother's wing when the falcon is in the air. In the morning, before you leave your room, put yourself definitely into His hands, persuaded He is able to keep that which you commit unto Him. Go from your home with the assurance that He will cover you with His feathers, and under His wings shall you trust. And when the tempter comes, look instantly up and say, "Jesus, I am trusting Thee to keep me."

F. B. MEYER

A CLOSED DOOR

He is despised and rejected of men.
ISAIAH 53:3

You read of His going up to the annual feast at Jerusalem; you never read of Jerusalem giving Him a welcome. Although Christ had wrought many miracles, and many parables had fallen from His lips, although the most wonderful sermons that were ever preached on this earth were preached by Him, there was hardly anyone speaking a kind word for Him. Almost a universal hiss was going up against Him.

In one place you read that He looked around Him and saw death and woe and misery, while so few people were willing to let Him bless them, and then looked to that world where all knew Him and honoured Him and loved Him, where He had never been mistrusted or called a blasphemer or impostor, which was common all around Him when He was on earth. I can just imagine how, as He looked toward that world, He sighed and longed to get back. In another place it says he had been lifting up the standard very high, and many of His disciples "went back, and walked no more with Him." It is one of the sad scenes in His life.

In another place it says: "Every man went to his own house, and Jesus went to the Mount of Olives." He didn't have any house to go to. He that was once rich became poor for your sake and mine. He that created all things had emptied Himself and become one of the poorest of the land. On an occasion like that He uttered the words: "The foxes have holes, and the birds of the air have nests; but the Son of man has nowhere to lay His head." His cradle was a borrowed one. He hadn't an inch of ground that He could call His own. When He went to the Mount of Olives, the ground was His bed, the sod was His pillow. I can see Him with His locks wet with the dew of the night.

I often think that if I had been living in those days I would like to have had a home in Jerusalem, I would have liked that very night to have asked Him to my home. But I presume my house would have been closed against Him like the others in the city of Jerusalem.

D. L. MOODY

A BETTER COUNTRY

He looked for a city which hath foundations,
whose builder and maker is God.
HEBREWS 11:10

Perhaps it will be asked, should we think as much and as often about spiritual things as about the lawful things of this life? To that I say we should, and more and more often, if we are to be truly spiritually minded. What would you think of a person who pretends that he is journeying to another country where he has an inheritance and yet whose whole conversation is about the trifling things he has to leave behind when he goes? The Saviour forbids us to be anxious about the things of this life, as though our heavenly Father could not care for us. Nor should the things of this life occupy our thoughts as fully as spiritual things (Matthew 6:31-33).

There is a land of pure delight,
Where saints immortal reign;
Infinite day excludes the night
And pleasures banish pain.

There everlasting spring abides
And never-withering flowers;
Death, like a narrow sea, divides
This heavenly land from ours.

O could we make our doubts remove,
These gloomy doubts that rise,
and see the Canaan that we love
With unbeclouded eyes.

JOHN OWEN

SEPTEMBER 4

SOMETHING PERSONAL

What must I do to be saved?
ACTS 16:30

The first thing to remember about being saved is that salvation is a personal matter. "Seek ye the Lord." That means every one must seek for himself. It won't do for the parent to seek for the children; it won't do for the children to seek for the parent. If you were sick, all the medicine that I might take wouldn't do you any good. Salvation is a personal matter that no one else can do for you; you must attend to it yourself.

Some persons lack but one thing - open confession of the Lord Jesus Christ. Some think that they must come to Him in a certain way - that they must be stirred by emotion or something.

Some people have a deeper conviction of sin before they are converted than after they are converted. With some it is the other way. Some know when they are converted and others do not.

Some people are emotional. Some are demonstrative. Some will cry easily. Some are cold and can't be moved to emotion. A man jumped up in a meeting and asked whether he could be saved when he hadn't shed a tear in forty years. Even as he spoke he began to shed tears. It's all a matter of how you're constructed. I am vehement, and I serve God with the same vehemence that I served the devil when I went down the line.

Some of you say that in order to accept Jesus you must have different surroundings. You think you could do it better in some other place. You can be saved where you are as well as any place on earth. I say, "My watch doesn't run. It needs new surroundings. I'll put it in this other pocket, or I'll put it here, or here on these flowers." It doesn't need new surroundings. It needs a new mainspring; and that's what the sinner needs. You need a new heart, not a new suit.

What can I do to keep out of Hell? "Believe on the Lord Jesus Christ and thou shalt be saved."

The Philippian jailer was converted. He had put the disciples into the stocks when they came to the prison, but after his conversion he stooped down and washed the blood from their stripes.

BILLY SUNDAY

SECRET STRENGTH

So run, that ye may obtain.
1 CORINTHIANS 9:24

In some there is a painful fear that they shall not persevere in grace because they know their own fickleness. Certain persons are constitutionally unstable. Some men, are by nature conservative, not to say obstinate; but others are as naturally variable and volatile. Like butterflies, they flit from flower to flower, till they visit all the beauties of the garden and settle upon none of them. They are never long enough in one stay to do any good, not even in their business nor in their intellectual pursuits. Such persons may well be afraid that ten, twenty, thirty, forty, perhaps fifty years of continuous religious watchfulness will be a great deal too much for them. We see man joining first one church and then another, till they box the compass. They are everything by turns and nothing long. Such have a double need to be made not only steadfast but unmovable, or otherwise they will not be found "always abounding in the work of the Lord."

All of us, even if we have no constitutional temptation to fickleness, must feel our own weakness if we are really made alive by God. Dear reader, do you not find enough in any one single day to make you stumble? You that desire to walk in perfect holiness, as I trust you do; you that have set before you a high standard of what a Christian should be - do you not find that before the breakfast things are cleared away from the table, you have displayed enough folly to make you ashamed of yourselves? If we were to shut ourselves up in the lone cell of a hermit, temptation would follow us; for as long as we cannot escape from ourselves we cannot escape from incitements to sin. There is that within our hearts which should make us watchful and humble before God. If he does not confirm us, we are so weak that we shall stumble and fall, not overturned by an enemy but by our own carelessness. Lord, be our strength. We are weakness itself.

Besides that, there is the weariness that comes of a long life. When we begin our Christian profession, we mount up with wings as eagles, further on we run without weariness; but in our best and truest days we walk without fainting. Our pace seems slower, but it is more serviceable and better sustained. I pray God that the energy of our youth may continue with us so far as it is the energy of the Spirit and not the mere fermentation of proud flesh.

CHARLES H. SPURGEON

A FAITHFUL HEART

They that sow in tears shall reap in joy.
PSALM 126:5

Work for the souls of men is undoubtedly attended by great discouragements. The heart of natural man is very hard and unbelieving. The blindness of most men to their own lost condition and peril of ruin is something past description. "The carnal mind is enmity against God" (Romans 8:7). No one can have any just idea of the desperate hardness of men and women until he has tried to do good. No one can have any conception of the small number of those who repent and believe until he has personally endeavoured to "save some" (1 Corinthians 9:22). To suppose that everybody who is told about Christ and entreated to believe will become a true Christian is mere childish ignorance. "Few there be that find the narrow way!" The labourer for Christ will find the majority of those among whom he labours unbelieving and impenitent, in spite of all that he can do. The "many" will not turn to Christ. These are discouraging facts. But they are facts and facts that ought to be known.

The true antidote against despondency in God's work is an abiding recollection of such promises as that before us. There are "wages" laid up for faithful reapers. They shall receive a reward at the last day, far exceeding anything they have done for Christ - a reward proportioned not to their success, but to the quantity of their work. They are gathering "fruit" which shall endure when this world has passed away - fruit in some souls saved, if many will not believe, and fruit in evidences of their own faithfulness, to be brought out before assembled worlds. Do our hands ever hang down and our knees wax faint? Do we feel disposed to say, "My labour is in vain and my words without profit"? Let us lean back at such seasons on this glorious promise. There are "wages" yet to be paid. One single soul saved shall outlive and outweigh all the kingdoms of the world.

J. C. RYLE

SHEEP AND SWINE

The younger son gathered all together, and
took his journey into a far country.
LUKE 15:13

From the moment the prodigal decided to remain in the far country, it was line upon line, precept upon precept. The hand of his father was against him - in love it is true - but still against him - and the position became worse and worse. *"Behold I am against thee"* is an awful scripture, yet it occurs very often in the Bible; and not only is the hand of God against the reprobate - against those who are given up and let alone - but against every man who, feeling himself to be a wanting, needy creature, endeavours to supply his wants with anything that is not God. If God be for us, who can be against us? but if God be against us, who can be for us? Vain, then, is all human aid; vain is the help of any citizen of this country. If God be against us, utterly vain and worse than useless is every device and plan of man to do good to himself.

By joining himself to a citizen of this country the prodigal made his position worse than ever; *he sent him into his fields to feed swine!*

No son of the father ever yet joined himself to a citizen of this country who did not send him into his fields to feed swine.

Let me try and explain what I mean.

The world is divided into two classes, and only two: the children of God and the children of the wicked one - the clean and the unclean, the sheep and the swine. Those who are washed in the blood of the Lord Jesus Christ are the sheep - the clean - the children of God; those who are not washed in the blood of the Lord Jesus Christ are the swine - the unclean, the children of the wicked one. And not only does everybody belong to one or other of the two classes mentioned, but from every one of us there is an influence constantly going forth, which is feeding sheep or feeding swine - an influence which has a power for good or evil over those with whom we associate, and which is helping forward the cause, either of God or the devil in the world.

BROWNLOW NORTH

SEPTEMBER 8

OUR MONEY FOR JESUS

Your liberality.
1 CORINTHIANS 16:3

"The silver is mine, and the gold is mine," saith the Lord of Hosts. Yes, every coin we have is literally our Lord's money. Simple belief of this fact is the stepping-stone to full consecration of what He has given us, whether much or little.

"Then you mean to say we are never to spend anything on ourselves?"

Not so. Another fact must be considered - our Lord has given us our bodies as a special personal charge, and we are responsible for keeping these bodies - according to the means given and the work required - in working order for Him. This is part of our "own work". A master entrusts a worker with a delicate machine for the assigned task. He also provides him with a sum of money to keep the machine in thorough repair. Is it not obvious that it is the man's distinct duty to see to this faithfully? Would not the worker be failing in duty if he chose to spend it all on something for somebody else's work or on a present for his master, fancying that would please him better, while the machine is creaking and wearing for want of a little oil or working badly for the want of a new band or screw? Just so, we are to spend what is really needful on ourselves, because it is our charge to do so; but not for ourselves, because we are not our own but our Master's.

He knows our frame, knows its need of rest and medicine, food and clothing; and the securing of these for our own entrusted bodies should be done just as much "for Jesus" as the greater pleasure of obtaining them for someone else. Therefore, the assertion is true: consecration is not real and complete while we are looking upon a single penny as our own to do what we like with. Also the principle is exactly the same, whether we are spending pennies or pounds. It is our Lord's money and must not be spent without reference to Him.

Take my silver and my gold,
Not a mite would I withhold:
Take my intellect, and use
Every power as Thou shalt choose.

FRANCES R. HAVERGAL

SEPTEMBER 9

CHRIST ALONE

Neither is there salvation in any other.
ACTS 4:12

In the evening I went very unwillingly to a society in Aldersgate Street, where one was reading Luther's preface to the Epistle to the Romans. About a quarter before nine, while he was describing the change which God works in the heart through faith in Christ, I felt my heart strangely warmed. I felt I did trust in Christ, Christ alone, for my salvation; and an assurance was given me that he had taken away my sins, even mine, and saved me from the law of sin and death .. But it was not long before the enemy suggested, "This cannot be faith; for where is thy joy?" Then was I taught that ... as to the transports of joy ... in those who have mourned deeply, God sometimes giveth, sometimes withholdeth them, according to the counsels of His own will.

> *To save what was lost, from Heaven He came;*
> *Come, sinners, and trust in Jesus' name;*
> *He offers you pardon, He bids you be free;*
> *If sin be your burden, O come unto Me!*
>
> *Then let us submit His grace to receive,*
> *Fall down at His feet and gladly believe;*
> *We all are forgiven for Jesus' sake;*
> *Our title to Heaven His merits we take.*

JOHN WESLEY

THE WELL BELOV'D SON

He shall offer it without blemish.
LEVITICUS 3:6

The Father's delight in His Son seems plainly exhibited in the ever-recurring direction - *"without blemish."* The eye of God rested with infinite complacency on the spotlessness of Jesus. "Behold my servant whom I have chosen, mine elect (my chosen Lamb) , in whom my soul delighteth." It is an expression that teaches us, by its frequent repetition, both the holy delight which the Father had in "the holy child Jesus" and the delight He will have in His unblemished Church.

It is a holy God that speaks; it is the Author of the holy law. The Lawgiver is He who prescribes the type of a fulfilled and satisfied law. We recognise the God and Father of our Lord and Saviour, "just while He justifies". It is truly pleasant, unspeakably precious, to see God's thorough demand for spotlessness; for thus we are assured that, beyond all doubt, our reconciliation is solid. It is full reconciliation to a God who is fully satisfied.

Guilty, vile and helpless we:
Spotless Lamb of God was He;
"Full atonement" can it be?
Hallelujah! what a Saviour.

ANDREW BONAR

THE CROSS OF CHRIST SPEAKS
OF THE LOVE OF GOD

The Son of God, who loved me, and gave himself for me.
GALATIANS 2:20

After I became a father, and for years had an only son, as I looked at my boy I thought of the Father giving His Son to die, and it seemed to me as if it required more love for the Father to give His Son than for the Son to die. Oh, the love that God must have had for the world when He gave His Son to die for it! "God so loved the world, that he gave his only begotten Son, that whosoever believeth in him should not perish, but have everlasting life" (John 3:16). I have never been able to preach from that text. I have often thought I would, but it is so high that I can never climb to its height; I have just quoted it and passed on. Who can fathom the depth of those words: "God so loved the world"? We can never scale the heights of His love or fathom its depths. Paul prayed that he might know the height, the depth, the length and the breadth of the love of God, but it was past his finding out. It "passeth knowledge" (Ephesians 3:19).

Nothing speak to us of the love of God like the cross of Christ. Come with me to Calvary and look upon the Son of God as He hangs there. Can you hear that piercing cry from His dying lips: "Father, forgive them; for they know not what they do!" and say that he does not love you? "Greater love hath no man than this, that a man lay down his life for his friends" (John 15:13). But Jesus Christ laid down His life *for His enemies.*

Another thought is this: He loved us long before we even thought of Him. The idea that He does not love us until we first love Him is not to be found in Scripture. In 1 John 4:10 it is written: "Herein is love, not that we loved God, but that he loved us, and sent his Son to be the propitiation for our sins." He loved us before we even thought of loving Him. You loved your children before they knew anything about your love. And so, long before we ever thought of God, we were in His thoughts.

What brought the prodigal home? It was the thought that his father loved him. Suppose the news had reached him that he was a cast-off and that his father did not care for him anymore. Would he have gone back? Never! But the thought dawned upon him that his father loved him still: so he rose up, and went back to his home.

D. L. MOODY

THE HOPE OF HIS CALLING

The riches of the glory of his inheritance in the saints.
EPHESIANS 1:18

Several advantages are to be expected from regularly thinking about heaven. In the same way as when one looks at a bright light and the image of that brightness afterwards blinds one to other sights for a while, so whoever meditates on heavenly glories will find desire for earthly things lessened ... Faith will grow stronger by thoughts about heaven. The more that believers think about heaven, the more they will look forward to being there. Those who do not think of heaven frequently, do not think of it sincerely. As a result of strong faith, believers have a bright hope ... The reason why believers sometimes lack hope is because they do not think often enough about the things hoped for.

On Jordan's stormy banks I stand,
And cast a wishful eye
To Canaan's fair and happy land,
Where my possessions lie.

O sweet and blessed country,
The home of God's elect!
O sweet and blessed country,
That eager hearts expect!

Jesus, in mercy bring us
To that dear land of rest,
Who art, with God the Father
And Spirit, ever blest!

JOHN OWEN

THE SECRET OF GUIDANCE

He will be our guide.
PSALM 48:14

We must wait the gradual unfolding of God's plan in providence. God's impressions within and His Word without are always corroborated by His providence around, and we should quietly wait until these three focus into one point.

Sometimes it looks as if we are bound to act. Everyone says we must do something; and, indeed, things seem to have reached so desperate a pitch that we must. Behind are the Egyptians; right and left are inaccessible precipices; before is the sea. It is not easy at such times to stand still and see the salvation of God; but we must. When King Saul compelled himself and offered sacrifice, because he thought that Samuel was too late in coming, he made the greatest mistake of his life.

God may delay to come in the guise of His providence. There was delay while Sennacherib's host lay like withered leaves around the Holy City. There was delay while Jesus came walking on the sea in the early dawn or hastened to raise Lazarus. There was delay before the angel sped to Peter's side on that night before his expected martyrdom. He stays long enough to test patience of faith, but not a moment behind the extreme hour of need. "The vision is yet for an appointed time, but at the end it shall speak, and shall not lie; though it tarry, wait for it, because it will surely come, it will not tarry."

It is very remarkable how God guides us by circumstances. At one moment the way may seem utterly blocked, and then shortly afterward some trivial incident occurs, which might not seem much to others but which to the keen eye of faith speaks volumes. Sometimes these sings are repeated in different ways in answer to prayer. They are not haphazard results of chance, but the opening up of circumstances in the direction in which we should walk. And they begin to multiply as we advance toward our goal, just as lights do as we near a populous town when darting through the land by night express.

My Wisdom and my Guide,
My Counsellor Thou art;
O never let me leave Thy side,
Or from Thy paths depart!

F. B. MEYER

SEPTEMBER 14

OUR TEST AND TOUCHSTONE

Then shall two be in the field; the one shall be taken, and the other left.
MATTHEW 24:40

I t is written that Abraham had two sons, the one by a bondmaid, the other by a freewoman. But he who was of the bondwoman was born after the flesh; but he of the freewoman was by promise" (Galatians 4:22-23).

Abraham had two sons. Ishmael and Isaac were beyond all dispute veritable sons of Abraham. Yet one of them inherited the covenant blessing, and the other was simply a prosperous man of the world. See how close these two are together! They were born in the same society, called the same great patriarch "father" and sojourned in the same encampment with him. Yet Ishmael was a stranger to the covenant, while Issac was the heir of the promise. How little is there in blood and birth!

A more remarkable instance than this happened a little afterward; for Esau and Jacob were born of the same mother, at the same birth, yet it is written, "Jacob have I loved, and Esau have I hated." One became gracious and the other profane. So closely may the two come together and yet so widely may they be separated! Verily, it is not only that two shall be in one bed, and the one shall be taken, and the other left; but two shall come into the world at the same moment and yet one of them will take up his inheritance with God, and the other will for a morsel of meat sell his birthright. We may be in the same church, baptized in the same water, seated at the same Communion table, singing the same psalm, and offering the same prayer; and yet we may be of two races as opposed as the seed of the woman and the seed of the serpent.

Abraham's two sons are declared by Paul to be types of two races of men, who are much alike and yet widely differ. They are unlike in their origin. They were both sons of Abraham; but Ishmael, the child of Hagar, was the offspring of Abraham upon ordinary conditions; he was born after the flesh. Isaac, the son of Sarah, was not born by the strength of nature; for his father was more than a hundred years old, and his mother was long past age. He was given to his parents by the Lord and was born according to the promise of faith. This is a grave distinction, and it marks off the true child of God from him who is only so by profession. The promise lies at the bottom of the distinction, and the power that goes to accomplish the promise creates and maintains the difference. Hence the promise, which is our inheritance, is also our test and touchstone.

CHARLES H. SPURGEON

THE LIFE OF FAITH

He that cometh to God must believe that he is.
HEBREWS 11:6

Remember that Christ Jesus is the Teacher as well as the Saviour of His people and that believing Him, or laying hold of Him by faith, includes belief in what *He teaches*, as well as in what *He promises*. The distinguishing mark of the true Christian is not merely that he professes to believe in Jesus, but that he evidences his faith by his conduct; Christ has become his Teacher; and he no longer walks in the imaginations of his own heart, but *he walks by faith*. "Not everyone who saith unto Me, Lord, Lord, shall enter in the kingdom of heaven, but he that doeth the will of my Father which is in heaven."

"Come unto Me all ye that labour and are heavy laden, and I will give you rest."

"Take my yoke upon you, and learn of Me, and ye shall find rest unto your souls." These are all the words of Jesus, and the promise in this last quotation is positive. Christ says, "ye shall"; but the command explains the promise; it is made to those *who take His yoke, and learn of Him*. Do you think that a soul disquieted and in search of rest can be said to be bearing Christ's yoke, or learning of Him, who seeks relief and peace in the things of this world, or in the society of its god-forgetting citizens?

If religion does not make you happy without the things of the world, I say again it is not because there is not enough in religion to satisfy you, but because you have not got *enough of religion*. "Acquaint thyself with God, and be at peace," is the prescription given by God Himself, the Good Physician, to those who are in search of happiness; and the happiest man at this moment on earth, is the man who knows most of God. We become acquainted with God *by faith* - have you got it? A man without faith is spiritually dead; but when faith comes, life comes; and where there is real faith and real life, there follows of necessity the *life of faith*. Faith first, and then the life of faith, after that, but never till that - happiness.

BROWNLOW NORTH

SEPTEMBER 16

OUR EXAMPLE

Ye also ought to wash one another's feet.
JOHN 13:14

Chirstians must never be ashamed of doing anything that Christ has done. We read, "Verily, I say unto you, the servant is not greater than his Lord; neither he that is sent greater than he that sent him."

There seems little doubt that our Lord's all-seeing eye saw a rising unwillingness in the minds of the apostles to do such menial things as they had just seen Him do. Puffed up with their old Jewish expectation of thrones and kingdoms in this world, secretly self-satisfied with their own position as our Lord's friends, these poor Galileans were startled at the idea of washing people's feet! They could not bring themselves to believe that Messiah's service entailed work like this. They could not yet take in the grand thought that true Christian greatness consisted in doing good to others. And hence they needed our Lord's word of warning. If He had humbled himself to do humbling work, His disciples must not hesitate to do the same.

The lesson is one of which we all need to be reminded. We are all to apt to dislike any work which seems to entail trouble, self-denial and going down to our inferiors. We are only too ready to depute such work to others and to excuse ourselves by saying, "It is not in our way." When feelings of this kind arise within us we shall find it good to remember our Lord's words in this passage, no less than our Lord's example. We ought never to think it beneath us to show kindness to the lowest of men. We ought never to hold our hand because the objects of our kindness are ungrateful or unworthy. Such was not the mind of Him who washed the feet of Judas Iscariot as well as Peter. He who in these matters cannot stoop to follow Christ's example gives little evidence of possessing true love or true humility.

J. C. RYLE

AT THE CROSSROADS

With the heart man believeth unto righteousness; and with the mouth
confession is made unto salvation.
ROMANS 10:10

Right where the two roads through life diverge God has put Calvary. There He put up a cross, the stumbling block over which the love of God said, "I'll touch the heart of man with the thought of father and son." He thought that would win the world to Him but for nineteen hundred years men have climbed the Mount Calvary and trampled into the earth the tenderest teachings of God.

You are on the devil's side. How are you going to cross over?

So you cross the line and God won't issue any extradition papers. Some of you want to cross. If you believe, then say so, and step across. There are hundreds that are on the edge of the line and many are standing straddling it. But that won't save you. You believe in your heart - confess Him with your mouth. With his heart man believes and with his mouth he confesses. Then confess and receive salvation full, free, perfect and eternal. God will not grant any extradition papers. A man isn't a soldier because he wears a uniform, or carries a gun. He is a soldier when he makes a definite enlistment. All of the others can be bought without enlisting. When a man becomes a soldier he goes out on muster day and takes an oath to defend his country. It's the oath that makes him a soldier. Going to church doesn't make you a Christian any more than going to a garage makes you an automobile, but public definite enlistment for Christ makes you a Christian.

"Oh," a woman said to me out in Iowa, "Mr. Sunday, I don't think I have to confess with my mouth." I said, "You're putting up your thought against God's."

M-o-u-t-h doesn't spell intellect. It spells mouth and you must confess with your mouth. The mouth is the biggest part about most people, anyhow.

What must I do?

Philosophy doesn't answer it. Infidelity doesn't answer it. First, "believe on the Lord Jesus Christ and thou shalt be saved." Believe on the Lord. Lord - that is His kingly name. That's the name He reigns under. "Thou shalt call his name Jesus." It takes that kind of a confession. Give me a Saviour with a sympathetic eye to watch me so I shall not slander. Give me a Saviour with a strong arm to catch me if I stumble. Give me a Saviour that will hear my slightest moan.

BILLY SUNDAY

A FEAST FOR FALLEN MAN

The Lord's passover.
LEVITICUS 23:5

*T*he *Lamb slain,* is the first object held up to the view of Israel about to be redeemed. "Behold the Lamb of God!" is still the cry that first reaches a sinner's ear and a sinner's heart. Here is the first feast for fallen man. What grace meets the sinner! God meets him with the *Lamb,* and that Lamb is His beloved Son; and shows him in that Lamb life out of death, even life to the sinner out of the death of the Son of God. The first altar we read of exhibited a *Lamb slain;* the first deed of the new dispensation was, presenting the true Lamb to the view of all, and the offering it up to God (John 1:29); and the first opening of the sanctuary above (Revelation 14:1) where the coming glory is preparing, exhibits the *Lamb that was slain,* loved, adored, ruling, reigning, with all heaven gazing on Him in unutterable transports of delight and thankfulness.

We should notice, however, that *a people delivered* is essentially connected with the passover. The Lamb is not slain in vain. Behold a people going forth in perfect freedom in the fresh joy of recent deliverance from imminent peril. A people thus escaped, cheerful, thankful, solemn, with a heavenward eye, and a step lifted up to tread on Canaan's kingdom - this is as essential to the full idea of the passover as the lamb.

> *Not all the blood of beasts,*
> *On Jewish altars slain,*
> *Could give the guilty conscience peace,*
> *Or wash away the stain.*
>
> *But Christ, the heavenly Lamb,*
> *Takes all our sins away;*
> *A sacrifice of nobler name*
> *And richer blood than they.*

ANDREW BONAR

OUR GREAT CALLING

Having made known unto us the mystery of his will.
EPHESIANS 1:9

The epistle to the Ephesians is the epistle of "In-ness". That is, it is the epistle in which from first to last Paul uses the little preposition "in" and tells us what we are in Christ Jesus. Just as this whole creation slept in the mind of God to be elaborated step by step to its consummation, so the whole church of Jesus Christ lay in the mind of God before the mountains were brought forth or ever He had formed the earth. And you and I were appointed to a definite place in that wonderful body. What that place was will not be made fully clear to us until we stand before God in the eternal light, but it is comforting to know that there was a definite place in the purpose of God for you and me.

Doesn't that give a new meaning and dignity to your life, that it is the working out of the conception of God and that every day you must try so to walk as to realise the purpose that was in the mind of God when he created you in Christ Jesus? As one looks out upon men and women and things, life seems so full of commonplaces and little anxieties, worries, troubles and misfortunes that one is apt to get into the way of supposing it does not matter very much how he lives. But if we remember that there is an eternal purpose in Christ in our regeneration, we shall always try to act worthily of our great calling in Christ Jesus.

The greatest thing you can do in this world is to live a saintly, holy, lovely life. All the small things of your life - the worries, anxieties, the troubles, your location and environment, the lines you are compelled to follow - all these have been contrived by God to give you the best possible opportunity to become what He wants you to be. God could have made you anything He liked. He could have made that woman a queen; He could have made that man a millionaire or a prince. But out of all the myriad opportunities of this world God Almighty chose for you just that position in which you find yourself today because He knew that was the one place in which you could come nearest His ideal.

F. B. MEYER

SEPTEMBER 20

"FOR CHARLIE'S SAKE"

And whatsoever ye do in word or deed, do all in the name of the Lord Jesus.
COLOSSIANS 3:17

Some years ago at a convention, an old judge was telling about the mighty power Christians summon to their aid in the petitions "for Christ's sake" and "in Jesus' name", and he told a story that made a great impression on me. When the war came on, the judge said, his only son left for the army and he suddenly became interested in soldiers. Every soldier that passed by brought his son to remembrance; he could see his son in him. He went to work for soldiers. When a sick soldier came there to Columbus one day, so weak he couldn't walk, the judge took him in a carriage and got him into the Soldier's Home.

Soon the judge became president of the Soldier's Home in Columbus, and would go down every day and spend hours in looking after those soldiers and seeing that they had every comfort. He spent on them a great deal of time and money.

One day he said to his wife, "I'm giving too much time to these soldiers. There's an important case coming on in court, and I've got to attend to my own business."

He said he went down to the office that morning, resolved in the future to let the soldiers alone. He went to his desk and then to writing. Pretty soon the door opened, and he saw a soldier hobble slowly in. He stared at the sight of him. The man was fumbling at something in his breast, and pretty soon he got out an old soiled paper. The father saw it was his own son's writing.

Dear father: This young man belongs to my company. He has lost his leg and his health in defence of his country, and he is going home to his mother to die. If he calls on you, treat him kindly,

For Charlie's sake.

"For Charlie's sake." The moment he saw that, a pang went into his heart. He sent for a carriage, lifted the maimed soldier in, drove home, put him into Charlie's room, When the young soldier got well enough to go to the train to go home to his mother, he took him to the railway station, put him in the nicest, most comfortable place in the carriage and sent him on his way. "I did it," said the old judge, "for Charlie's sake."

Now, whatsoever you do, my friends, do it for the Lord Jesus' sake. Do and ask everything in the name of Him "who loved us and gave himself for us."

D. L. MOODY

THE HAPPINESS OF HEAVEN

He that followeth after righteousness and mercy findeth life.
PROVERBS 21:21

Holiness and happiness, joined in one, are sometimes styled, in the inspired writings, "the kingdom of God" ... because it is the immediate fruit of God's reigning in the soul. So soon as ever He takes unto Himself His mighty power, and sets up His throne in our hearts, they are instantly filled with this "righteousness and peace and joy in the Holy Ghost" (Romans 14:17). It is called "the kingdom of heaven" because it is, in a degree, heaven opened in the soul. For whosoever they are that experience this, they can say before angels and men: "Everlasting life is won, Glory is on earth begun."

Eternal life to all mankind
Thou hast in Jesus given,
And all who seek, in Him shall find
The happiness of Heaven.

Faith in Thy power Thou seest I have,
For Thou this faith hast wrought;
Dead souls Thou callest from their grave
And speakest worlds from nought.

Thy name to me, Thy nature grant;
This, only this be given:
Nothing beside my God I want,
Nothing in earth or Heaven.

JOHN WESLEY

PERSONAL PURITY

Wash me, and I shall be whiter than snow.
PSALM 51:7

A full atonement is as much required for our inward secret sins as for open and flagrant sins. The sinful vision that our fancy spread out before us for a moment must be washed away by blood. The tendency which our soul felt to sympathise in that act of resentment or revenge must be washed away by blood. The hour or minutes we spent in brooding over our supposed hard lot must be redeemed by blood. The selfish wish we cherished for our own special prosperity, in some undertaking that was to reflect its credit on us only, is to be washed away by blood. The proud aspiration, the sensual impulse, the world-loving glance our soul casts on earth's glories, must be washed away by blood. The darkness, ignorance, suspicion, and misconception we entertain toward God and His salvation, must be washed in the blood. "Behold, thou desirest truth in the inward parts; and in the hidden part (hidden region of the soul) thou shalt make me to know wisdom" (Psalm 51:6)

Father, I have wandered from Thee,
Often has my heart gone astray;
Crimson do my sins seem to me:
Water cannot wash them away.
Jesus, to that fountain of Thine
Leaning on Thy promise I go,
Cleanse me by Thy washing divine,
And I shall be whiter than snow.

ANDREW BONAR

SEPTEMBER 23

OUR VOICES FOR JESUS

While I live will I praise the Lord.
PSALM 146:2

If you only knew, dear hesitating friends, what strength and gladness the Master gives you when you loyally sing forth the honour of His name, you would not forgo it. Oh, if you only knew the difficulties it saves! For when you sing "always and only for your King" you will not get much entangled by the King's enemies. Singing an out-and-out sacred song often clears one's path at a stroke as to many other things. If you only knew the rewards He gives, very often then and there, the recognition that you are one of the King's friends by some lonely and timid one, the natural openings to speak a word for Jesus to hearts which, without the song, would never have given you the chance of the word.

If you only knew the joy of believing that His sure promise "My word shall not return unto me void" will be fulfilled as you sing that word for Him! If you only tasted the solemn happiness of knowing that you have indeed a royal audience, that the King Himself is listening as you sing! If you only knew - and why should you not know? Shall not the time past of your life suffice you for the miserable, double-hearted calculating service? Let Him have the whole use of your voice at any cost, and see if He does not put many a totally unexpected new song in your mouth.

I am not writing all this to great and finished singers, but to everybody who can sing at all. Those who think they have only a very small talent are often most tempted not to trade with it for their Lord. Whether you have much or little natural voice, there is reason for its cultivation and room for its use. Place it at your Lord's disposal, and He will show you how to make the most of it for Him, for not seldom His multiplying power is brought to bear on a consecrated voice.

Take my voice, and let me sing,
Always, only for my King;
Take my lips, and let them be
Filled with messages from Thee.

FRANCES R. HAVERGAL

OUR THOUGHTS

Consider him ... lest ye be wearied and faint in your minds.
HEBREWS 12:3

Our peace with God depends on what Christ has done for us. We love Him for that. But more; we rejoice that He is now so glorious in heaven. We look forward to being with Him, but we will not enjoy being with Him there if we do not enjoy being with Him here. I know some people who are anxious if too long a time passes without having Him in their thoughts. Sadly I know more who rarely have Him in their thoughts. It is important to think about Christ in a biblical way ... We must make sure that the means we use to help us meditate are themselves spiritual. Pray continually for the Holy Spirit's help. Read some passages of Scripture which teaches something about Christ, and think about that.

Jesu, Thy boundless love to me,
No thought can reach, no tongue declare;
O knit my thankful heart to Thee,
And reign without a rival there:
Thine wholly, Thine alone, I am,
Be Thou alone my constant flame.

O grant that nothing in my soul,.
May dwell but Thy pure love alone;
O may Thy love possess me whole,
My joy, my treasure, and my crown:
Strange flames far from my heart remove;
My every act, word, thought, be love.

JOHN OWEN

REMISSION OF SINS

This cup is the new testament in my blood.
1 CORINTHIANS 11:25

See brothers and sisters, to what the blood of your Lord destines you. Oh, my soul, bless God for that one cup, which reminds you of the great sacrifice and prophesies to you - your glory at the right hand of God forever!

We are told in Matthew 26:28 that his blood is shed "for many for the remission of sins". In that large word "many" let us exceedingly rejoice. Christ's blood was not shed for the handful of apostles alone. There were but eleven of them who really partook of the blood symbolised by the cup. The Saviour does not say, "This is My blood which is shed for you, the favoured eleven."; but, "shed for many," Jesus did not die for the ministers alone. I recollect in Martin Luther's life that he saw, in one of the churches, a picture of the pope and the cardinals and bishops and priests and monks and friars, all on board a ship. They were all safe, every one of them. As for the laity, poor wretches, they were struggling in the sea, and many of them drowning. Only those were saved to whom the good men in the ship were so kind as to hand a rope or a plank. That is not our Lord's teaching. His blood is shed "for many" and not for the few. He is not the Christ of a caste, or a class but the Christ of all conditions of men.

Those in the upper room were all Jews, but the Lord Jesus Christ said to them: "This blood is shed for many," to let them see that He did not die alone for the seed of Abraham but for all races of men that dwell upon the face of the earth. "Shed for many!" His eye, I doubt not, glanced at these far-off islands, and at the vast lands beyond the western sea. He thought of Africa, and India, and the land of Siam. A multitude that no man can number gladdened the farseeing and foreseeing eye of the Redeemer. He spoke with joyful emphasis when He said, "Shed for many for the remission of sins."

Believe in the immeasurable results of redemption. Whenever we are making arrangements for the preaching of this precious blood, let us make them on a large scale. The mansion of love should be built for a large family. The masses must be compelled to come in. A group of half dozen converts makes us very glad, and so it should; but oh, to have half a dozen thousand at once! Why not? This blood is shed for many.

CHARLES H. SPURGEON

SEPTEMBER 26

GOD'S MEDICINE

Jesus saith unto him, Go thy way; thy son liveth.
JOHN 4:50

What benefits affliction can confer on the soul! We read that anxiety about a son led the nobleman to Christ, in order to obtain help in time of need. Once brought into Christ's company, he learned a lesson of priceless value. In the end, "He believed, and his whole house." All this, be it remembered, hinged upon the son's sickness. If the nobleman's son had never been ill, his father might have lived and died in his sins.

Affliction is one of God's medicines. By it He often teaches lessons which would be learned in no other way. By it He often draws souls away from sin and the world, which would otherwise have perished everlastingly.

Let us beware of murmuring in the time of trouble. Let us settle it firmly in our minds that there is a meaning, a needs-be and a message from God in every sorrow that falls upon us. There are no lessons so useful as those learned in the school of affliction.

Christ's word is as good as Christ's presence. We read that Jesus did not come down to Capernaum to see the sick young man, but only spoke the work: "Thy son liveth." Almighty power went with that little sentence. That very hour the patient began to amend. Christ only spoke and the cure was done. Christ only commanded and the deadly disease stood fast.

The fact before us is singularly full of comfort. It gives enormous value to every promise of mercy, grace and peace which ever fell from Christ's lips. He that by faith has laid hold on some word of Christ has got his feet upon a rock. What Christ has said, he is able to do, and what he has undertaken, he will never fail to make good. The sinner who has really reposed his soul on the word of the Lord Jesus Christ is safe to all eternity. He could not be safer, if he saw the book of life and his own name written in it.

J. C. RYLE

HE DIED FOR ME

Who his own self bare our sins.
1 PETER 2:24

In the war there was a band of guerillas, Quantrell's band, that had been ordered to be shot on sight. They had burned a town in Iowa and they had been caught. One long ditch was dug and they were lined up in front of it and blindfolded and tied. Just as the firing squad was ready to present arms a young man dashed through the bushes and cried, "Stop!" He told the commander of the firing squad that he was as guilty as any of the others. He had escaped and had come of his own free will, and pointing to one man in the line he asked to take his place. "I'm single," he said, "while he has a wife and babies." The commander of the firing squad was an usher in one of the cities in which I held meetings, and he told me how the young fellow was blindfolded and bound and the guns rang out and he fell dead.

Time went on and one day a man came upon another in a graveyard in Missouri weeping and shaping the grave into form. The first man asked who was buried there and the other said, "The best friend I ever had." Then he told how he had not gone far away but had come back and taken the body of his friend after he had been shot. He buried it; so he knew he had the right body. And he had brought a withered bouquet all the way from his home to put on the grave. He was poor then and could not afford anything costly, but he had placed a slab of wood on the pliable earth with these words on it: "He died for me."

Major Whittle stood by the grave some time later and saw the monument. The man became rich and today there is a marble monument fifteen feet high and on it this inscription:

SACRED TO THE MEMORY OF
WILLIE LEE
HE TOOK MY PLACE IN THE LINE
HE DIED FOR ME

Sacred to the memory of Jesus Christ. He took our place on the cross and gave His life that we might live, and go to heaven and reign with Him.

Believe on the Lord Jesus Christ, confess Him with your mouth, and you shall be saved and your house.

BILLY SUNDAY

GRACES OF THE CHURCH

Frankincense; myrrh and aloes, with all the chief spices.
SOLOMON'S SONG 4:14

The frankincense, fragrant in its smell, denoted the acceptableness of the offering. As a flower or plant - the rose of Sharon or the balm of Gilead- would induce any passing traveller to stoop down over them, and regale himself with their fragrance, so the testimony borne by Christ's work to the character of Godhead brings the Father to bend over any to whom it is imparted, and to rest over him in His love. The Lord Jesus says to His Church, in Song 4:6, "Until the day breaks, and the shadows flee away, I will get me to the mountain of myrrh, and the hill of frankincense." This spot must be the Father's right hand. In like manner, then, it ought to be the holy purpose of believing souls who are looking for Christ, to dwell so entirely amid the Redeemer's merits, that, like the maidens of king Ahasuerus (Esther 2:12), they shall be fragrant with the sweet odours, and with these alone, when the Bridegroom comes.

> *Tis the church triumphant singing,*
> *Worthy the Lamb!*
> *Heaven throughout with prayers ringing,*
> *Worthy the Lamb!*
> *Thrones and powers before Him bending,*
> *Odours sweet with voice ascending*
> *Swell the chorus never ending,*
> *Worthy the Lamb!*

ANDREW BONAR

SEPTEMBER 29

TRUST HIM WITH ALL YOUR HEART

Trusting in the Lord.
PSALM 112:7

God is my Saviour and my Redeemer; not prayers or feelings or works or tears or anything in or of myself. "God is my salvation; I will trust, and not be afraid: for the Lord Jehovah is my strength and my song; he also is become my salvation." There is salvation in front of you and salvation behind you; salvation to begin with and salvation to end with. So now, just pray to the Lord to help you to trust Him from this hour - from this minute - trust Him with your body and with your soul.

There is a grand proverb teaching us how to trust: "Trust in the Lord with all thine heart; and lean not unto thine own understanding. In all thy ways acknowledge him, and he shall direct thy paths" (Proverbs 3: 5-6). I never knew a man who was willing to trust the Lord with all his heart but the Lord saved him, and delivered him from all his doubts. The great trouble is that we do not trust Him with all our heart. God says, "Ye shall seek me, and find me, when you search for me with all your heart." God says, "Trust me with all your heart." Is there anything to hinder you from putting your whole trust in Him?

If Satan comes to you and wants to hear you explain some mysterious sayings in the Bible, do not lean on your own understanding; tell him you are going to trust the Lord and not yourself. If God cannot be trusted, who can? Trust Him without any doubts. There cannot be true faith where there is doubt; the very fact that you doubt should show you that you do not trust with all your heart.

It is said that Alexander the Great had a favourite physician who followed him through all his battles. This favourite doctor had an enemy who wanted to get him out of the way. The latter wrote a letter to Alexander, stating that the favourite physician intended to give him a poison cup on the following morning. The man through the Emperor would order the physician to be put to death. Next morning, however, the Emperor took the message and read it out loud; and, before the physician had time to reply, he drank what was in the cup before his eyes to show his friend that he did not believe one word that his enemy had said.

That is believing with all the heart; and when Satan comes with some insinuation about God not being love, tell him that you believe God with all your heart.

D. L. MOODY

ALL THE KEYS

Present your bodies a living sacrifice, holy, acceptable unto God,
which is your reasonable service.
ROMANS 12:1

I knelt by my bed, with the door of my room locked, and resolved that I would not sleep until I had settled the matter and surrendered everything to Jesus. It seemed as though Jesus was by my side and that I took from my pocket a large bunch of keys. From that bunch I took one tiny key, which I kept, and then held to Jesus the bunch with the one missing.

"Here are the keys of my life," I said. He looked at me sadly and asked, "Are all there?" "All but one tiny one, to a small cupboard. It is so small that it cannot amount to anything." He replied, "Child, if you cannot trust Me with everything, you cannot trust me with anything."

Satan whispered to me: "You cannot give up that thing. Besides if you let Christ have His way, you don't know what He will ask of you next. Don't give it to Him!"

Then the thought came to me of my only child, who at that time was somewhat wayward. Supposing she were to come to me and say, "Father, I give my whole life up to you; you may choose anything you want for me." I know I would not call her mother and say, "Now here is our chance. What can we do to make her life miserable and unhappy?"

Instead I would say, "Wife, let's now take away everything that hurts her, and we will make her life one long summer day."

Christ would not be harder on me than I on my child, and at last I said, "Lord, I cannot give the key, but I am willing to have you come and take it."

It was as I expected. I seemed to hold out my hand, and He came and opened the fingers and took the key from me. Then He went straight to that cupboard, unlocked and opened it and saw there a thing that was terrible and hideous. He said: "This must go out. You must never go that way again." And the moment He took the thing from me, He took the desire for it out of my soul, and I began to hate it. Then I yielded myself absolutely to Him and said, "From this night I want You to do as You will with my life."

The next morning I awoke expecting a sort of hallelujah feeling, but I was as calm and quiet as I am now. I only had a delightful sense that I did belong to Jesus Christ, and a hundred times that day I said to myself: "I am His! I am absolutely His!"

F. B. MEYER

OCTOBER 1

HOW TO ABIDE

When thou prayest, enter into thy closet.
MATTHEW 6:6

What has the branch to do? You know that precious inexhaustible word that Christ used in John 15: Abide. Your life is to be an abiding life. And how is the abiding to be? It is to be just like the branch in the vine, abiding every minute of the day. There are the branches, in close communion, in unbroken communion, with the vine, from January to December. And cannot I live every day - it is to me an almost terrible thing that we should ask the question - cannot I live in abiding communion with the heavenly vine?

You say, "But I am so much occupied with other things."

You may have ten hours' hard work daily, during which your brain has to be occupied with temporal things: God orders it so. But the abiding work is the work of the heart, not of the brain or the muscle, the work of the heart clinging to and resting in Jesus, a work in which the Holy Spirit links us to Christ Jesus. Oh, do believe that deeper down than the brain, deep down in the inner life, you can abide in Christ, so that every moment you are free the consciousness will come: "Blessed Jesus, I am still in Thee." If you will learn for a time to put aside other work and to get into this abiding contact with the heavenly vine, you will find that fruit will come.

What is the application to our life of this abiding communion? What does it mean? It means close fellowship with Christ in secret prayer. I am sure there are Christians who do long for the higher life and who sometimes have got a great blessing and have at times found a great inflow of heavenly joy and a great outflow of heavenly gladness; and yet after a time it has passed away. They have not understood that close personal actual communion with Christ is an absolute necessity for daily life. Take time to be alone with Christ. Nothing in heaven or earth can free you from the necessity for that, if you are to be happy and holy Christians.

Many Christians look upon it as a burden and a tax and a duty and a difficulty to get much alone with God. That is the great hindrance to our Christian life everywhere. We need more quiet fellowship with God, and I tell you in the name of the heavenly vine that you cannot be healthy branches, branches into which the heavenly sap can flow, unless you take plenty of time for communion with God.

ANDREW MURRAY

OCTOBER 2

OUR PRAYERS ARE TOO FEEBLE

Let us therefore come boldly unto the throne of grace.
HEBREWS 4:16

Our prayers are too little and too feeble to execute the purposes or to claim the promises of God with appropriating power. Marvellous purposes need marvellous praying to execute them. Miracle-making promises need miracle-making praying to realise them. Only divine praying can operate divine promises or carry out divine purposes. How great, how sublime, and how exalted are the promises God makes to His people! How eternal are the purposes of God!

Why are we so impoverished in experience and so low in life when God's promises are so 'exceeding great and precious'? Why do the eternal purposes of God move so tardily? Why are they so poorly executed? Our failure to appropriate the divine promises and rest our faith on them, and to pray believing is the solution. 'We have not because we ask not'. 'We ask and receive not because we ask amiss.'

Furnish thyself with arguments from the promises,
to enforce thy prayers,
and make them prevalent with God.
The promises are the ground of faith,
and faith, when strengthened, will make thee fervent,
and such fervency ever speeds and returns with victory,
out of the field of prayer.
The mightier any is in the Word,
the more mighty he will be in prayer.

E. M. BOUNDS

CHRIST FOR US

Your life is hid with Christ in God.
COLOSSIANS 3:3

Creation and providence are but the whisper of its power, but redemption is its music, and praise is the echo which shall yet fill His temple. The whisper and the music, yes, and the thunder of His power, are all for thee. For what is the good pleasure of His will? (Ephesians 1:5). Oh, what a grand list of blessings purposed, provided, purchased and possessed, all flowing to us out of it! And nothing but blessings, nothing but privileges, which we never should have imagined, and which, even when revealed, we are slow of heart to believe - nothing but what should even now fill us with joy unspeakable and full of glory!

Think of this will as always and altogether on our side - always working for us and in us and with us, and if we will only let it. Think of it as always and only synonymous with infinitely wise and almighty love. Think of it as undertaking all for us, from the great work of our eternal salvation down to the momentary details of guidance and supply. As we think of those things, do we not feel utter shame and self-abhorrence at ever having hesitated for an instant to give up our tiny, feeble, blind will to be - not crushed, not even bent - but blended with His glorious and perfect will?

His heart for thee. "Behold, God is mighty ... in [heart]," said Job (Job 36:5, margin). And this mighty and tender heart is for you! If He had only stretched forth His hand to save us from bare destruction and said, "My hand for thee!" how could we have praised Him enough? But what shall we say of the unspeakably marvellous condescension which says, "Thou hast ravished my heart, my sister, my spouse!" The very fountain of His divine life, light and love, the very centre of His being, is given to His beloved ones, who are not only set as a seal upon His heart but taken into His heart, so that our life is hid there. We dwell there in the very centre of all safety and power and love and glory.

What will be the revelation of that day, when the Lord Jesus promises, "Ye shall know that I am in my Father, and ye in me?" For He implies that we do not yet know it and that our present knowledge of this dwelling in Him is not knowledge at all compared with what He is going to show us about it.

Now shall we, can we, reserve any corner of our hearts from Him?

FRANCES R. HAVERGAL

NO MORE DEATH

They shall reign for ever and ever.
REVELATION 22:5

The kiss of reunion at the gate of Heaven is as certain as the goodbye kiss when you drift out with the tide. Death is a cruel enemy. He robs the mother of her baby, the wife of her husband, the parents of their children, the love of his intended wife. He robs the nation of its President.

Death is a rude enemy. He upsets our best plans without an apology. He enters the most exclusive circles without an invitation.

Death is an international enemy. There is no nation which he does not visit. The islands of the seas where the black-skinned mothers rock their babies to the lullaby of the ocean's waves. The restless sea. The majestic mountains. All are his haunts.

Death is an untiring enemy. He continues his ghastly work spring, summer, autumn and winter. He never tires in his ceaseless rounds, gathering the spoils of human souls.

But death is a vanquished enemy. Jesus arose from the dead and abolished death although we may be called upon to die.

Death to the Christian is swinging open the door through which he passes into heaven.

"Aren't you afraid?" said the wife to a dying miner.

"Afraid, lassie? Why should I be? I know Jesus and Jesus knows me."

The house in which we live, "our body", is beginning to lean. The windows rattle. The glass is dim. The shingles are falling off.

Thank God for the rainbow of hope that bends above the graves of our loved ones.

We stand on this side of the grave and mourn as they go. They stand on the other side and rejoice as they come.

On the Resurrection morning
Soul and body meet again;
No more sorrow, no more weeping,
No more pain.

BILLY SUNDAY

MORE ABOUT JESUS

That I may know him.
PHILIPPIANS 3:10

That I may know him, and the power of his resurrection, and the fellowship of his sufferings; being made conformable unto his death. If by any means I might attain unto the resurrection of the dead." This was Paul's aim in life, and it was passionately pursued. He already knew something of Christ but was longing to know more. It was no mere intellectual knowledge which he aimed at but personal acquaintance with Christ. This knowledge cannot be acquired in schools, nor gleaned from books. In this way we may get to know many things about Him, but to know Himself we need to live in communion with Him. To deepen our knowledge of Christ in this way is a worthy aim for the whole of life. Some knowledge puffs up but this knowledge will make us humble. Most of the subjects which we study down here will be forgotten in the world to come, but the knowledge of Christ will abide with us for ever. It will still be pursued amid eternal glories. Christ Himself will be our lesson for eternity.

The Apostle also desired to know the power of His resurrection. This expression refers to the power that flows from the resurrection of Christ. There are several distinct powers ascribed to it in the New Testament. It is spoken of as an evidencing power in reference to our Lord's person and work, for He is by it declared to be the Son of God with power. His resurrection has also a justifying power - "He was raised again for our justification". Christ's resurrection has also a comforting power as to all departed saints. As surely as He rose, all those who are His shall rise also. When the trumpet blast shall wake the dead the graves shall give up their spoils. This assurance comes to us through Jesus' empty tomb, "Hallelujah, Christ arose."

WILLIAM GILMORE

OCTOBER 6

MEDITATE ON HEAVEN

Are not even ye in the presence of our Lord Jesus Christ at his coming.
I THESSALONIANS 2:19

Have we a good hope of going to heaven, a hope that is scriptural, reasonable, and will bear investigation? Then let us not be afraid to meditate often on the subject of "heaven" and to rejoice in the prospect of good things to come. I know that even a believer's heart will sometimes fail when he thinks of the last enemy and the unseen world. Jordan is a cold river to cross at the very best, and not a few tremble when they think of their own crossing. But let us take comfort in the remembrance of the other side. Think, Christian believer, of seeing your Saviour, and beholding your King in His beauty. Faith will be at last swallowed up in sight and hope in certainty. Think of the many loved ones gone before you, and of the happy meeting between you and them. You are not going to a foreign country; you are going home. You are not going to dwell amongst strangers, but amongst friends. You will find them all safe, all well, all ready to greet you, all prepared to join in one unbroken song of praise. Then let us take comfort and persevere. With such prospects before us, we may well cry, "It is worthwhile to be a Christian!"

I conclude all with a passage from *"Pilgrim's Progress,"* which well deserves reading. *Said Pliable to Christian, "What company shall we have in heaven?"*

Christian replied, "There we shall be with seraphim and cherubim, creatures that will dazzle your eyes to look upon. There, also, you shall meet with thousands and ten thousands that have gone before us to that place; none of them hurtful, but loving and holy; every one walking in the sight of God, and standing in His presence with acceptance for ever. In a word, there we shall see the elders with their golden crowns; there we shall see holy virgins with their golden harps; there we shall see men that by the world were cut in pieces, burnt in flames, eaten of beasts, drowned in the seas, for the love they bore to the Lord of the place; all well, and clothed with immortality as with a garment.

Then said Christian, "The Lord, the Governor of the country, hath recorded that in this book; the substance of which is, if we be truly willing to have it. He will bestow it upon us freely,"

Then said Pliable, "Well, my good companion, glad am I to hear of these things. Come on, let us mend our pace."

J. C. RYLE

STRENGTH FOR THE JOURNEY

Be strong in the Lord and in the power of his might.
EPHESIANS 6:10

W e are in a great spiritual warfare and moving against a great spiritual foe, and let me say this, especially to the young people, that when you face the enemy you will need to be filled with the truth of God's Word. Always remember that when the Lord Jesus met the tempter in the wilderness He defeated him each time by quoting from the Book. He just dipped into Deuteronomy three times and said, "It is written". Never try to fight the enemy with human reasoning, or lean on your own understanding, because you will fail. Always lean on God's Word. When you can open the Book and say, this is what God's Word says, you will often find that the devil will leave you alone.

As we go through this world walking as servants of God, not one of us is faultless, and as we march through this waste howling wilderness we get defiled day after day in our walk. Of course we are being made whiter than the snow by the application of the blood of Jesus, and in that sense we are really washed, but when we defile ourselves in any little way it breaks the fellowship between us and the One we love, and we must get this dust of the journey removed.

Then sometimes we see a brother or sister in the Lord and they are getting into soft sand or they are going to defile themselves, and we may try to help them to get back into fellowship, and in that sense we would be washing their feet. But the trouble with some of us is that when we go to help a brother we either make the water so cold that we freeze him, or we make it so hot that we roast him, and then we find that we are not very good at this feet-washing business after all.

Nevertheless, we do need to wash one another's feet, but let us be very careful how we do it. The Book teaches us that if we see someone overtaken in a fault we have to restore such a one in the spirit of meekness.

WILLIE MULLAN

OCTOBER 8

HOLINESS TO THE LORD

Ye have your fruit unto holiness.
ROMANS 6:22

Never forget that holiness is not an attainment but an attitude. It is the opening of the heart to the balmy air and sunlight of God's nature, which entering in, fill the spirit of man or woman.

In Exodus 28:36, the high priest stands before you vested in his full white robes with breastplate of gold. On the frontlet of his forehead, the legend *Holiness to the Lord* is inscribed, so that wherever he goes to and fro, he bears upon his brow that sacred text.

Suppose I should turn from him and, speaking to you, say that I want you to meet Christ in glory bearing that frontlet upon your brow and have that holy legend inscribed upon you. It might be you would shrink back and say, "No, no, I will never be a hypocrite. I do trust in Christ and desire to be like Him. But I dare not arrogate to myself that sacred frontlet, that holy legend. I am not *Holiness to the Lord.*"

Then, my friend, you are putting away from you the privilege of this dispensation, of which Zechariah says that in this age there shall be so much Holy Spirit given to the men and women who believe in Christ that Holiness to the Lord shall be engraved upon their heads, that the common vessel in their homes shall have the same legend upon them, and be as holy as the vessels in the Lord's house: "In that day shall there be upon the bells of the horses, HOLINESS UNTO THE LORD; and the pots in the Lord's house shall be like the bowls before the altar" (Zechariah 14:20).

I remember so well spending some winter days in the city of Boston. I shall never forget the blue sky and the crisp white snow, the absence of the rumbling of wheels, and everywhere the sweet music of the sleigh bells. The bells of all our life - the dinner bell, the rising bell, the bell summoning us to our daily work, the telephone bell asking us to hold conversation with another - all the bells ringing in our lives are to have these words inscribed so that our whole life shall have this as its keynote.

F. B. MEYER

LOVE AND DEVOTION

A full reward be given thee of the Lord God of Israel.
RUTH 2:12

True service is the outcome of devotion, and this is what our Master values. Though Ruth had given up much she did not dwell on it like some would, but marvelled that Boaz should take notice of her and that she should find grace in his sight. Humility characterised all her actions, but what she hid from the servants was known unto the Lord of the Harvest. "It hath fully been shewed me all that thou hast done." That which was done in secret was rewarded openly.

How wonderfully this self-renunciation is seen in our Lord Jesus, who is the ideal of a true servant. Never did He seek His own will, never did He seek His own glory. His meat and drink was to do the will of Him who sent Him. "I have glorified Thee, I have finished the work Thou gavest Me to do." "Who pleased not Himself." "For I do always those things that please Him." (John 8:29) And again, "He made Himself of no reputation, but took upon Him the form of a servant."

The mountain top, the solitary place, the wilderness were His hiding places. There He could pour out His heart to His Father, there He could hear His Father's voice and get fresh comfort and fresh power for the coming strife. "All men do seek Thee" said His disciples, but the one object of His ministry was to lead them to the Father. If the Father's mansion was magnificent, He was the door. If they looked for Him, He desired that they should see the Father. How He sought to instil this lesson of self-effacement into His disciples' minds. "Ye know that they which think good to rule over the Gentiles, exercise lordship over them, and their great ones exercise authority upon them. But so shall it not be among you: but whosoever shall be great among you shall be your minister; and whosoever of you shall be the chiefest, shall be servant of all. For even the Son of Man came not to be ministered unto, but to minister, and to give His life a ransom for many." (Mark 10:42-45).

The Master called with words of love,
It won our hearts, it set us free;
Then came His voice so wondrous sweet
"Who, who will go and work for Me?"

SPENCER WALTON

THE MEN WHO WOULDN'T
STOP AT ANYTHING

Present your bodies a living sacrifice.
ROMANS 12:1

L ook at the three worthies who brought water from the well of Bethlehem.
was harvest-time, so David was tired and hot and thirsty. Then he longe
for one more draught of the water that tasted so cool and sweet to his memor
Doubtless many things were struggling through his mind when he gave expres
sion to this gust of desire from the very depths of his spirit. Doubtless he wante
the water to quench his thirst, but there was more than this in that irresistible lon;
ing that swept across him.

He may have been thinking of some early spiritual experience associated wi
that same old well. Don't we all sigh sometimes for the water of the well of Bethl
hem. In memory we go back to where we started and think of the days of first lov
and that early devotion to the Saviour. But whatever may have been the feelin;
that lay behind David's desire, it was quite sufficient for these heroes to know th.
he longed for a drink from the well of Bethlehem. They said, "He shall have it." B
the ranks of the Philistines stood between them and Bethlehem - how were they
get through? How could three men outmanoeuvre an army? Love never stops
calculate. It laughs at impossibilities and cries, "it shall be done". These were th
men who wouldn't stop at anything. They were ready to die to win for David th
draught he desired. So they slipped away and broke through the ranks of th
Philistines and brought back the sparkling water. Surely this is a sweet sample of
what we ought to be - loving not our own lives unto death for Christ's sake. Oh tha
the spirit of God may kindle in our hearts a flame of ardent love for the Person of
Christ. Then it will be our delight to know His will and seek grace to do it.

Take my love; my Lord, I pour
At Thy feet its treasure store.
Take myself and I shall be
Ever, only, all for Thee.

WILLIAM GILMOR

OCTOBER 11

OUR HEARTS KEPT FOR JESUS

Surely he shall not be moved for ever.
PSALMS 112:6

We find it both the means and the result of the keeping in the 112th Psalm: "His heart is fixed." Whose heart? Of an angel? Of a saint in glory? No! Simply the heart of the man who fears the Lord and delights greatly in His commandments. Therefore yours and mine, as God would have them be; just the normal idea of a God-fearing heart, nothing extremely and hopelessly beyond attainment.

Fixed! How does that tally with the deceitfulness and waywardness and fickleness about which we really talk as if we were rather proud of them that utterly shamed of them?

Does our heavenly Bridegroom expect nothing more of us? Does His mighty all-constraining love intend to do no more for us than to leave us in this deplorable state, when He is undoubtedly able to heal the desperately wicked heart (compare verses 9 and 14 of Jeremiah 17), to rule the wayward one with His peace, and to establish the fickle one with His grace? Are we not without excuse?

Fixed, trusting in the Lord! Here is the means of the fixing - trust. He works the trust in us by sending the Holy Spirit to reveal God in Christ to us as absolutely, infinitely, worthy of our trust. When we see Jesus by Spirit-wrought faith, we cannot but trust Him. We distrust our hearts more truly than ever before, but we trust our Lord entirely, because we trust Him only. For, entrusting our trust to Him, we know that He is able to keep that which we commit (i.e. entrust) to Him. It is His own way of winning and fixing our hearts for Himself. Is it not a beautiful one? Thus his heart is established.

But we have not quite faith enough to believe that. So what is the very first doubting, and therefore sad thought, that crops up?

"Yes, but I am afraid it will not remain fixed."

That is your thought. Now see what is God's thought about the case: "His heart is established, he shall not be afraid."

Is that not enough? What is, if such plain and yet divine words are not?

FRANCES R. HAVERGAL

OCTOBER 12

BELLS OF GOLD

His sound shall be heard when he goeth in ... and when he cometh out.
EXODUS 28:35

Our blessed Lord Jesus came into this world to save sinners and, bless God, He lived without spot or stain, and even the old devil couldn't make rend in His character. Then there came a time when He offered Himself without spot to God, and there was a day when wicked men took Him and stripped Him stark naked (because the Bible says, 'He despised the shame') and they laid His body on the cross, and as they put the nails through his hands (and remember he felt the pain) His lips moved and He said,*"Father, forgive them for they know not what they do."*

Then they lifted the cross and rattled it into its sockets and His bones were pulled out of joints. Then when man had done his worst God smote Him and all the waves and billows of God's wrath passed over His Holy Head. Yes, He went into the depths where there was no standing, and He went right out of fellowship with God. His cry now is,*"My God, My God, why hast thou forsaken me?"*

We shall never be able to understand this, nor shall we ever be able to probe the depths of Calvary ...

"None of the ransomed ever knew
How deep were the waters crossed
Nor how dark was the night
That the Lord passed through
E're He found the sheep that was lost."

Yes, He took my sins and your sins upon Him and God struck Him for us and He became the substitutionary sacrifice and He made an atonement. Then He cried,*"IT IS FINISHED"* and immediately He uttered these three words, He said,*"Father, into thy hands I commend my spirit."*

Our blessed Lord Jesus went right through for us. As He stepped into death the bells were ringing, and then there was silence for three days; but, praise God, on resurrection morning He arose and the bells are ringing again. Yes, He was accepted, He was alive and praise God He is alive for evermore. Yes, the One who died and rose again, the One who finished the work, the One who never fails, is alive today and we have a real, living Saviour.

WILLIE MULLAN

OCTOBER 13

SET APART

The Holy Ghost sent down from heaven.
I PETER 1:12

That is now the will of God as the Holy Spirit reveals it? It is contained in one word: separation unto the Holy Spirit. That is the keynote of the message from heaven.

"Separate unto me Barnabas and Saul for the work whereunto I have called them. The work is mine, and I care for it, and I have chosen these men and called them, and I want you who represent the church of Christ upon earth to set them apart unto me."

Look at this heavenly message in its twofold aspect. The men were to be set apart to the Holy Spirit, and the church was to do this separating work. The Holy Spirit could trust these men to do it in a right spirit. There they were abiding in fellowship with the heavenly, and the Holy Spirit could say to them, "Do the work of separating these men." And these were the men the Holy Spirit had prepared, and He could say to them, "Let them be separated unto me."

Here we come to the very root, to the very life of the need of Christian workers. The question is: What is needed that the power of God should rest upon us more mightily, that the blessing of God should be poured out more abundantly among those poor wretched people and perishing sinners among whom we labour? And the answer from heaven is: "I want men separated unto the Holy Spirit."

What does that imply? You know that there are two spirits on earth. Christ said, when He spoke about the Holy Spirit: "The world cannot receive Him." Paul said: "We have received not the spirit of the world, but the Spirit that is of God." That is the great want in every worker - the spirit of the world going out, and the Spirit of God coming in to take possession of the inner life and of the whole being.

I am sure there are workers who often cry to God for the Holy Spirit to come upon them as a Spirit of power for their work, and when they feel that measure of power and get blessing, they thank God for it. But God wants something more and something higher. God wants us to seek for the Holy Spirit as a Spirit of power in our own heart and life, to conquer self and cast out sin, and work the blessed and beautiful image of Jesus into us.

ANDREW MURRAY

OCTOBER 14

THE ONLY WAY TO HEAVEN

How can we know the way?
JOHN 14:5

You must know the password if you ever enter Heaven. Jesus said, "I am the way, the truth and the life; no man cometh unto the Father, but by me." Here comes a crowd. They cry: "Let me in. I was very useful on earth. I built churches. I endowed colleges. I was famous for my charities. I have done many wonderful things."

"I never knew you."

Another crowd shouts: "We were highly honoured on earth. The world bowed very low before us. Now we have come to get our honours in Heaven."

"We never knew you."

Another crowd approaches and says: "We were sinners, wanderers from God. We have come up, not because we deserve Heaven, but because we heard of the saving power of Jesus; and we have accepted Him as our Saviour."

They all cry, "Jesus, Jesus, Thou Son of God, open to us."

They all pass through the pearly gates.

One step this side and you are paupers for eternity. One step on the other side and you are kings and queens for eternity. When I think of Heaven and my entering it, I feel awkward.

Sometimes when I have been exposed to the weather, shoes covered in mud, coat wet and soiled with mud and rain, hair dishevelled, I feel I am not fit to go in and sit among the well-dressed guests.

So I feel that way about Heaven. I need to be washed in the blood of the Lamb and clothed in the robe of Christ's righteousness. I need the pardoning waves of God's mercy to roll over my soul. And, thank God, they have.

A saint lay dying. She said: "My faith is being tried. The brightness of which you speak I do not have. But I have accepted Jesus as my Saviour; and if God wishes to put me to sleep in the dark, His will be done."

BILLY SUNDAY

THE SURE FOUNDATION OF PRAYER

The Lord will receive my prayer.
PSALM 6:9

Prayer is based on the purpose and promise of God. Prayer is submission to God. Prayer has no sigh of disloyalty against God's will. It may cry out against the bitterness and the dread weight of an hour of unutterable anguish: "If it be possible, let this cup pass from me." But it is surcharged with the sweetest and promptest submission. "Yet not my will, but thine be done."

But prayer in its usual uniform and deep current is conscious conformity to God's will, based upon the direct promise of God's Word, and under the illumination and application of the holy Spirit. Nothing is surer than that the Word of God is the sure foundation of prayer. We pray just as we believe God's Word. Prayer is based directly and specifically upon God's revealed promises in Christ Jesus. It has no other ground upon which to base its plea. All else is shadowy, sandy, fickle. Not our feelings, not our merits, not our works, but God's promise is the basis of faith and the solid ground of prayer.

> *Now I have found the ground wherein*
> *Sure my soul's anchor may remain;*
> *The wounds of Jesus - for my sin,*
> *Before the world's foundation slain.*

The converse of this proposition is also true. God's promises are dependent and conditioned upon prayer to appropriate them and make them a conscious realisation. The promises are inwrought in us, appropriated by us, and held in the arms of faith in prayer. Let it be noted that prayer gives the promises in their efficiency, localises and appropriates them and utilises them. Prayer puts the promises as the seed in the fructifying soil. Promises, like the rain, are general. Prayer embodies, precipitates, and locates them for personal use. Prayer goes by faith into the great fruit orchard of God's exceeding great promises, and with hand and heart picks the ripest and richest fruit. The promises, like electricity, may sparkle and dazzle and yet be impotent for good till these dynamic, life-giving currents are chained by prayer, and are made the mighty forces which move and bless.

E. M. BOUNDS

OCTOBER 16

I TRUST IN GOD

He is faithful that promised.
HEBREWS 10:23

October 21, 1868 - As the days come, we make known our requests to Him for our outgoings have now been for several years at the rate of more than one hundred pounds each day; but though the expenses have been so great, He has never failed us. We have been, as to the outward appearance, like the "Burning Bush in the Wilderness"; yet we have not been consumed. Moreover, we are full of trust in the Lord, and therefore of good courage, though we have before us the prospect, that, year by year, our expenses will increase more and more.

If all my beloved fellow disciples, who seek to work for God, knew the blessedness of looking truly to God alone, and trusting in Him alone, they would soon see how soul refreshing this way is, and how entirely beyond disappointment, so far as He is concerned. Earthly friends may alter their minds regarding the work in which we are engaged; but if indeed we work for God, whoever may alter his mind regarding our service, He will not. Earthly friends may lose their ability to help us, however much they may desire so to do; but He remains throughout eternity the infinitely rich one. Earthly friends may have their minds after a time diverted to other objects, and, as they cannot help everywhere, much as they may desire it, they may have to discontinue to help us; but He is able, in all directions, though the requirements were multiplied a million times, to supply all that can possibly be needed. And He does it with delight, where His work is carried on and where He is confided in. Earthly friends may be removed by death, and thus we may lose their help, but He lives for ever; He cannot die.

In this latter point of view I have especially, during the past 40 years, in connection with this instruction, seen the blessedness of trusting in the living God alone. Not one or two, nor even five or ten, but many more, who once helped me much with their means, have been removed by death; but have the operations of the institution been stopped on that account? No. And how came this? Because I trusted in God, and in Him alone.

GEORGE MUELLER

OCTOBER 17

FELLOWSHIP WITH CHRIST
IN SERVICE

If any man will come after me, let him deny himself,
and take up his cross, and follow me.
MATTHEW 16:24

It is a beautiful privilege to work along with Christ, but we shall not serve in that blessed apprenticeship long without learning this lesson: that He has no pleasure in service rendered to Himself or others that does not cost us blood! This is characteristic of His own service to the world, and you will find that he will soon drop you out unless you are prepared, in your measure, to surrender yourself to the blood-letting, which alone counts in the service of humanity.

As we look out on society today we can understand why so many lives are unhappy. They have never learned that the one secret of happiness is to give to the point of self-denial and self-sacrifice. As Phillips Brooks has put it, "They need something to happen which shall force them out on the open ocean of complete self-sacrifice. If only a slow quiet tide or a furious storm would come and break every rope that binds them to the wooden wharves of their own interests and carry them clear out to sea! The soul that trifles and toys with self-sacrifice can achieve neither its true joy nor power. Only the soul that gives itself up forever to the life of others can know the delight and peace which surrender gives."

This trace of blood in our actions is a matter that we can never talk about. When it is being shed, we must anoint our head and wash our face, that men may have no inkling of what is happening. Neither the right hand nor the left hand must know, nor divulge the secret. It should be remembered, also, that we have no right to deprive wife or child of whatever is necessary. It must be a personal act, affecting no one but yourself. You must be the one who gives the blood, not they! Keep happy and smiling! When Jesus was performing this miracle, there was no strain or effort, no wrinkle on His forehead, no cloud upon His smile. He drew no attention to Himself, needed no thanks, and stole away unrecognised, at least for the moment, as the giver.

Of course, there is no merit in such actions. The blood we shed cannot atone, cannot save, cannot cleanse. Only His blood can do that. But, also, it is true that the great soulwinners of the world have faced the blood of martyrdom and counted not their lives dear unto themselves.

F. B. MEYER

OCTOBER 18

OUR FUTURE HOME

What is our hope, or joy, or crown of rejoicing?
1 THESSALONIANS 2:19

Now what will Heaven be like? The question, no doubt, is a deep one, but there is nothing presumptuous in looking at it. The man who is about to sail for Australia or New Zealand as a settler, is naturally anxious to know something about his future home, its climate, its employments, its inhabitants, its ways, its customs. All these are subjects of deep interest to him. You are leaving the land of your activity, you are going to spend the rest of your life in a new hemisphere. It would be strange indeed if you did not desire information about your new abode. Now surely, if we hope to dwell for ever in that "better country, even a heavenly one," we ought to seek all the knowledge we can get about it. Before we go to our general home we should try to become acquainted with it.

There are many things about Heaven revealed in Scripture. That all who are found there will be of one mind and of one experience, chosen by the same Father, washed in the same blood of atonement, renewed by the same Spirit; that universal and perfect holiness, love and knowledge will be the eternal law of the kingdom - all these are ancient things, and I do not mean to dwell on them at the moment. Suffice it is to say, that Heaven is the eternal presence of everything that can make a saint happy, and the eternal absence of everything that can cause sorrow. Sickness, and pain, and disease, and death, and poverty, and labour, and money, and care, and ignorance, and misunderstanding, and slander and lying and strife, and contention, and quarrels, and envies, and jealousies, and bad tempers, and infidelity, and skepticism, and irreligion, and superstition, and heresy, and schism, and wars, and fightings, and bloodshed, and murders, and law suits - all, all these things shall have no place in Heaven. On earth, in this present time, they may live and flourish. In Heaven even their footprints shall not be known.

Hear what the glorious dreamer, John Bunyan says: "*I saw in my dream that these two men, Christian and Hopeful, went in at the gate. And lo! as they entered they were transfigured, and they had raiment put on that shone like gold. There were also that met them with harps and crowns and gave them to them; the harps to praise withal, and the crowns in token of honour. Then I heard in my dream that all the bells in the city rang again for joy, and that it was said unto them, "Enter ye into the joy of your Lord."*

J. C. RYLE

OCTOBER 19

GOD'S MAN

Who through faith subdued kingdoms.
HEBREWS 11:33

The Book of Judges is a record of man's failures and of God's faithfulness. Again and again they sinned and fell under the power of their foes. Again and again God heard their cries and raised them up a deliverer. Consider the story of their oppression by the Midianites. From early times they had shown themselves the enemies of God's people. It was the Midianites who first tried to get the curse of God upon them through Baalim. The Midianites were also masters in the art of plundering, and in the time of Gideon they settled down upon the land like the plague of locusts, destroying all food and sustenance. But God raised up a deliverer in the person of Gideon, the youngest son of an obscure family in a small tribe. His name stands among the heroes of faith in the eleventh chapter of Hebrews, and his conduct throughout this story proves his right to be there. His character has never been sufficiently admired. Preachers have given more attention to names less brilliant than his. He was a truly great man and deserves far better treatment than he has yet received. Despite his failings he was one of the greatest of the men of faith. A careful study of the life and work of Gideon would teach us many lessons of permanent value in the service of the Lord. Most of the incidents in his pathway to victory took place at night. We, too, are passing through the night, and like him we are surrounded by foes, but Gideon will show us how to overcome these foes and win the battle by the sword of the Lord and of Gideon.

We in ourselves are nothing,
A small and feeble host,
Nor have we aught of prowess
Wherein to make our boast.
Our stronghold is Christ Jesus,
His grace alone we plead,
His name our shield and banner,
Himself - just all we need.

WILLIAM GILMORE

OCTOBER 20

PRAYER AND THE PROMISE

The effectual, fervent prayer of a righteous man availeth much.
JAMES 5:16

Without the promise prayer is eccentric and baseless. Without prayer, the promise is dim, voiceless, shadowy, and impersonal. The promise makes prayer dauntless and irresistible. The Apostle Peter declares that God has given to us "exceeding great and precious promises." "Precious" and "exceeding great" promises they are, and for this very cause we are told to "add to our faith," and supply virtue. It is the addition which makes the promises current and beneficial to us. It is prayer which makes the promises weighty, precious and practical. The Apostle Paul did not hesitate to declare that God's grace so richly promised was made operative and efficient by prayer. "Ye also helping together by prayer for us."

The promises of God are "exceeding great and precious," words which clearly indicate their great value and their broad reach, as grounds upon which to base our expectations in praying. Howsoever exceeding great and precious they are, their realisation, the possibility and condition of that realisation, are based on prayer. How glorious are these promises to the believing saints and to the whole Church! How the brightness and bloom, the fruitage and cloudless midday glory of the future beam on us through the promises of God! Yet these promises never brought hope to bloom or fruit to a prayerless heart. Neither could these promises, were they a thousandfold increased in number and preciousness, bring millennium glory to a prayerless Church. Prayer makes the promise rich, fruitful and conscious reality.

Prayer as a spiritual energy, and illustrated in its enlarged and mighty working, makes way for and brings into practical realisation the promises of God.

God's promises cover all things which pertain to life and godliness, which relate to body and soul, which have to do with time and eternity. These promises bless the present and stretch out in their benefactions to the illimitable and eternal future. Prayer holds these promises in keeping and in fruition. Promises are God's golden fruit to be plucked by the hand of prayer. Promises are God's incorruptible seed, to be sown and tilled by prayer.

E. M. BOUNDS

OCTOBER 21

DEGREES AND FIG LEAVES

No man cometh unto the Father but by me.
JOHN 14:6

In the church today far too much emphasis is placed upon occupying pulpits with men who have academic standing instead of trusting God to send a man whom He has gifted. I am not for one moment discrediting the work of the colleges and universities or despising those who have degrees; if God gives someone who has obtained a degree a gift from heaven I will say "Amen" and be the first to help him, and if God gifts a wee fellow from a back street I shall be his friend. God can take up whom He will and who are we to say, what doest thou? Yes He took a Hebrew of Hebrews like Paul and he also took a rough fisherman like Peter and He used both men to His Glory. Sidlow Baxter said once "With all their degrees they are emptying the churches by degrees".

The first time the word "coat" is mentioned in the Bible is in the garden of Eden (Genesis chapter 3). You remember that when Adam sinned and fell he was enlightened enough to know that he wasn't fit to meet God and so he began to prepare to meet Him. He made a covering of fig leaves, and there are a great many people in this world who are working at this fig leaf business. They are preparing, by the works of their own hands, to meet God. They don't go after the degrees, but they give money into the church and pray night and day and run here and there and yonder and they are really trying to work their way to heaven. But neither degrees nor fig leaves are any substitute for Jesus Christ. If you could work your way to heaven God would never have sent His Son to this earth to die on Calvary.

So Adam tried this way, but when he heard God's voice in the garden in the cool of the day he was afraid and he knew then that his fig leaves had failed. Yes they were just dead works and already they were perishing on his body. But bless God He did not leave Adam in his perishing state, but in Genesis chapter 3 verse 21 we read these words … "Unto Adam also and his wife did the Lord God make coats of skins, and clothed them".

This word "clothed" is very interesting, because the word used for "clothed" is the same as that used for "atonement" and the word for "atonement" is the word "kaffer" and in every case it means "covering". Of course the atonement of Calvary is the sinner's covering and the "coat" was the covering.

WILLIE MULLAN

HEAVEN IS A PLACE

In my Father's house are many mansions.
JOHN 14:2

Oh, what a place Heaven is! The Tuileries of the French, the Windsor Castle of the English, the Alhambra of the Spanish, the Schonbrunn of the Austrians, the White House of the United States - these are all dungeons compared with Heaven.

There are mansions there for the redeemed - one for the martyrs with blood-red robes; one for you ransomed from sin; one for me plucked like a brand from the fire.

Look and see - who are climbing the golden stairs, who are walking on the golden streets, who are looking out of the windows? Some whom we knew and loved here on earth. Yes, I know them. My father and mother, blithe and young as they were on their wedding day. Our son and daughter, sweet as they were when they cuddled down to sleep in our arms. My brother and sister, merrier than when we romped and roamed the fields and plucked wild flowers and listened to the whippoorwill as he sang his lonesome song away over in Sleepy Hollow on the old farm in Iowa where we were born and reared.

Cough gone, cancer gone, consumption gone, erysipelas gone, blindness gone, rheumatism gone, lameness gone, asthma gone, tears gone, groans and sighs gone, sleepless nights gone.

I think it will take some of us a long time to get used to Heaven.

Heaven will be free from all that curses us here.

No sin - no sorrow - no poverty - no sickness - no pain - no want - no aching heads or hearts - no war - no death. No watching the undertakers screw the coffin lid over our loved ones.

When I reach Heaven I won't stop to look for Abraham, Isaac, Jacob, Moses, Joseph, David, Daniel, Peter or Paul. I will rush past them all saying, "Where is Jesus? I want to see Jesus who saved my soul one dark, stormy night in Chicago in 1887."

If we could get a real appreciation of what Heaven is, we would all be so homesick for Heaven the Devil wouldn't have a friend left on earth.

BILLY SUNDAY

OCTOBER 23

AT HIS FEET

I fell at his feet to worship him.
REVELATION 19:10

When David, the man after God's own heart, summoned Mephibosheth into his presence (2 Samuel 9) and commenced to tell him the kindness he was going to show him and the possessions he was to have, even promising him a seat at the King's table (verse 7), poor Mephibosheth was overwhelmed and could only fall down and say "What is thy servant that thou shouldest look upon such a dead dog as I am?" (verse 8). From that point David's "I wills" were changed into "haves," "I have given" (verse 9). Not only is this lowly attitude one of blessing but in it we are in the proper position of soul to hear God's Word and God's secrets. St. John in Patmos found it so - falling at His feet as one dead. In the awe-inspiring presence of Divine majesty and glory he still recognised the voice of the One upon whose bosom he used to lay his head - no longer the Man of Sorrows in Him humility but the Man Christ Jesus in His glory - the Conqueror, the Victor who had passed through the uplifted gates - the Lord mighty in battle. What secrets he heard, giving him an insight into the very purposes of God! It is there, at His feet, my dear reader, that our Lord can speak to us. Let us bow down to that place of self-abnegation, let His very feet be put on us that self may be crushed out by the power of love (for His feet are pierced). Then He can tell us what He sees and knows, and we can bear it. How often, through the assertion of self, we prevent Him speaking. We talk of what we have done, and what we have said, and what we can do, and that word "we" keeps Him out or mars the sweetness of His voice.

It was down at the feet of Jesus
Where I found such perfect rest;
Where the light first dawned on my spirit,
And my soul was truly blest.

SPENCER WALTON

OCTOBER 24

GOD WILL SUPPLY ALL OUR NEEDS

God is able.
ROMANS 14:4

My comfort was that, if it were His will, He would provide not merely the means but also suitable individuals to take care of the children. The whole of those two weeks I never asked the Lord for money or for persons to engage in the work.

On December 5, however, the subject of my prayer all at once became different. I was reading Psalm 81 and was particularly struck, more than any time before, with verse 10: "Open thy mouth wide, and I will fill it." I thought a few moments about these words, and then was led to apply them to the case of the orphan house. It struck me that I had never asked the Lord for anything concerning it, except to know His will, respecting its being established or not; and then I fell on my knees and opened my mouth wide, asking Him for much.

I asked in submission to His will, without fixing a time when He should answer my petition. I prayed that He would give me a house, either as a loan or that someone might be led to pay the rent for one or that one might be given permanently for this object; further, I asked him for 1,000 pounds; and likewise for suitable individuals to take care of the children. Besides this, I have been since led to ask the Lord to put into the hearts of His people to send me articles of furniture for the house and some clothes for the children. When I was asking the petition, I was fully aware what I was doing - that I was asking for something that I had no natural prospect of obtaining from the brothers whom I know, but which was not too much for the Lord to grant.

December 10, 1835 - This morning I received a letter in which a brother and sister wrote thus: "We propose ourselves for the service of the intended orphan house, if you think us qualified for it; also to give up all the furniture, etc., which the Lord has given us, for its use; and to do this without receiving any salary whatever; believing that if it be the will of the Lord to employ us, He will supply all our needs."

GEORGE MUELLER

BROKENNESS OF HEART

When I would do good, evil is present with me.
ROMANS 7:21

He is utterly unhappy and miserable; and what is it that makes him so utterly miserable? It is because God has given him a nature that loves Himself. He is deeply wretched because he feels he is not obeying his God. He says, with brokenness of heart, "It is not I that do it, but I am under the awful power of sin, which is holding me down. It is I, and yet not I: alas! it is myself; so closely am I bound up with it, and so closely is it intertwined with my very nature." Blessed be God when a man learns to say: "O wretched man that I am!" from the depth of his heart. He is on the way to the eighth chapter of Romans.

There are many who make this confession a pillow for sin. They say that Paul had to confess his weakness and helplessness in this way; what are they that they should try to do better? So the call to holiness is quietly set aside. Would God that every one of us had learned to say these words in the very spirit in which they are written here! When we hear sin spoken of as the abominable thing that God hates, do not many of us wince before the word? Would that all Christians who go on sinning and sinning would take this verse to heart. If ever you utter a sharp word say: "O wretched man that I am!" And every time you lose your temper, kneel down and understand that it was never meant by God that this was to be the state in which His child should remain. Instead, we are to take this word into our daily life and say it every time we are touched about our own honour, and every time we say sharp things, and every time we sin against the Lord God and against His self-sacrifice. Forget everything else and cry out: "O wretched man that I am! Who shall deliver me from the body of this death?"

Why should you say this whenever you commit sin? Because it is when a man is brought to this confession that deliverance is at hand.

And remember it was not only the sense of being impotent and taken captive that made him wretched, but it was above all the sense of sinning against his God. The law was doing its work, making sin exceedingly sinful in his sight. The thought of continually grieving God became utterly unbearable - it was that this brought forth the piercing cry: "O wretched man!"

ANDREW MURRAY

OUR WILLS KEPT FOR JESUS

Teach me to do thy will; for thou art my God.
PSALM 143:10

It is most comforting to remember that the grand promise "Thy people shall be willing in the day of thy power" (Psalm 110: 3) is made by the Father to Christ Himself. The Lord Jesus holds this promise, and God will fulfil it to Him. He will make us willing because He has promised Jesus that He will do so. And what is being made willing but having our wills taken and kept?

All true surrender of the will is based upon love and knowledge of confidence in the one to whom it is surrendered. We have the human analogy so often before our eyes, that it is the more strange we should be so slow to own even the possibility of it as to God. It is thought anything so extraordinary and high flown when a bride deliberately prefers wearing a colour that was not her own taste of choice, because her husband likes to see her in it? Is it very unnatural that it is no distress to her to do what he asks her to do, or to go with him where he asks her to come, even without question of explanation, instead of doing what or going where she would undoubtedly have preferred if she did not know and love him? Is it very surprising if this lasts beyond the wedding day, and if year after year she still finds it her greatest pleasure to please him, quite irrespective of what used to be her own ways and likings? Yet in this case she is not helped by any promise or power on his part to make her wish what he wishes.

But He who so wonderfully condescends to call Himself the bridegroom of His church, and who claims our fullest love and trust, has promised and has power to work in us to will. Shall we not claim His promise and rely on His mighty power and say, not self-confidently, but looking only unto Jesus -

Keep my will, for it is Thine;
It shall be no longer mine!

Only in proportion as our own will is surrendered are we able to discern the splendour of God's will.

Conversely, in proportion as we see this splendour of His will, we shall more readily or more fully surrender our own. Not until we have presented our bodies a living sacrifice can we prove what is that good and perfect and acceptable will of God.

FRANCES R. HAVERGAL

THE MIND

Thou wilt keep him in perfect peace, whose mind is stayed on thee.
ISAIAH 26:3

When we begin to think about the mind it is really a tremendous faculty, and as we think about it more deeply the truth of God's Word breaks in upon us with real meaning when we read that: "we are fearfully and wonderfully made".

For example, let us take the face. The face is enclosed within a comparatively small circumference and contains a brow, two eyes, a nose, a mouth and a chin, and yet inside that small circle God has made millions, and millions of faces that are all different. That proves to me just how wonderful our God really is. But when we come to consider the mind it is even more wonderful than the face, and of course we all have different minds. All of us have imagination, and some have greater imagination than others. Then we have memory, and a good memory can be a real asset to us. Then there is understanding and we know that one and one makes two and so on. Then there is knowledge and some are more knowledgable than others. Then there is our thought life, and where these thoughts come from and how we can turn them over in our mind and how they bless us at times and how they disturb us at times. Yes it is all very wonderful.

We must however differentiate between the mind of a saved man and the mind of an unsaved man. Remember that when Adam fell there was total depravity as a result of the fall and the understanding became darkened and the mind became vain in its imagination. That is why so many believers were fools in their unsaved days. But when a man gets saved his mind becomes renewed by the Holy Ghost and he begins to receive light and to see and understand things he never understood before. Let me say however that Christ's mind was never tarnished. When we look at the pure gold we see here something that is unchanging, something that is everlasting - it is the mind of God - it was divine. There are those of course who would not agree with this, they would try to limit the Lord and say that there are certain things He doesn't know. Well if my Lord doesn't know more than some of the modernists that I know then we are to be pitied. But I know beyond any shadow of doubt whatsoever that my Lord was never limited in His knowledge.

WILLIE MULLAN

OCTOBER 28

DIVINE DISCIPLINE

I went out full, and the Lord hath brought me home again empty.
RUTH 1:21

Three widows standing weeping around open graves, but Naomi's sorrow was deepest, husband and sons had gone and she was bereft; she "went out full," but she is now desolate, broken, empty! "Then she arose with her daughters-in-law that she might return from the country of Moab; for she had heard in the country of Moab how that the Lord had visited His people in giving them bread, wherefore she went forth out of the place where she was."

A very decided step, for she not only arose that she might return, but she went forth. We must notice that it was for the Lord's bread, and not for the Lord, so she had no influence over one daughter-in-law. When a point in the road was reached, her entreaties were listened to by Orpah but set aside by Ruth. Naomi's was an influence for evil - "Go, return," she said. How could she recommend the Lord she had forsaken? Her conduct had estranged her from Him. He changed not, as we shall see, and yet she sought to make out that He would be found in Moab, the land of idols. Oh, the subtlety of a backsliding heart! "The Lord deal kindly with you," she said, and later on she speaks of Orpah as having gone back to her people and her gods, thus contradicting her own words. How this brings out the awful hindrance a backslider becomes, and shows us that such conduct is the great cause of infidelity, and a stumbling-block to thousands.

The people of Sodom listened not to the voice of Lot. "But he seemed as one that mocked unto his sons-in-law." (Gen 19:14). How could he seem anything else? His life was inconsistent, and thus his preaching was a mockery.

SPENCER WALTON

APOSTOLIC TEARS

And now tell you even weeping.
PHILIPPIANS 3:18

Paul was no soft piece of sentiment and seldom shed a tear even under griev-ous trials. Do we ever read of him weeping when he was persecuted? When he was cast into prison, we read of his singing but never of his sighing. Then why does this courageous man weep now? Ah, he was thinking of some professed followers of Christ who had gone far astray, and of whom he had warned the Philippians often. As he thought of their unholy conduct and their awful doom, it drew the tears from his eyes even in the midst of his joys. Who these unworthy professors were is somewhat obscure. They are characterised as enemies of the Cross of Christ. They seem to have shaken off the restraints of common morality and were living for self-indulgence. They were also out and out worldlings - they minded earthly things, Little wonder the Apostle wept as he thought of them. If we had more of his tender-heartedness we might weep too. There are still many who bear the name of Christ who by their ways show that there is not a breath of divine life in them. Professing to know God in works then deny Him. In these last days profession is made easy, and it is not difficult to be formally in fellowship with the people of God. But let us not be deceived. If the main current of a life is in the direction of worldliness and sin, there can be only one end to that life, and that is destruction.

O safe to the Rock that is higher than I
My soul in its conflict and sorrows would fly;
So sinful, so weary, Thine, Thine would I be'
Thou blest Rock of Ages, I'm hiding in Thee.

WILLIAM GILMORE

OCTOBER 30

WAITING FOR GOD'S WILL

Understanding what the will of the Lord is.
EPHESIANS 5:17

December 11, 1850 - The special burden of my prayer is that God would be pleased to teach me His will. My mind had also been especially pondering how I could know His will satisfactorily concerning this particular. Sure I am that I shall be taught. I therefore desire patiently to wait for the Lord's time, when He shall be pleased to shine on my path concerning this point.

December 26 - Fifteen days have elapsed since I wrote the preceding paragraph. Every day since then I have continued to pray about this matter, and that with a goodly measure of earnestness, by the help of God. There has passed scarcely an hour during these days, in which, while awake, this matter has not been more or less before me. But all without a shadow of excitement. I converse with no one about it. Hitherto have I not even done so with my dear wife. From this I refrain still and deal with God alone about the matter, in order that no outward influence and no outward excitement may keep me from attaining unto a clear discovery of His will. I have the fullest and most peaceful assurance that He will clearly show me His will.

This evening I have had again an especially solemn season for prayer, to seek to know the will of God. But while I continue to entreat and beseech the Lord, that He would not allow me to be deluded in this business, I may say I have scarcely any doubt remaining on my mind as to what will be the result, even that I should go forward in this matter.

Since this, however, is one of the most momentous steps that I have ever taken, I judge that I cannot go about this matter with too much caution, payerfulness, and deliberation. I am in no hurry about it. I could wait for years, by God's grace, were this His will, before even taking one single step towards this thing, or even speaking to anyone about it; and on the other hand, I would set to work tomorrow, where the Lord to bid me so.

This calmness of mind, this having no will of my own in the matter, this only wishing to please my heavenly Father in it - this state of heart, I say, is the fullest assurance to me that my heart is not under a fleshly excitement and that, if I am helped thus to go on, I shall know the will of God to the full.

GEORGE MUELLER

OCTOBER 31

BREATHING EXERCISES

Be filled with the Spirit.
EPHESIANS 5:18

L et us then take the following steps suggested by Andrew Murray: *1. I believe that there is a Pentecostal blessing to be received - the anointing of the Holy Spirit and the enduement with power [a filling of Holy Spirit-power described in Ephesians 5:18]. 2. I believe it is for me! 3. I have never received it; or, if I received it once, I have lost it. 4. I long and desire to secure it at all cost; and am prepared to surrender whatever hinders. 5. I do now humbly and thankfully open my heart to receive all that I believe my Saviour is waiting to give; and even if there be no resulting emotion, I will still believe that I have received according to Mark 11:24.*

If there is any difficulty in making a full surrender (see step 4 above), I suggest that if you have not been willing to give up the key of some special door, tell Him that you are willing to be made willing, and cast on him the responsibility of dealing with that special difficulty. When dealing with your own case or the case of others, the one matter that claims imperative and primary consideration is the will. When that takes Christ's side, you may trust Him to deal with every hindrance or sin; and He will.

As to steps, I trust that I may not be charged with egotism, if I reprint part of a tract by Dr. Chapman: "Two or three years ago Mr. Moody invited me to breakfast at his home in Northfield. I got to the house before the breakfast hour and met Dr. Meyer beneath a great tree in front of the house. I said to him, 'What is the matter with me? So many times I seem half empty, and so many times utterly powerless; what is the matter?' He put his hand on my shoulder, and said: 'Have you ever tried to breathe out three times without breathing in once?' I wondered if he was referring to some new breathing exercise, so I said, 'I do not think I have,'

"'Well,' he said, 'try it.' So I breathed out once, and then I had to breath in again. Then he said: 'You must always breathe in before you can breathe out, and your breathing out must always be in proportion to your breathing in.' Then he said: 'Good morning,' and I went on into Mr. Moody's house. But I had had my lesson and knew that I had been trying to breathe out more than I had breathed in."

There must be a constant inhalation of the Spirit of Pentecost!

F. B. MEYER

WRONG ... UNTIL JESUS
MAKES IT RIGHT

Having made peace through the blood of his cross, by him to reconcile
all things unto himself ... whether they be things in earth, or things in heaven.
COLOSSIANS 1:20

Men and women without God are helpless and hopeless human beings. We do well to remember that sin is to the human nature what cancer is to the human body!

Who can argue with the fact that sin has ruined us?

Our feverish activity is only one sign of what is wrong with us - sin has plunged us into the depths and so marked us with morality that we have become brother to the clay - but God never meant it to be so.

I recall being invited to speak at a summer conference where much of the emphasis is upon fun and amusement and jokes, something like Hollywood, I suppose. After my sessions there, the pastor-director told me frankly of his wife's reaction: "Honey, after listening to Dr Tozer, can it be true that there isn't anything good in this world?"

Well, I know she had a Bible in her house and I consider her query one of the foolish questions of our times. Of course the world makes its own argument that there are things that can be considered good on the human level - but they belong to us only for a brief day. Nothing is divinely good until it bears the imprint of our Lord Jesus Christ!

Men and women may argue and make excuses, but it does not change the fact that in our human society we are completely surrounded by three marks of the ancient curse: everything is recent, temporal and transient! That is why the Holy Spirit whispers faithfully, reminding us of the Christ of God, eternity walking in flesh, God Almighty come to live among us and to save - actually to give us eternity!

A. W. TOZER

NOVEMBER 2

OVERCOMING THE WORLD

Who is he that overcometh the world, but he that
believeth that Jesus is the Son of God.
1 JOHN 5:5

Christ had spoken strongly on the world hating Him. His Kingdom and the kingdom of this world were in deadly hostility. John had understood the lesson and summed up all in the words: "We know that we are of God, and the whole world lieth in wickedness." "Love not the world, nor the things that are of the world." "If any man love the world, the love of the Father is not in him."

John also teaches us what the real nature and power of the world is: *the lust of the flesh,* with its self-pleasing; *the lust of the eyes,* with its seeing and seeking what there is in the glory of the world; and *the pride of life,* with its self-exaltation. We find these three marks of what the World is in Eve in Paradise. She "saw that the tree was good for food, and that it was pleasant to the eyes, and a tree to be desired to make one wise." Through the body and the eyes and the pride of wisdom, the world acquired the mastery over her and over us.

The world still exerts a terrible influence over the Christian who does not know that in Christ he has been crucified to the world. In the pleasure in eating and drinking, in the love and enjoyment of what there is to be seen of its glory, and in all that constitutes the pride of life, the power of this world proves itself. And most Christians are either utterly ignorant of the danger of a worldly spirit or feel themselves utterly powerless to conquer it.

Christ left us with the great far-reaching promise: *"Be of good cheer, I have overcome the world."* As the child of God abides in Christ and seeks to live the heavenly life in the power of the Holy Spirit, he may confidently count on the power to overcome the world. *"Who is he that overcometh the world, but he that believeth that Jesus is the Son of God?"* *"I live by the faith of the Son of God, who loved me, and gave Himself for me"*; this is the secret of daily, hourly victory over the world and all its secret, subtle temptation. But it needs a heart and a life entirely possessed by the faith of Jesus Christ to maintain the victor's attitude at all times. Oh, my brothers and sisters, take time to ask whether you do with your whole heart believe in the victory that faith gives over the world.

ANDREW MURRAY

THE PROMISES OF GOD

Having therefore these promises.
2 CORINTHIANS 7:1

It is the unspeakable privilege of all believers to have, as a certain possession, the previous promises of God. But under what notion have we the promises of God?

1. We have them as manifest tokens of God's favour towards us; and every one of them are yea, amen, in Christ Jesus our Lord.

2. We have them as fruits of Christ's purchase. The Lord having purchased us with His own blood we have these promises produced by that inestimable grace.

3. They are plain and ample declarations of the good-will of God towards men, and therefore as God's part of the covenant of grace.

4. They are a foundation of our faith, and we have them as such; and also of our hope, on these we are to build all our expectations from God; and in all temptations and trials we have them to rest our souls upon.

5. We have them as the directions and the encouragements of our desires in prayer. Seek and you shall find, knock and it shall be opened unto you. Wherefore they are the guide of our desires, and the ground of our hope in prayer.

6. We have them as the means by which the grace of God works for our holiness and comfort, for by these we are made partakers of a divine nature, and faith, applying these promises, is said to work by love.

7. We have the promises as the earnest and assurance of future blessedness. By these eternal life and glory is secured to all true believers.

MATTHEW HENRY

THE IMPORTANCE OF BEING EARNEST

Go out into the highways and hedges, and compel them to come in
LUKE 14:23

Real Christianity is, in its very nature and essence, aggressive. We get this principle fully exhibited and illustrated in the parables of Jesus Christ. If you will study them you will find that He has not given us anything to be used merely for ourselves, but that we hold and possess every talent which He has committed to us for the good of others and for the salvation of man.

How wonderfully this principle was exhibited in the lives of the apostles and early Christians! How utterly careless they seemed to be of everything compared with this - this was the first thing with them everywhere! How Paul, at the very threshold, counted nothing else of any consequence, but willingly, cheerfully, gave up every other consideration to live for this. And so with the early Christians, who were scattered through the persecutions - how they went everywhere preaching the word; how earnest and zealous they were. Even after the apostolic age, we learn from ecclesiastical history how they pushed themselves in everywhere; how they made converts and won real, self-denying followers, even in king's courts: how they would not be kept out, and would not be kept down, and would not be hindered or silenced.

Like their Master, they could not be hid; they could not be repressed - so aggressive, so constraining, was the spirit which inspired and urged them on.

Live for something - God and angels
Are thy watchers in the strife,
And above the smoke and conflict
Gleams the victor's crown of life
Live for something; God has given
Freely of His stores divine;
Richest gifts of earth and Heaven,
If thou willest, may be thine.

CATHERINE BOOTH

NOVEMBER 5

LAW AND LIBERTY

The perfect law of liberty.
JAMES 1:25

Law and liberty. Mark the conjunction of these two words. Men often oppose these terms, as being contrary to one another - law as opposed to liberty, and liberty as opposed to law. But the apostolic conjoins them.

Right and proper law is not bondage, but is liberty; true liberty is not lawlessness, is not self-will, but is lawful, well regulated liberty - "the law of liberty." And that law which unites thoroughly these two often contrasted things, law and liberty, such law is a perfect law.

And such a law God's law is - a perfect law of liberty. Law, standing simply, and as law, is the expressed will of a superior, who has the right to command, and the power to see to it that his law, his expressed will, be complied with. Such is law in the width of its meaning. And law, thus defined, may be right or wrong. It is the expressed will of a superior, of one who has power to see to it that what he wills and commands be done.

But God's law, like its Author, has certain qualities flowing from His perfections. He is holy, just and good; His law likewise is holy, just and good. And from this we may be able to see in some degree how it unites the idea of law and liberty, if we take first of all the character of the Legislator, and if we take secondly the character of the being to whom this law is given, as that being came from Jehovah's hand.

The law is the law of Jehovah, not only infinitely wise and powerful, but also infinitely holy, just, and good. Therefore there can be in His will - His will existing in Him, or as given forth and expressed by Him when it becomes law - nothing contrary to the essential perfections of His nature. His law must be holy, just, and good.

But He who is absolute perfection - who is not only Creator and Preserver, and so absolute Lord over all the earth, but absolutely and infinitely perfect in wisdom, power, holiness, justice, goodness, and truth - He, from the perfections of His nature, hath a right to be absolute Lord, for He cannot will wrong, any more than He can be wrong. He cannot but will holily, justly, and wisely; He can give no law but what is at once for His own glory, and for the good of His obedient subjects. So, to serve Him, to be altogether subject to Him, is to be absolutely free.

JOHN DUNCAN

COMING AGAIN

Our conversation is in heaven; from whence also we look for the Saviour.
PHILIPPIANS 3:20

Little is mentioned between Christ's ascent to heaven and His descent to come. True, a rich history comes between; but it lies in a valley between two stupendous mountains: we step from Alp to Alp as we journey in meditation from the ascension to the second advent.

Both His ascension and second coming are possible because of what happened during His first coming. Had He not come a first time in humiliation, born under the law, He could not come a second time in amazing glory "without a sin offering unto salvation". Because he died once, we rejoice that He dies no more. Death has no more dominion over Him, and therefore He will come again to destroy that last enemy whom He has already conquered. It is our joy, as we think of our Redeemer as risen, to feel that in consequence of His rising, the trump of the archangel shall assuredly sound for the awaking of all His slumbering people, when the Lord Himself shall descend from heaven with a shout.

As for His ascension, He could not a second time descend if He had not first ascended; but having perfumed heaven with His presence, and prepared a place for His people, we may fitly expect that He will come again and receive us unto Himself, that where He is there we may be also.

He will come again, for *He has promised to return*. We have His own word for it. That is our first reason for expecting Him. Among the last of the words that He spoke to His servant John are these, "Surely I come quickly." You may read it. "I am coming quickly. I am even now upon the road. I am travelling as fast as wisdom allows. I am always coming, and coming quickly."

Glorious day when we stand in His presence,
All of our heartaches and sorrows are past,
No more burden too heavy to carry-
We shall see Jesus at last!

CHARLES H. SPURGEON

THE POWER WE NEED

Endued with power from on high.
LUKE 24:49

A *great promise of God for the Bible student and soul winner* is found in Acts 1:8: "But ye shall receive power, after that the Holy Ghost is come upon you: and ye shall be witnesses unto me both in Jerusalem, and in all Judea, and in Samaria, and unto the uttermost part of the earth." The greatest need of a missionary, a minister and personal worker, or a father and a mother, when they study God's Word and when they go out to win souls, is power - power to penetrate the sacred cloisters of God's Word where such abundant treasures of truth are stored and power to present to others the truth discovered in such a way as to convict of sin and reveal Jesus Christ and to bring men to accept Jesus as their Lord and Saviour.

This verse reveals the great secret of that power: "Ye shall receive power, *after that the Holy Ghost is come upon you*." We need power, a power not from this earth, not from human culture, not the power learned in schools of oratory, nor the power that comes from the tricks of the world, not the power to draw crowds learned from Douglas Fairbanks, Mary Pickford, or Charlie Chaplin. No! No! No! We need "power from on high" (Luke 24: 49).

This promise tells us how to get such power. It tells us how any child of God can get it. Listen again, "Ye shall receive power, *after that the Holy Ghost is come upon you*: and ye shall be witnesses unto me both in Jerusalem, and in all Judea, and in Samaria, and unto the uttermost part of the earth." The source of all power is the Holy Spirit within us. "For the promise is unto you, and to your children, and to all that are afar off, even as many as the Lord our God shall call unto Him."

Holy Spirit, dwell with me;
I myself would holy be;
Separate from sin, I would
Choose and cherish all things good,
And whatever I can be
Give to Him who gave me Thee!

R. A. TORREY

ANATHEMA MARANATHA

The Lord is at hand.
PHILIPPIANS 4:5

"If any man love not the Lord Jesus Christ, let him be Anathema Maranatha" (1 Corinthians 16:22) This is one of the most incisive and challenging statements in all the Bible. Incisive because there is no possibility of misunderstanding it. In the fewest possible words, it declares the inevitable doom of all who do not love the Lord Jesus. Challenging, first because of its very incisiveness; and second, because of the fact that it contains two untranslated foreign words, *Anathema Maranatha*, taken from two different languages, and which by their very strangeness compel our attention.

Anathema is Greek and means "accursed" or "devoted to judgment". It is the same word that the apostle uses in Galatians 1:8-9: "But though we, or an angel from heaven, preach any other gospel unto you than that which we have preached unto you, let him be accursed. As we said before, so say I now again, If any man preach any other gospel unto you than that ye have received, let him be accursed." The man or angel who misleads others with a false gospel is under the ban of eternal God - Anathema, "accursed," "devoted to judgment". He uses the same word again when speaking of himself: he says, "I could wish that I myself were accursed (Anathema) from Christ for my brethren, my kinsmen according to the flesh." It implies, then, clearly a definite separation from Christ, banishment from God, without any hope of restoration.

The other word, *Maranatha*, is a compound word, an Aramaic expression of Chaldean origin, translated "our Lord come!" or "the Lord comes!" It is a vivid reminder that the rejected Christ is to return in glory as judge of the living and the dead.

So, then, the strange compound expression, this Greco-Aramaic term, "Anathema Maranatha," might really be rendered, "devoted to judgment; our Lord cometh." Slightly paraphrasing the entire sentence, it would read, "If any man love not our Lord Jesus Christ, he will be devoted to judgment at the coming of the Lord." What a tremendously solemn statement and how seriously we should consider it.

HARRY IRONSIDE

GRACE TO SERVE

I thank Christ Jesus our Lord ... for that he counted me faithful,
putting me into the ministry.
1 TIMOTHY 1:12

Isaiah 6:8: "Here am I; send me." It is a signal instance of grace on the part of the Lord that I am allowed to be a volunteer. The Lord has a right, a dearly purchased right, to deal with me very differently. He might issue a peremptory command. He might utter His stern voice of authority, and at once, order me. But He knows what is in man better than to treat thus the broken and relenting heart of whom He has smitten by the brightness of His glorious holiness to the ground, and healed by the touch of His ever-living sacrifice of blood. He is considerate. He is generous. His servant is not coerced or constrained, as with a bit and bridle. He has the unspeakable privilege and happiness of giving himself voluntarily ... to the Lord, who willingly gave Himself for him.

O Lord, I pray
That for this day
I may not swerve
By foot or hand
From Thy command
Not to be served, but to serve.

And if I may,
I'd have this day
Strength from above
To set my heart
In heavenly art
Not to be loved, but to love.

ROBERT S. CANDLISH

STRETCH OR STARVE

*Every one that useth milk is unskilful in the word of
righteousness: for he is a babe.*
HEBREWS 5:13

You know it is always regarded a great event in the family when a child can feed himself. The child is propped up at the table, and at first perhaps he uses the spoon upside down. But by and by he handles it all right, and mother, or perhaps sister, claps her hands and says, "Just see, baby's feeding himself!" Well, what we need as Christians is to be able to feed ourselves. How many there are who sit helpless and listless, with open mouths, hungry for spiritual things, and the minister has to try to feed them, while the Bible is a feast prepared into which they never venture.

There are many who have been Christians for twenty years who have still to be fed with an ecclesiastical spoon. If they happen to have a minister who feeds them, they get on pretty well; but if they have not, they are not fed at all. This is the test as to your being a true child of God - whether you love and feed upon the Word of God. If you go out to your garden and throw down some sawdust, the birds will not take any notice; but if you throw down some crumbs, you will find they will soon sweep down and pick them up. So the true child of God can tell the difference, so to speak, between sawdust and bread. Many so-called Christians are living on the world's sawdust, instead of being nourished by the Bread that cometh down from heaven. Nothing can satisfy the longings of the soul but the Word of the living God.

The best law for Bible study is the law of perseverance. The psalmist says, "I have stuck unto thy testimonies." Application to the Word will tend to its growth within and its multiplication without. Some people are like express trains; they skim along so quickly that they see nothing.

I met a lawyer in Chicago who told me he had spent two years in study upon one subject; he was trying to smash a will. He made it his business to read everything on wills he could get. Then he went into court and he talked two days about that will; he was full of it; he could not talk about anything else but wills. That is the way with the Bible: study it and study it, one subject at a time, until you become filled with it.

Read the Bible itself; do not spend all your time on commentaries and helps. If a man spent all his time reading up the chemical constituents of bread and milk, he would soon starve.

D. L. MOODY

FREE FROM THE POWER OF SIN

Ye know that he was manifested to take away our sins; and in him is no sin. Whosoever abideth in him sinneth not.
1 JOHN 3:5-6

John had taken deep into his heart and life the words that Christ had spoken in the last night on abiding in Him. He ever remembered how the Lord had six times over spoken of loving Him and keeping His commandments as the way to abiding in His love and receiving the indwelling of the Father and the Son. And so in this Epistle in his old age the abiding in Christ is one of the key-words of the life it promises (John 2:6,24,28; 3:6,24; 4: 13,16).

In our text John teaches how we can be kept from sinning: "He that abideth in Christ sinneth not." Though there is sin in our nature, the abiding in Christ, in whom is no sin, does indeed free us from the power of sin and enables us day by day to live so as to please God. Of the Lord Jesus it is written that He had said of the Father (John 8:29): "I do always those things that please Him." And so John writes in the Epistle: "Beloved, if our heart condemn us not, we have boldness toward God; and whatsoever we ask, we receive of Him, *because we keep His commandments and do the things that are pleasing in His sight.*"

Let the soul that longs to be free from the power of sin take these simple but far-reaching words: "In Him is no sin," and "of God I am in Him." "He that establisheth us in Christ is God." As I seek to abide in Him in whom there is no sin, Christ will indeed live out His own life in me in the power of the Holy Spirit and fit me for a life in which I always do the things that are pleasing in His sight.

Dear child of God, you are called to a life in which faith, great faith, strong faith, continuous and unbroken faith in the Almighty power of God is your one hope. As you day by day take time and yield yourself to the God of peace who perfects you in every good work to do His will, you will experience that what the heart has not conceived is what God indeed works in them that wait for Him.

"He that abideth in Him, sinneth not," The promise is sure: God the Almighty is pledged that He will work in you what is well-pleasing in His sight through Christ Jesus. In that faith, abide in Him.

ANDREW MURRAY

UNCLEAN BY COMPARISON

And when I saw him, I fell at his feet as dead.
REVELATION 1:17

In the Old Testament, whenever the living God revealed Himself in some way to humankind, terror and amazement were the reactions. People saw themselves as guilty and unclean by comparison!

In the book of Revelation, the Apostle John describes the overwhelming nature of his encounter with the Lord of glory. Although a believer and an apostle, John sank down in abject humility and fear when the risen, glorified Lord Jesus appeared before him on Patmos.

Our glorified Lord did not condemn John. He knew that John's weakness was the reaction to revealed divine strength. He knew that John's sense of unworthiness was the instant reaction to absolute holiness. Along with John, every redeemed human being needs the humility of spirit that can only be brought about by the manifest Presence of God.

Jesus at once reassured John, stooping to place a nail-pierced hand on the prostrate apostle, and saying: "Do not be afraid. I am the Living One. I was dead, and behold I am alive for ever and ever, and I hold the keys of death and hades."

He walks among the golden lamps
On feet like burned bronze;
His hair as snow of winter white,
His eyes with fire aflame, and bright
His glorious robe of seamless light
Surpassing Solomon's

And in His hand the seven stars
And from His mouth a sword:
His voice the thunder of the seas;
All creatures bow to His decrees
Who holds the everlasting keys
And reigns as Sovereign Lord.

A. W. TOZER

THE WORTH OF THE SOUL

Blessed is the man that walketh not in the counsel of the ungodly.
PSALM 1:1

Those that take up with a cheap and easy religion despise their own souls; that are afraid of doing too much for their own souls. Did we put a right value upon our souls, we should object to no pains or care for the securing of their welfare. We should go from strength to strength; we should give diligence to add to our graces, and thus make our calling and election sure, 2 Peter 1:5-10. But those that only inquire, will not less serve manifest that they despise their souls: they labour at the world, and sleep at an ordinance; they crowd their religion into a corner, and make not a business, but a by-business of it. What account do such make of their souls who will scarce go over the threshold to hear a sermon? They "refuse instruction." He that is slothful in work for his soul is brother to him that is a great waster.

Those that are prodigal of their times despise their own souls. Time is an opportunity of doing something for the soul, and is to be redeemed accordingly, Ephesians 5:16, because there is an eternity depends upon it. Time may be well spent, either in doing something for God with the soul, or in getting something from God for the soul; yet with many their time is a drug. What value do those put upon their souls that fill up their time with mere recreation, and all this while neglect their souls? Every day might be a harvest day for the soul, but it is idled away; the time of the morning and evening sacrifice stolen away by one idle companion or other. Value your souls and you will value your time.

Those that make themselves drudges to the world despise their own souls. The soul should be our darling, but many make it a slave, and send it to feed swine, Luke 15:15, and to provide for the flesh, Romans 13:14. Those that are eager in pursuit of worldly wealth despise their souls, not only because the soul is neglected and the body preferred before it, but because it is employed in these pursuits, Psalm 127:2. Care about the world fills the soul and disquiets it. It is a great disparagement to an immortal soul to be thus wholly employed.

MATTHEW HENRY

BLESSED MATCH-MAKER

The marriage of the Lamb is come, and his wife hath made herself ready.
REVELATION 19:7

John in Patmos, being in the Spirit on the Lord's day, heard a voice; and when he had looked he beheld the Son of God, and fell at His feet. He saw visions; and among other visions he saw this: - an angel came and said to him, "Come hither, I will shew thee the bride, the Lamb's wife." O when the eye had seen the Lamb, it has seen the best sight; but next to that is the sight of the bride, THE LAMB'S WIFE. "I will shew thee the bride, the Lamb's wife," the espoused one. "I have espoused you as a chaste virgin to Christ."

Next to the sights of the Lamb I would like to see the Father of the Lamb; I would like to see the Spirit of the Lamb; but next to that I would like to see the Bride, the Lamb's wife. I would like to see her; I would like to *be* her.

I bless God for Paul. Blessed be God for all His holy prophets and apostles. I bless God for Paul, who said, "I have espoused you as a chaste virgin to Christ." Blessed match-maker! And blessed be God for Paul, who, by his words since his death, has espoused far more than all they whom he espoused in his life.

"I will shew thee the bride, the Lamb's wife;" a fretting, captious, quarrelsome bride! We speak of lovers' quarrels. O how many quarrels before this match is completed! Yet the Lord bears with it in His long-suffering.

"I will shew thee the bride, the Lamb's wife;" a singing people, and a weeping people; a people receiving and retaining the word of the Gospel "in much affliction, with joy of the Holy Ghost."

Now may the Lord shew you the Lamb more and more, and shew you the bride, the Lamb's wife! And may He carry on in you the objects of His espousals until the full consummation of the marriage. "I have espoused you," yea *married* you; yet awaiting the marriage supper of the Lamb.

The apostle in holy prophetic vision saw the end - "The marriage of the Lamb is come, and His wife hath made herself ready;" for "there are they which came out of great tribulation, and have washed their robes, and made them white in the blood of the Lamb." That in vision; but, meanwhile, the Bride is washing her robes, and making them white; working out the bestowed salvation, with fear and trembling, under the promise and experience of this that "it is God which worketh in us both to will and to do, of His good pleasure."

JOHN DUNCAN

THE GROUND OF OUR HOPE

Satisfied with favour, and full with the blessing of the Lord.
DEUTERONOMY 33:23

He has chosen to make His promises to elect persons, who in process of time are discovered by their exercising faith in Him. Those whom God has chosen are led by the Holy Spirit to choose God and His way of salvation by faith in Christ Jesus. Those of the elect who come to years of discretion are led to faith in Jesus; and all who have faith in Him may conclude beyond doubt that they are of the chosen number to whom the promises are given. To those who live and die in unbelief there is no absolute and personal promise of God: they are not under grace but under law, and to them belong the threatenings and not the promises. These prefer another method of dealing to that of gracious promise, and in the end they perish as the result of their foolish preference. The chosen of the Lord are led to relinquish the proud way of self and merit; they take to the road of faith, and so find rest unto their souls. To believe the Word of God and to trust in Him whom God has sent to be our Saviour may seem a small thing; but indeed it is not so. It is the sign of election, the token of regeneration, the mark of coming glory. So to believe that God is true as to rest one's eternal interests upon His promise bespeaks a heart reconciled to God, a spirit in which the germ of perfect holiness is present.

When we believe God as He is revealed in Christ Jesus, we believe all His promises. Confidence in the person of Christ involves confidence in all that He speaks: hence we accept all the promises of God as being sure and certain. We do not trust one promise and doubt another, but we rely upon each one as true, and we believe it to be true to us so far as it has respect to our condition and circumstances. We argue from general statements to particular applications. He who has said that He will save those who believe in Him will save me since I believe in Him; and every blessing which He has engaged to bestow upon believers He will bestow upon me as a believer.

This is sound reasoning, and by it we justify the faith by which we live and are comforted. Not because I deserve anything, but because God has freely promised it to me in Christ Jesus, therefore I shall receive it: this is the reason and ground of our hope.

CHARLES H. SPURGEON

NOVEMBER 16

TRUE DIGNITY

Looking unto Jesus ..who .. endured the cross, despising the shame
HEBREWS 12:2

When the Church and the world can jog along comfortably together you may be sure there is something wrong. The world has not altered. Its spirit is exactly the same as it ever was, and if Christians were equally faithful and devoted to the Lord, and separated from the world, living so that their lives were a reproof of all ungodliness, the world would hate them as much as ever it did. It is the Church that has altered, not the world. You say, *"We should be getting into endless turmoil. There would be uproar."* Yes. And the Acts of the Apostles is full of stories of uproar.

"But," you say, *"wouldn't it be inconsistent with the dignity of the gospel?"* That depends upon the standpoint from which you look at it, upon what really constitutes the dignity of the gospel. Is it human dignity or is it divine? It was a very undignified thing, looked at humanly, (for Christ) to die on a cross between two thieves. (So considered), it was the most undignified thing ever done in this world, and yet, looked at on the moral and spiritual grounds, it was the grandest spectacle that ever earth or Heaven gazed upon.

That dignity will never suffer even though you should have to be dragged through the streets with a howling mob at your heels, though you should be tied to a stake, as where the martyrs of old, and surrounded by laughing and taunting fiends that will be a dignity which shall be crowned in Heaven with everlasting glory.

Withstand the foe!
Die daily, that thou mayest forever live,
Be faithful unto death; thy Lord will give
The crown of life.

CATHERINE BOOTH

NOVEMBER 17

PLEASURES FOR EVERMORE

The Lamb which is in the midst of the throne shall feed them, and shall lead them unto living fountains of waters.
REVELATION 7:17

Some question whether heaven is a place or a state of the soul. Jesus Christ plainly declares that heaven is a place. In John 14:2 He says: "I go to prepare a *place* for you," and to make it even more plain He adds in the next verse that when the place is prepared He will come again and receive us unto Himself, that *where* He is we may be also.

Let's consider how the Scriptures describe heaven. Heaven is a place more beautiful than any of us can conceive. In our present state very sense and faculty of perception is blunted by sin and the disease that results from sin. In our redeemed bodies every sense and faculty will receive enlargement and exist in perfection. There may be new senses, but what they may be we cannot now imagine. The fairest sights that we have ever beheld on earth are nothing in beauty to what will greet us in that fair "city that hath no foundations."

Heaven will be free from everything that curses or mars our lives here. There will be no servile grinding toil, no sickness or pain (Revelation 21:4), no death, no funerals, and no separations. Above all, there will be no sin. It will be a place of universal and perfect knowledge (1 Corinthians 13:12), of universal and perfect love (1 John 3:2, 4:8), and of perpetual praise (Revelation 7:9-12). It will be a land of melody and song.

There is just one thing that anyone needs to do to get to heaven, that is, to accept Jesus Christ as his personal Saviour, surrender to Him as his Lord and Master, and openly confess Him before the world. Jesus Christ says: "I am the way, the truth, and the life. No man cometh unto the Father but by me" (John 14:6). Again He says: "I am the door. By me if any man enter in he shall be saved" (John 10:9). Any one who receives Jesus becomes at once a child of God, an heir of God, a joint-heir with Jesus Christ (John 1:12; Romans 8:16,17).

Anyone can know whether he is already on the way to heaven or not by asking himself the questions: "Have I received Jesus Christ? Have I taken Him as my Sin-bearer, the One who bore my sins in His own body on the cross (Isaiah 53:6; 1 Peter 2:24; Galatians 3:13)? Am I trusting God to forgive my sins because Jesus bore them for me?" If any one can answer yes to these simple questions he may know he is on the way to heaven.

R. A. TORREY

NOVEMBER 18

KNOWING GOD PERSONALLY

There arose not a prophet ... like unto Moses, whom the Lord knew face to face.
DEUTERONOMY 34:10

To believe that God is omnipotent ... when that belief is the mere admission of a dogma in theology ... will go but a little way toward strengthening you in that faith which glorifies God. But let me again remind you that the faith in question is believing God; not believing something about God, but believing God. It is a personal dealing of God with you, and of you with God. He and you come together; He to speak, you to hear; He to promise, you to believe; you to ask, He to give.

To walk with God, O fellowship divine!
Man's highest state on earth - Lord, be it mine!
With Thee, may I a close communion hold;
To Thee, the deep recesses of my heart unfold.

With Thee hold converse sweet where'er I go;
Thy smile of love my highest bliss below!
With Thee transact life's business -doing all
With single aim for Thee - as Thou dost call.

Oh, may this high companionship be mine,
And all my life by its reflection shine,
My great, my wise, my never-failing Friend,
Where love no change can know, or turn, nor end.

ROBERT S. CANDLISH

DOUBTING CHRISTIANS

Sin shall not have dominion over you.
ROMANS 6:14

Many uninstructed believers become discouraged because of their own failures, and Satan takes advantage of these to inject into their minds doubts as to whether they are not deceiving themselves after all in supposing they are Christians. But a knowledge of the truth as to the believer's two natures will often help here. It is important to understand that sin in the flesh, inherent in the old nature, is not destroyed when one is born again. On the contrary, that old sin principle remains in the believer as long as he is in the body. What takes place at new birth is that a new and divine nature is communicated. These two natures are in conflict with each other.

But the Christian who walks in the spirit will not fulfil the desires of the flesh, even though at times those desires may be manifested. In order to so walk, one must take sides with God against this principle of evil which belongs to the old Adamic nature. God reckons it as executed at the cross of Christ; for the Lord Jesus died, not only for what we have done but for what we are by nature. Now faith accepts this as true, and the believer can exclaim, "I live by the faith of the Son of God who loved me and gave himself for me—" (Galatians 2:20).

Carefully consider what is taught here: I, the responsible I, the old man, all that I was as a man in the flesh, including my entire sinful nature - "I have been crucified with Christ." When was that? It was when Jesus died on Calvary's tree nineteen hundred years ago. He was there for me. I was there in Him. He was my representative, my substitute. He died the death I deserved to die. Therefore in God's eyes His death was my death. So I have died with Him.

Now I am called upon to make this real in my personal experience. I am to reckon myself as dead indeed unto sin but alive unto God (Romans 6:11). The old nature has no claim upon me. If it asserts itself and endeavours to bring me into bondage, I am to take sides with God against it. He has condemned sin in the flesh. I must condemn it too. Instead of yielding to it, I am to yield myself unto God as one alive from the dead, for I have been crucified in Christ's crucifixion, but I live anew in His resurrection.

HARRY IRONSIDE

KEEP NOTHING BACK

All things are possible to him that believeth.
MARK 9:23

After the transfiguration on the mountain, Jesus and the disciples came down and met a father who had a son possessed with a devil (Mark 9:14-29). When the father went to bring his son to Jesus the devil tripped him up. Like a bad tenant, he tried to do as much harm as he could before leaving. The devil knew that he was going to get orders to leave, so he gave the boy such a throw that he nearly killed him. The disciples could not cast the devil out. The boy was deaf and dumb, and I presume the disciples said: "Oh, you know, that is a hopeless case. If he could only tell us how he feels, or if we could only shout into his ear, we might get at him; but we cannot make him hear or speak, and we cannot do anything."

They lacked faith. But the Lord came down, and that father came to Christ. "Mark you," Spurgeon says, "he (the father) was a poor theologian when he came to Christ. He came and said, "If thou canst do anything," and the Lord rebuked him right there. He said, "If thou canst believe." He put the 'if' in the right place. 'All things are possible to him that believeth; bring him unto me.'"

You may have some brother or father or friend whom you want to be converted. You have brought them to Christians, and the devil has not been cast out. Listen! What did Christ say to His Father? "Bring him unto me."

There is a great deal of joy in the thought that Christ has power over the devils. Remember that "all power in heaven and earth" is given to Him, and don't think for a moment that any man is beyond the reach of God's mercy. Don't you think that your brother who is a slave to strong drink is beyond the reach of God. "Bring him to Me," says Christ. Get beyond your church, your society and go right to the master Himself.

When that mother came and told Elisha that her child was dead (2 Kings 4:8-37), the prophet said to his servant, "Take that stick and lay it out on that dead child." Away went the servant. But that woman was wiser than Elisha; she would not leave him. She was not going to trust in that staff or that servant, she wanted the prophet himself. Some people think that it will do to love Christ without giving themselves to the work. No. Sometimes your whole life must be given to win a person. Make up your mind that if it costs you your life, you are going to do it.

D. L. MOODY

THE WONDER OF CREATION

The heavens declare the glory of God: and the firmament sheweth his handywork.
PSALM 19:1

Reading my Bible, I am greatly impressed by the manner in which godly men of old revealed in their writings an intense love for every natural beauty round them. They saw nature as the handiwork of an all-powerful and all-glorious Creator!

The Old Testament is a marvellous rhapsody on the creation. Start with Moses, and when you get beyond the Levitical order you will find him soaring in his acute consciousness of the presence of God in all creation.

Go to the book of Job. In the closing section you will be amazed at the sublimity of the language describing the world around us. Then go to the Psalms, with David literally dancing with ecstatic delight as he gazes out upon the wonders of God's world. Go to Isaiah, where imagery is neither fanciful nor flighty but a presentation of the wonders of creation.

In our generation, how rarely we get into a situation where we can feel the impulses of nature communicated to us. We seldom have time to lift our eyes to look at God's heaven - except when we are wondering if we should wear our boots!

So soberly and softly
The seasons tread their round,
So surely seeds of autumn
In spring-time clothe the ground,
Amid their measured music
What watchful ear can hear
God's voice amidst the garden?
Yet, hush! For He is here.

A. W. TOZER

DAILY COMMUNION WITH GOD

The desire of our soul is to thy name.
ISAIAH 26:8

It is to live a life of desire toward God; to wait on Him as the beggar waits on his benefactor, with earnest desire to receive supplies from him; as the sick and sore in Bethesda's pool waited for the stirring of the water, and attended in the porches with desire to be helped in and healed. When the prophet had said, "Lord, in the way of thy judgments we have waited for thee," he explained himself thus in the next words, "The desire of our soul is to thy name, and to the remembrance of thee; and with my soul have I desired thee," Isaiah 26:8-9. Our desire must not be only towards the good things that God gives, but towards God Himself, His favour and love, the manifestation of His name to us, and the influence of His grace upon us. Then we wait on God, when our souls pant after Him, and His favour, when we thirst for God, for the living God; Oh that I may behold the beauty of the Lord! Oh that I may taste His goodness! Oh that I may bear His image, and be entirely conformed to His will! for there is none in heaven or earth that I can desire in comparison of Him. Oh that I may know Him more and love Him better, and be brought nearer to Him, and made fitter for Him. Thus upon the wings of holy desire should our souls be still soaring upward towards God, still pressing forward, forward towards Heaven.

We must not only pray solemnly in the morning, but that desire which is the life and soul of prayer, like the fire upon the altar, must be kept continually burning, ready for the sacrifices that are to be offered upon it. The bent and bias of the soul, in all its motions, must be toward God, the serving of Him in all we do, and the enjoying of Him in all we have. And this is principally intended in the commands given us to pray always, to pray without ceasing, to continue in prayer. Even when we are not making actual addresses to God, we must have habitual inclinations toward Him; as a man in health, though he is not always eating, yet has always a disposition in him towards the nourishment and delights of the body. Thus must we be always waiting on God, as our chief good, and moving toward Him.

MATTHEW HENRY

NOVEMBER 23

THE HOLY TRINITY

Elect according to the foreknowledge of God the Father; through sanctification of the Spirit, unto obedience and sprinkling of the blood of Jesus Christ.
1 PETER 1:2

Here we have one of the texts in which the great truth of the blessed Trinity is seen to lie at the very root of our spiritual life. In this book we have spoken especially of the adoration of God the Father and the need of time, sufficient time each day, to worship Him in some of His glorious attributes. But we must remind ourselves that, for all our communion with God, the presence and the power of the Son and the Spirit are absolutely necessary.

What a field this opens for us in the inner chamber. We need time to realise how all our communion with the Father is conditioned by the active and personal presence and working of the Lord Jesus. It takes time to become fully conscious of what need I have of Him in every approach to God, what confidence I may have in the work that He is doing for me and in me, and what the holy and intimate love is in which I may count upon His presence and all-prevailing intercession. But oh to learn the lesson that it needs time and that that time will be most blessedly rewarded!

Even so too is it with the divine and almighty power of the Holy Spirit working in the depth of my heart as the One who alone is able to reveal the Son within me. Through Him alone I have the power to know what and how to pray and, above all, how to plead the name of Jesus and to receive the assurance that my prayer has been accepted.

Dear Christian reader, have you not felt more than once that it was as it were a mockery to speak of five minutes to be alone with God, to come under the impression of His glory? And now does not the thought of the true worship of God in Christ through the Holy Spirit make you feel more than ever that it needs time to enter into such holy alliance with God as shall keep the heart and mind all the day in His peace and presence? *It is in tarrying in the secret of God's presence that you receive grace to abide in Christ and all the day to be led by His Spirit.*

Just pause and think: "Elect according to the foreknowledge of God the Father, through sanctification of the Spirit, unto obedience and sprinkling of the blood of Jesus Christ!" What food for thought - and worship!

ANDREW MURRAY

JESUS AND THE PROMISES

Preserved in Jesus Christ.
JUDE 1

Jesus is the confirmer of the promises. They are "in him yea, and in him, Amen." His coming into our nature, His standing as our head, and His fulfilling of all the stipulations of the covenant have made all the articles of the divine compact firm and enduring. Now, is it not only kind but just with God to keep His promises to men? Since Jesus has rendered, on man's behalf, a full recompense to the divine honour that sin has assailed, the justice of God unites with His love in securing the carrying out of every word of promise.

As the rainbow is our assurance that the world shall never be destroyed by a flood, so is Jesus our assurance that the floods of human sin shall never drown the faithful kindness of the Lord. He has magnified the law and made it honourable; He must be rewarded for His soul-travail, and therefore all good things must come to those for whom He died. It would be an unhinging and dislocation of all things if the promises were now to become of no effect after our Lord has done all that was required to make them sure. If we are indeed one with the Lord Jesus Christ, the promises are as sure to us as the love of His Father is to Him.

Jesus remembers the promises. He pleads with God on our behalf, and His pleads is the divine promise. "He made intercession for the transgressors." For the good things that He has promised the Lord will be inquired of us by that He may do them for us; and that this inquiry may be carried out under the most encouraging circumstances, behold, the Lord Jesus Himself becomes the intercessor for us. For Zion's sake He does not hold His peace, but day and night He makes remembrance of the everlasting covenant and of the blood whereby it was sealed and ratified. At the back of every promise stands the living, pleading, and prevailing high priest of our profession.

We may forget the faithful promise, but He will not. He will present the incense of His merit, and the engagements of God on our behalf, in that place within the veil where He exercises omnipotent intercession.

CHARLES H. SPURGEON

ALTOGETHER APART

Sit ye here, while I go and pray yonder.
MATTHEW 26:36

Notice the prayer life of our blessed Lord. Because He became man, He prayed to the Father. He took the place of a dependent. He trod the path of faith and drew His strength from above. He was often found at night on a hillside or in a garden, pouring out His heart in prayer. But His prayer never took the character of confession. Hence He always prayed alone. He never prayed in fellowship with anyone else. He prayed for others. He did not pray with them. We never find Him kneeling with Peter, James, and John, His intimate disciples, and joining together with them in intercession, or with anyone else. We who serve Christ today have some of our most blessed experiences as we mingle our prayers and supplications with those of our fellow believers and bow together before God in acknowledgment of our common sinfulness and our common need. He never did this with anyone. He taught His disciples to pray, "Forgive us our trespasses, as we forgive those who trespass against us," but He could not, in the very nature of things, pray that prayer with them. He stood altogether apart. They were sinners; He was sinless, the Saviour of sinners. "He knew no sin."

The Word of God teaches that He not only never made the acquaintance of sin by actual failure, by transgression, by disobedience in thought, word, or deed, but He knew no sin in the sense that His humanity was never contaminated by an inward tendency to sin. He was absolutely, from the moment of His incarnation, the holy One. The angel said to the blessed virgin mother: "That holy thing which shall be born of thee shall be called the Son of God." In Adam, unfallen, we see humanity innocent; in all his children since, we see humanity fallen; but in Christ Jesus we see humanity holy.

We are told that He was tempted in all points like as we are, yet without sin. Some people have taken this last expression to mean, "Yet without sinning." That was true as we have seen, but it is not all of the truth. That verse really means this: He was tempted in all points like as we are, apart from sin. He was never emptied by inbred sin. He could say, "The prince of this world cometh, and hath nothing in me." You cannot say that; I cannot. When the enemy comes at me from without, there is a traitor inside who would gladly surrender the citadel, if he could, but with my Lord it was quite otherwise.

HARRY IRONSIDE

THE GREATEST IS HOPE

And now abideth faith, hope, charity, these three; but the
greatest of these is charity.
1 CORINTHIANS 13:13

Love is of two kinds - the love of benevolence and the love of delight. The one is without regard to the qualities of those who are loved - without regard to return, without regard to any attractive quality. Such is the love of God and Christ to us - pure benevolence. And it is this which sends out the city missionary, the Christian man, to the outcasts of society, not on account of any good they *have*, but because of God they *need*, which he instrumentally and God effectively can impart. But there is also the love of delight, which is a moral quality. Such is the love of God to His Son, and such also, because of the fruit of His own grace, is the affection of God and Christ. This love, we see, is not blind, it is discriminating - "it rejoiceth not in iniquity." To the iniquity as iniquity it cannot extend itself; but in the proclamation of the word of grace God has made provision for evil-doers being, by God's grace, turned unto Him in true repentance, in newness of heart and life; and thus love can extend, and does extend, even to the workers of iniquity.

But it rejoiceth not in iniquity. It is a false love which is extended to iniquity, which goes out to a man in the way of cloaking and countenancing his iniquity. To love a man and to love his sin, is to love a man and to love his ague, to love his fever. I cannot love a man and love his disease - I cannot love a man and love his sin. Yes, but blessed be God, through His grace love has something to give it joy, even in this world, where there is so much sin, and which is for the most part joyless. There is truth - it "rejoiceth in the truth." "Truth shall spring out of the earth, and righteousness shall look down from heaven." There is truth on earth God has a people; there are righteous ways of God, and there are men walking in them. There are things by grace taking place in this world in which love can have joy, and it does rejoice, "rejoiceth in the truth".

"Love beareth all things, believeth all things, hopeth all things, endureth all things." Love does not say, "This is insupportable." Love has a way to bear it: it bears all bearable things, and it believes all believable things. Of course, not such as are actually incredible; but it is ready to believe. It easily believes good; and it needs great proof to make it believe what is bad.

JOHN DUNCAN

NOVEMBER 27

OUR INFLUENCE FOR GOD

Your faith should not stand in the wisdom of men, but in the power of God.
1 CORINTHIANS 2:5

While the early Christians were true to the example and teaching of their Master we never find them bemoaning their lack of ability to attract or to convert people. So mighty was their influence, though comparatively few in number, and insignificant in social position, that wherever they went they were said to have *"turned the world upside down"*, and large and flourishing churches sprang up in all directions.

They did not feel the necessity for any half-way meeting place between themselves and the world; they did not lower the tone of the Christian morality in order to meet the corrupt and heathenish notions of those around them; neither did they abjure their spirituality lest it should disgust them. On the contrary, the apostles and early Christians seemed to have had the conviction that the more complete their devotion to their Master - the more separate from the world, the more truly spiritual and divine they were - the greater would be their influence for God, and the greater their success in winning men to Christ. Their preaching was *"with demonstration of the Spirit and power"* consequently multitudes listened, believed, and turned to the Lord.

Lord of all power and might,
Father of love and light,
Speed on Thy Word:
O let the Gospel sound
All the wide world around,.
Wherever man is found;
God speed His Word.

CATHERINE BOOTH

NOVEMBER 28

ALL GOD'S CREATURES

In him we live, and move, and have our being.
ACTS 17:28

Would an earthly father consign his child to everlasting suffering? And if he would not, can we believe that God is not as good as we are and that He would treat His children in a way that we would not treat ours?

This question takes it for granted that all men are God's children. The Bible teaches that this is not true. All men are God's creatures and were created originally in His likeness, and in this sense they are all His offspring (Acts 17:26-29), but men become God's children in the fullest sense by being born again of the Holy Spirit (John 3:3-6) through the personal acceptance of Jesus Christ as their Saviour (John 1:12, Galatians 3:26).

Second God is something besides the Father even of the believers. He is the moral governor of this universe. As a righteous moral governor of the universe He must punish sin, and if sin is eternally persisted in He must eternally punish it. Even a wise earthly father would separate one of his own children who persisted in sin from contact with his other children. If a man had a dearly beloved son who was a moral monster he certainly would not allow him to associate with his daughters. If one whom you greatly loved should commit a gross wrong against someone you loved more, and should persist in it eternally, would you not consent to his eternal punishment?

Third, it is never safe to measure what an infinitely holy God would do by what we would do. As we look about us in the world today do we not see men and women suffering agonies that we would not allow our children to suffer if we could prevent it? What one of us could endure to see our children suffering some of the things that the men and women in the slums of the great city are suffering today? Why a God of love permits this to go on may be difficult for us to explain, but that it does go on we know. What men and women suffer even in the life that now is as a result of their disobedience to God and their persistence in sin and their rejection of Jesus Christ ought to be a hint of what men will suffer in the eternal world if they go on in sin as the result of their having rejected the Saviour in the life that now is.

R. A. TORREY

RICHES OF GRACE

God ... hath in these last days spoken unto us by his Son ...
by whom also he made the worlds.
HEBREWS 1:2

Would it startle you if I dared to say that the living God has never done anything in His universe apart from Jesus Christ? Christians seem to be woefully unaware of the full meaning and measure of the grace of God. Why should we question God's provision when the Holy Spirit tells us through the Apostle John that the Word who became flesh is "full of grace and truth"? Brethren, the stars in their courses, the frogs that croak beside the lake, the angels in heaven above and men and women on earth below - all came out of the channel we call the eternal Word!

In the book of Revelation, John bears record of the whole universe joining to give praise to the Lamb that was slain. Under the earth and on the earth, and above the earth John heard creatures praising Jesus Christ, all joining in a great chorus: "Worthy is the Lamb that was slain to receive power, and riches, and wisdom, and strength, and honour, and glory and blessing!"

Yes, surely the entire universe is beneficiary of God's rich grace in Jesus Christ!

Of the Father's love begotten
Ere the worlds began to be,
He is Alpha and Omega,
He the source, the ending, He.
Of the things that are, that have been,
And that future years shall be.

By His word was all created;
He commanded and 'twas done;
Earth and sky and boundless ocean,
Universe of there in one,
All that sees the moon's soft radiance,
All that breathes beneath the sun.

A. W. TOZER

THE INDWELLING CHRIST

That Christ may dwell in your heart by faith.
EPHESIANS 3:17

The great privilege that separated Israel from other nations was this: they had God dwelling in their midst, His Home in the Holiest of all, in the tabernacle and the temple. The New Testament is the dispensation of the indwelling God in the heart of His people. As Christ said (John 14:21,23) "If a man keep My words, he it is that loveth me; and My Father will love him, and I will love him, and we will come to him, and make our abode with him" - what Paul calls "The riches of the glory of this mystery among the Gentiles, which is Christ in you, the hope of glory." Or, as he says of himself, "Christ liveth in me".

The Gospel - the dispensation of the indwelling Christ. How few Christians there are who believe or experience it! Come and let us listen to Paul's teaching as to the way into the experience of this crowning blessing of the Christian life.

1. *"I bow my knees to the Father, that He would grant you."* The blessing must come from the Father to the supplicant on the bended knee, for himself or for those for whom he labours. It is to be found in much prayer.
2. *"That He would grant you according to the riches of His glory"* - something very special and divine - *"to be strengthened by His Spirit in the inner man,"* to separate from sin and the world, to yield to Christ as Lord and Master, and to live that live of love to Christ and keeping His commandments to which the promise has been given: "The Father and I will come to him, and make our abode with him."
3. *"That Christ may dwell in your heart by faith."* It is in the very nature of Christ, in His divine omnipresence and love, to long for the heart to dwell in. As faith sees this and bows the knee and pleads with God for this great blessing, it receives grace to believe that the prayer is answered and in that faith accepts the wonderful gift so long thirsted for - Christ dwelling in the heart by faith.
4. *"That ye being rooted and grounded in love may be filled with all the fullness of God,"* as far as it is possible for man to experience it.

ANDREW MURRAY

DECEMBER 1

NO COMPARISON

He is precious.
1 PETER 2:7

"As all the rivers run into the sea, yet the sea is not full" (Ecclesiastes 1:7). All enjoyment centres in our Beloved. The glances of His eyes outshine the sun and the beauties of His face are fairer than the choicest flowers, No fragrance is like the breath of His mouth. Gems of the mine and pears from the sea are worthless when compared to His preciousness.

Peter tells us that Jesus is precious, but he did not and could not describe how precious. No one can compute the value of "'God's indescribable gift (2 Corinthians 9:15). Words cannot depict the preciousness of the Lord Jesus, nor can words portray how essential He is to our satisfaction and happiness.

Believer, in the midst of plenty there is a famine if your Lord is absent. The sun may shine, but if Christ is hidden all your world is dark and it is night. Is the bright and morning star gone and there is no other star to yield a ray of light in its place?

What a howling wilderness this world is without our Lord! If we do not see Him our flowers wither, our enjoyable fruits decay, the birds stop singing, and storms overturn our hopes. All the lights of earth cannot produce daylight if the Sun of Righteousness is eclipsed. He is the soul of our soul, the light of our light, the life of our life.

Dear believer, what would you do with the temptations and cares of this world if you did not have Him? What would you do when you awaken and prepare for the day's battle if you did not have Him? What would you do at night when you arrive home exhausted and weary if there were no door of fellowship between you and Christ?

Blessed be His name. He will not leave you. His promise is sure, "I will never leave you nor forsake you" (Hebrews 13:5).

When you think what life would be like without Him, it magnifies His preciousness.

CHARLES H. SPURGEON

DECEMBER 2

A SPECIAL TIME

To everything there is a season, and a time to every purpose under the heaven.
ECCLESIASTES 3:1

It should be the aim of every Christian to set aside a little time each day for quiet communion with God. A time for everything - and shall there be no time to spend in the presence of the Creator of all things? No time to contemplate His will and purposes for us? The holy, loving God is indeed worthy of the best of our time - of all of our time. We should live in constant fellowship with Him, but each day there should be a special time of quiet when we are with Him alone.

We need a period daily for secret fellowship. Time to turn from daily occupation and search our hearts in His presence. Time to study His Word with reverence and godly fear. Time to seek His face and ask Him to make Himself known to us. Time to wait until we know that He sees and hears us so that we can make our wants known to Him in words that come from the depth of our hearts, to let ourselves be filled with His Spirit!

What do you think? Will it be possible to give a quarter of an hour each day for this purpose? If you are unwilling to make such an arrangement, you must not be surprised if your spiritual life is enfeebled and becomes ineffective. Fellowship with God should have a first claim on your time, and if you will only arrange for this brief time with God, you will soon learn to value it. It will not be long before you feel ashamed that there was ever a time when you thought fifteen minutes would suffice.

Everything on earth needs time. Think of the hours per day for so many years that a child spends at school gathering the rudiments of knowledge that he may cope with this life. How much longer then should we spend in learning from God for life everlasting?

O Christian, give the holy, gracious God all the time you can until His light and life and love fill your whole life and you abide in Christ and His love through His Word and through prayer.

ANDREW MURRAY

DECEMBER 3

THE WORSHIP OF THE REDEEMED

And the four and twenty elders fell down and worshipped God that sat on the throne, saying, Amen; Alleluia.
REVELATION 19:4

"Amen; hallelujah." These are not the empty words of an idle song. They are the expressions of dispositions, not of the transient day, but of the endless life. In those two days, if only we look at them aright, we may see the two great features of the heavenly life, the life that is lived in the immediate presence of God. "Amen," a note of resignation and submission, not sung with reluctance, but with a glad and eager consent. To all the revelations of God's will the angels send the response, "Amen"; "Hallelujah," the note of praise. The angels obey, but not sullenly: they submit, but cheerily. They love and praise; they serve and sing. God's love shines upon them as the sunlight falls upon our busy birds in spring, and like the birds they cannot help but sing. They bow to the Lord's will in "Amen". They sing to the Lord's praise in "Hallelujah". The two together make the unbroken harmony of the eternal song.

Now, need we wait for the great unveiling before we learn the song? This heavenly harmony may be in our lives even while we walk the ways of earth. To the cry of "Amen," "So be it," "Thy will be done," the angels kneel and lay their crowns at the King's feet. They kneel there, not as monarchs, but as subjects, listening for the King's will, in order that, as deputy kings, they may hasten away to perform it. May we not, even now, adopt the angel's posture and the angel's speech? We are too prone to stand in stiff rebelliousness when we ought to bow in resignation and submission. We keep our crowns upon our brows, as kings and queens whose rights and dignities we jealously guard against infringement, when our truest nobility would be gained in laying our crowns at the feet of our God. What crowns have we? We have the crown of thought and the crown of will, the power to think and the power to rule; but these powers only attain their highest efficiency and glory when they are constrained into obedience to the all-loving King.

J.H. JOWETT

DECEMBER 4

SURPRISING GRACE

Nevertheless I am continually with thee.
PSALM 73:23

Nevertheless: notwithstanding all the foolishness and ignorance that David had been confessing to God, by not one atom less was it true and certain that David was still saved and accepted by God.

The blessing of being constantly in God's presence was undoubtedly his. David was fully conscious of his own lost estate and the deceitfulness and vileness of his nature. Yet David, by a glorious outburst of faith sings, "*Nevertheless* I am continually with thee."

Believer, you are forced to confess and acknowledge with Asaph, "*Nevertheless*, since I belong to Christ I am continually with God!" You are continually on His mind. He is always thinking of you for your own good (Isaiah 49:15-16). You are continually before His eye, and His eye never sleeps but perpetually watches over you Psalm 121:3. You are continually in His hand, so that none can snatch you away (John 10:28). You are continually on His heart, worn there as a memorial, just as the priest bore the names of the twelve tribes on his heart (Exodus 39:14).

You always think of me, O God. The heart of Your love yearns towards me. You are always making providence work for my good. You have "set me as a seal upon Your heart, as a seal upon Your arm. Your love is strong as death … many waters cannot quench love, nor can the floods drown it" (Song of Solomon 8:6,7).

Surprising grace! You see me in Christ. Though in myself abhorred. You see me wearing Christ's righteous garments and washed in His blood. Thus I stand accepted in Your presence. I am continually in Your favour, "continually with You." This is comfort for the tried and afflicted soul who is pestered by the tempest within. Look at the calm without.

Nevertheless. Oh say it in your heart and receive the peace it gives. "*Nevertheless* I am continually with you."

CHARLES H. SPURGEON

DECEMBER 5

WHAT GOD IS

Behold, God is great, and we know him not.
JOB 36:26

The attribute of God as a Spirit whose being and glory are entirely beyond our power of apprehension is one that we ponder all to little. And yet in the spiritual life it is of the utmost importance to feel deeply that, as the heavens are high above the earth, so God's thoughts and ways are infinitely exalted beyond all our thoughts.

With what deep humility and holy reverence it becomes us to look up to God and then with childlike simplicity to yield ourselves to the teaching of His Holy Spirit.

"Oh the depth of the riches both of the wisdom and knowledge of God! how unsearchable are his judgments and his ways past finding out!" (Rom 11:33)

Let our hearts respond, "O Lord, O God of gods, how wonderful art Thou in all Thy thoughts, and Thy purposes how deep." The study of what God is, ought ever to fill us with holy awe and the sacred longing to know and honour Him aright.

Just think -

His Greatness ... Incomprehensible.

His Might ... Incomprehensible.

His Omnipresence ... Incomprehensible.

His Wisdom ... Incomprehensible.

His Holiness ... Incomprehensible.

His Mercy ... Incomprehensible.

His Love ... Incomprehensible.

As we worship, let us cry out: What an inconceivable glory is in this Great Being who is my God and Father! Confess with shame how little you have sought to know Him aright or to wait upon Him to reveal Himself.

"Mine eyes are unto thee, O God the Lord; in thee is my trust" (Ps 141:8).

"Be still and know that I am God" (Ps 46:10).

ANDREW MURRAY

DECEMBER 6

STEADFAST IN PRAYER

*She took for him an ark of bulrushes ... and she laid it in the
flags by the river's brink.*
EXODUS 2:3

The mother of Moses laid the ark in the flags by the river's brink. But before doing so, she laid it on the heart of God! She could not have laid it so courageously upon the Nile if she had not first devoutly laid it upon the care and love of God.

We are often surprised at the outward calmness of men who are called upon to do unpleasant and most trying deeds; but could we have seen them in secret, we should have known the moral preparation which they underwent before coming out to be seen by men.

Be right in the sanctuary if you would be right in the marketplace. Be steadfast in prayer if you would be calm in affliction. Start your race from the throne of God itself if you would run well and win the prize.

Go, bury thy sorrow,
The world hath its share;
Go, bury it deeply,
Go, hide it with care;
Go, think of it calmly,
When curtained by night;
Go, tell it to Jesus
And all will be right.

JOSEPH PARKER

DECEMBER 7

THE CORONET OF BEAUTY

That he may set him with princes.
PSALM 113:8

Our spiritual privileges are of the highest order. "With princes," is the place of select society. Truly our fellowship is with the Father and His Son Jesus Christ (1 John 1:3).

Speaking of select society, there is none like this! "You are a chosen generation, a royal priesthood, a holy nation. His own special people" (1 Peter 2:9). We have come "to the great assembly and church of the first born who are registered in heaven" (Hebrews 12:23).

Saints are admitted to the throne room. Princes enter when common people must stand at a distance. The child of God has free access to the inner courts of heaven. "For through Him we both have access by one Spirit to the Father" (Ephesians 2:18). "Let us therefore come boldly to the throne of grace" (Hebrews 4:16).

Among princes there is abundant wealth. But what is the abundance of princes compared with the riches of believers? "All things are yours, and you are Christ's, and Christ is God's" (1 Corinthians 3:23). "He who did not spare His own Son, but delivered Him up for us all, how shall He not with Him also freely give us all things?" (Romans 8:32).

Princes have distinctive power. Princes of heaven's empire have great influence. They wield a sceptre in their domains. They sit on Jesus' throne, for they "shall reign forever and ever" (Revelation 22:5) over the united kingdom of time and eternity.

Princes have special honour. We may look down on all earth-born dignity from the eminence where grace has placed us. What is human grandeur compared to this? He "raised us up together, and made us sit together in the heavenly places in Christ Jesus" (Ephesians 2:6). We share the honour of Christ. Compared to this, earthly splendours are not worth a thought.

Union with the Lord is a coronet of beauty outshining in all the blaze of imperial pomp.

CHARLES H. SPURGEON

TAKE IT INTO YOUR HEART

Thou shalt love the Lord thy God with all thy heart.
MARK 12:30

In this great command the Lord our God has tried to teach us how greatly He needs us wholly for Himself. Our love, our prayers, our consecration, our trust, our obedience - in all these there must be an unreserved surrender to God's will and service.

"With all thy heart" - with its longings, with its affections, with its attachments, with all its desires. "With all thy soul" - with its vital powers and the will as a royal master in the soul. "With all thy mind - its faculties of thought, of knowledge, of reasoning, and its powers of memory and imagination. "With all thy strength" - this is nothing less than the sacrifice of everything and the putting forth of our utmost endeavours. All for God, for God alone, and our one desire must be to love and serve Him perfectly.

What a wonderful God it is who has such a right to expect so much from us! Is He not the Creator who has made us to show forth His glory and for this purpose must possess us wholly? Is He not the Perfect and Glorious One who is worthy that we should forsake all to follow Him? Is He not the Everlasting Love and Goodness and Mercy, ever desirous of pouring out blessings upon us? Is He not indeed worthy, ten thousand times worthy, that all that is within us shall love and honour Him with all our strength and all our heart?

Think what it would mean in your prayer-life if you were strengthened with all might to call upon God each day! Take this commandment into your heart and make it the rule of your life and try to realise that God must have all. It will make a great difference in your life, and you will go from strength to strength until you appear before God in Zion.

God will assuredly work in our hearts that which He has promised in this command. We are unable to keep it in our own strength. The Almighty One will, through His Spirit, pour out His love in our hearts.

ANDREW MURRAY

DECEMBER 9

TREASURES OF LOVE

The secret of the Lord is with them that fear him.
PSALM 25:14

There are secrets of providence which God's dear children may learn. His dealing with them often seems, to the outward eye, dark and terrible. Faith looks deeper and says, "This is God's secret. You look only on the outside; I can look deeper and see the hidden meaning." Sometimes diamonds are done up in rough packages so that their value cannot be seen. When the tabernacle was built in the wilderness there was nothing rich in its outside appearance. The costly things were all within, and its outward covering of rough badger skin gave no hint of the valuable things which it contained. God may send you, dear friends, some costly packages. Do not worry if they are done up in rough wrappings. You may be sure there are treasures of love, and kindness, and wisdom hidden within. Do not be so foolish as to throw away a nugget of gold because there is some quartz in it. If we take what He sends, and trust Him for the goodness in it, even in the dark, we shall learn the meaning of the secrets of His providence.

A. B. SIMPSON

DECEMBER 10

THE SHEPHERD AND HIS SHEEP

I am the good shepherd, and know my sheep, and am known of mine.
JOHN 10:14

We should notice the name which Christ gives to true Christians. He uses a figurative expression which, like all His language, is full of deep meaning. He calls them "my sheep".

The word "sheep", no doubt, points to something in the character and way of true Christians. It would be easy to show that weakness, helplessness, harmlessness, usefulness are all points of resemblance between the sheep and the believer. But the leading idea in our Lord's mind was the entire dependence of the sheep upon its shepherd. Just as sheep hear the voice of their own shepherd and follow him, so do believers follow Christ. By faith they listen to His call. By faith they submit themselves to His guidance. By faith they lean on Him and commit their souls implicitly to His direction. The ways of a shepherd and his sheep are a most useful illustration of the relation between Christ and the true Christian.

The expression "my sheep" points to the close connection that exists between Christ and believers. They are His by gift from the Father, His by purchase, His by calling and choice and His by their own consent and heart-submission. In the highest sense they are Christ's property and, just as a man feels a special interest in that which he has bought at a great price and made his own, so does the Lord Jesus feel a peculiar interest in His people.

Expressions like these should be carefully treasured up in the memories of true Christians. They will be found cheering and heart-strengthening in days of trial. The world may see no beauty in the ways of a godly man and may often pour contempt on him. But he who knows that he is one of Christ's sheep has no cause to be ashamed. He has within him a "well of water springing up into everlasting life" (John 4:14).

J. C. RYLE

DECEMBER 11

A MIGHTY SAVIOUR

Mighty to save.
ISAIAH 63:1

With the words, "mighty to save," we can fully understand the great work of salvation. This indeed is total mercy. Christ is "might to save" those who call on Him. He is mighty to make sinners repent. He is mighty to give us new hearts and to work faith in us. He is mighty to make those who hate holiness love it and to make those who despise His name bow before Him. He is mighty to carry to heaven those who believe.

This is not all, for divine power is equally evident after conversion. The life of a believer is a series of miracles from "the mighty God". The bush burns but is not consumed (Exodus 3:2). He is mighty to keep His people holy and preserve them in His love until that day when He fulfils their spiritual existence in heaven.

Christ's might does not make people believers and then leave them to struggle alone. "Being confident of this very thing, that he which hath begun a good work in you will perform it" (Philippians 1:6). Jesus not only imparts the first germ of life in a dead soul, He also continues the divine existence and strengthens it until every bond of sin is broken Then the soul leaps from earth perfected in glory.

Here is some encouragement. Are you praying for someone you love? Oh don't stop praying. Remember Christ is "mighty to save". You are powerless to reclaim the rebel but your Lord is Mighty. Grab hold of that omnipotent arm and ask Him to put forth His strength.

Are you personally troubled? Fear not, "My grace is sufficient for thee, for my strength is made perfect in weakness" (2 Corinthians 12:9). Jesus is "mighty to save". The best proof is that He has saved you. What a thousand mercies that you did not find Him mighty to destroy!

CHARLES H. SPURGEON

DECEMBER 12

PRAY EVERY DAY

Give us day by day our daily bread.
LUKE 11:3

There are some Christians who are afraid of the thoughts of a promise to pray every day as altogether beyond them. They could not undertake it, and yet they pray to God to give them their bread day by day. Surely if the children of God themselves once yielded themselves with their whole lives to God's love and service, they should count it a privilege to avail themselves of any invitation that would help them every day to come into God's presence with the great need of His Church and Kingdom.

Are there not many who confess that they desire to live wholly for God? They acknowledge that Christ gave Himself for them, and that His love now watches over them and works in them without ceasing. They admit the claim that nothing less than the measure of the love of Christ to us is to be the measure of our love to Him. They feel that if this is indeed to be the standard of their lives, they ought surely to welcome every opportunity for proving day by day that they are devoting their heart's strength to the interests of Christ's Kingdom and to the prayer that can bring down God's blessing.

Our invitation to daily unite in prayer may come to some as a new and perhaps unexpected opportunity of becoming God's remembrancers who cry day and night for His power and blessing on His people and on this needy world. Think of the privilege of being thus allowed to plead every day with God on behalf of His saints, for the outpouring of His Spirit and for the coming of His Kingdom that His Will may indeed be done on earth as it is in Heaven. To those who have to confess that they have but little understood the high privilege and the solemn duty of waiting on God in prayer for His blessing on the world, the invitation ought to be most welcome. And even to those who have already their special circles of work for which to pray, the thought that the enlargement of their vision and their hearts to include all God's saints and all the work of His Kingdom and all the promise of an abundant outpouring of His Spirit should urge them to take part in a ministry by which their other work will not suffer, but their hearts be strengthened with a joy and a love and a faith that they have never known before.

ANDREW MURRAY

DECEMBER 13

THE REAL STIMULUS OF LIFE

Be not drunk with wine ... but be filled with the Spirit.
EPHESIANS 5:18

That is an extraordinary antithesis. The contrast would appear to be almost irrelevant. We are accustomed to oppose excessive drinking by the claims of abstinence; but here the alternative counsel is the reception of the Holy Ghost. "Be not drunken with wine, but be filled with the Spirit." Do not try to accomplish by one way what can only be attained by another. Do not seek the stimulus of life primarily through the senses, but through the heart. The fundamental need of life is not a sensation, but an inspiration. Man has a body; he is a soul. It is folly to seek to spur the essential powers of life by a stimulus of the flesh. The stimulus must be more inward, and must be given by the Holy Ghost in the soul. If a man wants buoyancy, power to contend with a "sea of troubles," and keep his head above the water; if he would be light-hearted, and have power to resist the awful, pressing weight of urgent care; if he would be optimistic, with reason that can pierce the new and frowning horizon, and realise the golden morrow beyond, the secret must be sought, not in the highways of the body, but in the deep recesses of the soul, And so the subject of the contrast expressed in the apostle's words is this - the real stimulus of life; what is it? What is it that reaches and quickens the innermost man? And the answer given is this - the inspiration of the Holy Ghost. Wine may excite a nerve; the Holy Ghost inspires and stimulates the life. "Be not drunken with wine, but be filled with the Spirit."

J.H. JOWETT

OUR SERVICE FOR GOD

In whom all the building, fitly framed together groweth unto
an holy temple in the Lord.
EPHESIANS 2:21

The life-tabernacle is a wondrous building; there is room for workers of all kinds in the uprearing of its mysterious and glorious walls. If we cannot do the greatest work, we may do the least.,

Our heaven will come out of the realisation of the fact that it was God's tabernacle we were building, and under God's blessing that we were working.

Are you busy in the corner
God entrusted to your care?
One small portion of God's vineyard
Is appointed as your share.

Each man has his work assigned him,
Each one has his special task
"What have you accomplished brother?"
Christ will soon return to ask.

Have you sown the seed, or watered
What another man has sown?
Have you brought some soul to Jesus?
Has God's love to him been shown?

Oh, God wants your little corner
To reflect His loving care;
and He wants its fruit to ripen
For the harvest "over there".

JOSEPH PARKER

DECEMBER 15

ALL TO GOD

I know him ... that they shall keep the way of the Lord.
GENESIS 18:19

God wants people that He can depend upon. He could say of Abraham, "I know him ... that the Lord may bring upon Abraham that which he hath spoken." God can be depended upon; He wants us to be just as decided, as reliable, as stable. This is just what faith means. God is looking for men on whom He can put the weight of all His love, and power, and faithful promises. When God finds such a soul there is nothing He will not do for him. God's engines are strong enough to draw any weight we attach to them. Unfortunately the cable which we fasten to the engine is often too weak to hold the weight of our prayer; therefore God is drilling us, disciplining us, and training us to stability and certainty in the life of faith. Let us learn our lessons, and let us stand fast.

God has His best things for the few
Who dare to stand the test;
God has his second choice for those
Who will not have His best.

Give me, O Lord, Thy highest choice,
Let others take the rest.
Their good things have no charm for me,
For I have got Thy best.

A.B. SIMPSON

DECEMBER 16

ALL FOR JESUS

Thou art worthy, O Lord.
REVELATION 4:11

In the fifth chapter of Revelation it has pleased God to reveal to us the song that the redeemed sing in heaven: "Worthy is the Lamb that was slain to receive power and riches, and wisdom, and strength, and honour, and glory, and blessing."

This is the song they all sing, all the redeemed; but every one of that great multitude - a multitude that no man can number - who now sings it before the throne of God and of the Lamb, first learned to sing it on earth. It was here on earth they not only first learned they were not their own, and had nothing they could call their own; but that even were the whole world their own, it could never make them happy. It was here on earth, taught by the Holy Ghost, they first learned that Christ, and Christ alone, was a satisfying portion; and that it was altogether worth their while to give all that they had for Him.

The price He cost each may have differed as to earthly value; but in every case, all that they had was the price that each paid, and that each thought it worth his while to pay. Matthew paid it, Peter paid it, Paul paid it and the penitent thief paid it. In one case it may have been the rich tables of the money changer, in another the comparatively valueless nets of the poor fisherman, in the third the righteousness of Paul, in a fourth the extenuating excuses of the sinner who had few advantages; but the main fact was the same with one and all of that vast multitude - each one had thought Him worth it, and so each forsook all that he had and gave it; and from that moment, but never until that moment, each begun to sing on earth what he now sings in heaven: *"Worthy is the Lamb that was slain to receive power, and riches, and wisdom, and strength, and honour, and glory, and blessing.*

BROWNLOW NORTH

DECEMBER 17

THE SACRED TREASURY

Thou hast bought me no sweet cane with money.
ISAIAH 43:24

Worshippers at the temple often brought presents of sweet perfume to be burned on God's altar. But Israel, in times of backsliding, was selfish and made few offerings to the Lord. This was evidence of their cold heart toward God and His house.

Reader, does this ever happen to you? Can the complaint in our text occasionally, if not frequently, be brought against you? Those who are poor in pocket but rich in faith will be accepted even if their gifts are small. But, my poor reader, do you give in fair proportion to the Lord, or is the widow's mite kept back from the sacred treasury (Mark 12:42)?

Wealthy believers should be thankful for the money entrusted to them, but they should never forget their larger responsibility, "for everyone to whom much is given, much will be required" (Luke 12:48). So, my wealthy reader, are you aware of your obligations? Are you giving to the Lord according to the benefits received?

Jesus gave His blood for us. What should we give Him? We, and all that we have, are His. He has purchased us, so can we act as if we were our own? Oh for more consecration! Oh for more love!

Blessed Jesus, how good of You to accept our sweet cane bought with money. Nothing is too costly for a tribute to Your unrivalled love. Yet You receive with favour the smallest sincere token of our affection. You accept our poor forget-me-nots as precious, even though they are only a bunch of wild flowers. May we never grow stingy toward You. From this hour may we never hear You complain of us because we withheld our gifts of love. Amen.

We will "Honour the Lord (with our) substance and with the first fruits of all (our) increase" (Proverbs 3:9). Then we will confess, "All things come of thee and of thine own have we given thee" (1 Chronicles 29:14).

CHARLES H. SPURGEON

DECEMBER 18

A CROSS OF LOVE

Father, forgive them; for they know not what they do.
LUKE 23:34

The seven words on the cross reveal what the mind of Christ is and show the dispositions that become His disciples. Take the three first words, all the expression of His wonderful love.

"Father, forgive them, for they know not what they do." He prays for His enemies. In the hour of their triumph over Him and of the shame and suffering which they delight in showering on Him, He pours out His love in prayer for them. It is the call to everyone who believes in a crucified Christ to go and do likewise, even as He has said, "Love your enemies, bless them that curse you. Do good to them that hate you, and pray for them which persecute you." The law of the Master is the law for the disciple; the love of the crucified Jesus, the only rule for those who believe in Him.

"Woman, behold thy son!" "Behold thy mother!" The love that cared for His enemies, cared too for His friends. Jesus felt what the anguish must be in the heart of His widowed mother and commits her to the care of the beloved disciple. He knew that for John there could be no higher privilege and no more blessed service, than that of taking His place in the care of Mary. Even so we who are the disciples of Christ must not only pray for His enemies, but prove our love to Him and to all who belong to Him, by seeing to it that every solitary one is comforted, and that every loving heart has some work to do in caring for those who belong to the blessed Master.

"Verily I say unto thee, today shalt thou be with Me in Paradise." The penitent thief had appealed to Christ's mercy to remember him. With what readiness of joy and love Christ gives the immediate answer to his prayer! Whether it was the love that prayed for His enemies, or the love that cared for His friends, or the love that rejoices over the penitent sinner who was being cast out by man - in all Christ proves that the Cross is a Cross of love, that the Crucified One is the embodiment of a love that passeth knowledge.

ANDREW MURRAY

COMPARE YOURSELF TO A DIAMOND

Better is the end of a thing than the beginning thereof.
ECCLESIASTES 7:8

Look at David's Lord and Master. See His beginning. "He is despised and rejected of men; a man of sorrows, and acquainted with grief" (Isaiah 53:3). See the end. "The Lord said unto my Lord, Sit thou on my right hand, till I make thine enemies thy footstool" (Matthew 22:44).

Like our Lord, you must bear the cross, or you will never wear the crown. You must wade through the mire, or you will never walk the golden pavement. Cheer up, Christian, for the end of a thing is better than its beginning.

See the creeping worm; its appearance is contemptible. It is the beginning of a thing. Mark the insect with gorgeous wings, playing in the sunlight, sipping at the flowers, full of happiness and life. The end of that thing was better than its beginning.

You are that caterpillar. Until you are wrapped in the chrysalis of death, be content to follow your Master. "It doth not yet appear what we shall be: but we know that, when he shall appear, we shall be like him; for we shall see him as he is." (I John 3:2). You will be satisfied when you wake in His likeness.

The rough diamond is put on the wheel of the lapidary. It is cut on all sides; it loses much that seems costly. Yet a glittering ray flashes from the diamond that was so roughly cut. Compare yourself to such a diamond, for you are one of God's people, and this is the time of the cutting process.

Let faith and patience have their perfect work. In the day when the crown will be set on the head of the King - Eternal, Immortal, Invisible (I Timothy 1:17) - one ray of glory will stream from you. "They shall be mine, saith the Lord of hosts, in that day when I make up my jewels'" (Malachi 3:17).

"Better is the end of a thing than the beginning thereof."

CHARLES H. SPURGEON

DECEMBER 20

THE FELLOWSHIP OF HIS SUFFERING

Unto you it is given in the behalf of Christ, not only to believe on him,
but also to suffer for his sake.
PHILIPPIANS 1:29

Paradox of Christianity which no man can explain - there is no joy like the fellowship of His suffering! What is the sense of sin that causes you pain, dear child of God? It is the outcome of purity. The measure of purity is the measure of suffering in the presence of sin. In the infinite mystery of pain there is the deeper heart and core of holy joy.

What is that suffering of your heart in the presence of misunderstanding of God? It is born of your perfect satisfaction in God. Why are you angry when that man libels God? Because you know Him. Your hot pain and great sorrow come out of the quiet rest of intimate knowledge. What is that pity for the sinner that throbs through your soul, fills your eyes, breaks your heart? It is the outcome of the love of God shed abroad in your heart.

G. CAMPBELL MORGAN

THE WORTH OF ONE

What man of you, having an hundred sheep, if he lose one of them, doth not ...
go after that which is lost ...?
LUKE 15:4

I thought perhaps he would not have troubled about one. If he had had only two sheep, and had lost one, I could have understood his concern, but to lose one out of a hundred would seem to be an almost insignificant loss. That is the line of reasoning which we sometimes introduce into our affairs. We reason as if the loss of one is lessened in its painfulness by the many that remain. We hear of some parents who have lost a little child, a fountain of joy and cheer. We compassionately inquire, "Have you any children left?" "Yes, they have four left." "Ah, well, it isn't as great a loss as if they had only one." That indicates a common principle of reasoning - the greater the family, the less the value of the individual soul. We carry the reasoning forward into the religious sphere, and it becomes the parent of depression and doubt. It creates the most terrible of all orphanhoods, the fear that there are so many of us that the individual does not count. God overlooks us, looks over us, and we cry, "My way is hid from the Lord."

Now this parable is intended to be an antidote to all such feelings of self-disparagement and doubt. The size of God's family does not affect the preciousness of the individual soul. The one sheep is not lost in the flock.

"He calleth His sheep by name." "He loved me and gave Himself for me." Let us hold fast to this inspiring truth - the infinite worth of the one in the esteem of the infinite God.

J.H. JOWETT

RIGHTEOUSNESS MADE POSSIBLE

The law of the Spirit of life in Christ Jesus hath made me free
from the law of sin and death.
ROMANS 8:2

Salvation is righteousness made possible. If you tell me that salvation is deliverance from hell, I tell you that you have an utterly inadequate understanding of what salvation is. If you tell me that salvation is forgiveness of sins, I shall affirm that you have a very partial understanding of what salvation is. Unless there be more in salvation than deliverance form the penalty and forgiveness of transgressions, then I solemnly say that salvation cannot satisfy my own heart and conscience.

Salvation, then, is making possible that righteousness. Salvation is the power to do right. However enfeebled the will may be, however polluted the nature, the gospel comes bringing to men the message of power enabling them to do right.

No condemnation now I dread;
Jesus, and all in Him is mine!
Alive in Him, my living Head,
And clothed in righteousness divine.
Bold I approach the eternal throne
And claim the crown, through Christ my own.

G. CAMPBELL MORGAN

SHOW FORTH THE LOVE OF GOD

By this shall all men know that ye are my disciples,
if ye have love one to another.
JOHN 13:35

We are taught in most of our creeds that the true Church is to be found where God's Word is rightly preached and the holy sacraments dispensed as instituted by Christ. Christ Himself took a much broader view. Not merely what the Church teaches through her ministers was, to Him, the distinguishing mark of His followers, but a life lived in love to other believers.

It is most important that we should understand this. In God, love reaches its highest point and is the culmination of His glory. In the man Christ Jesus on the cross, love is at its highest. We owe everything to this love. Love is the power that moved Christ to die for us. In love, God highly exalted Him as Lord and Christ. Love is the power that broke our hearts, and love is the power that heals them. Love is the power through which Christ dwells in us and works in us. Love can change my whole nature and enable me to surrender all to God. It gives me strength to live a holy, joyous life, full of blessing to others. Every Christian should show forth, as in a mirror, the love of God.

Alas, how seldom do Christians realise this! They seek, in the power of human love, to love Christ and other believers. And then they fail. They are sure it is impossible to lead such a life, and they do not even greatly desire it or pray for it. They do not understand that we may and can love with God's own love, which is poured forth unto our hearts by the Holy Spirit.

Oh, that this great truth might possess us: the love of God is shed abroad in our hearts by the Holy Spirit. If we fully believe that the Holy Spirit dwelling within us will maintain this heavenly love from hour to hour, we shall be able to understand the word of Christ: "All things are possible to him that believeth," and to love God and Christ with all our hearts; and, what is even hard, to love other Christians and even our enemies, while love flows from us as a stream of living water, "through the Holy Spirit."

ANDREW MURRAY

DECEMBER 24

IMMANUEL

Behold, a virgin shall conceive, and bear a son, and shall
call his name Immanuel.
ISAIAH 7:14

Let us go down to Bethlehem in the company of wondering shepherds and adoring Magi. Let us see Him who was born King of the Jews. By faith we can claim an interest in Him and can sing, "Unto us a Child is born, unto us a son is given" (Isaiah 9:6). Jesus is Jehovah incarnate, our Lord, our God, our brother, our friend. Let us adore and admire Him.

In our text we immediately notice His miraculous conception. That a virgin should conceive a child was unheard of. The first Messianic promise, however, was about "the seed of the woman" not the offspring of the man (Genesis 3:15). Since adventurous woman led the way in the sin, which brought forth Paradise lost, it is a woman who ushers in the Regainer of Paradise.

Our Saviour, though truly man, was the Holy One of God. Let us reverently bow before the holy Child whose innocence restores humanity to its ancient glory. Let us pray that He may be formed in us as the hope of glory (Colossians 1:27).

Don't miss His humble parentage. His mother was described simply as a virgin, not a princess, or prophetess, nor the heiress of a large estate. True, the blood of kings ran in her veins (Luke 3:23), and her mind was taught of God, but how humble was her position. How poor was the man she was engaged to marry. And how miserable were the accommodations for the newborn King!

Immanuel: God with us now in our nature, our sorrow, our lifework, our punishment, and our grave; and with us, or rather we with Him, in resurrection, ascension, triumph, and Second Advent splendour.

CHARLES H. SPURGEON

FROM THRONE TO MANGER

Unto you is born this day ... a Saviour.
LUKE 2:11

All praise to Jesus' hallowed name,
Who of virgin pure became
True man for us! The angels sing,
As glad news to earth they bring, Hallelujah!

The everlasting Father's Son
For a manger leaves His throne;
The mighty God, the eternal Good,
Hath clothed himself in flesh and blood. Hallelujah!

He whom the world could not inwrap
Yonder lies in Mary's lap;
He is become an infant small,
Who by His might upholdeth all. Hallelujah!

The eternal Light, come down from heaven,
Hath to us new sunshine given;
It shineth in the midst of night,
And maketh us the sons of light. Hallelujah!

The Father's Son, God ever blest,
In the world became a guest;
He leads us from this vale of tears,
And makes us in his kingdom heirs. Hallelujah!

He came to earth so mean and poor,
Man to pity and restore,
And make us rich in heaven above,
Equal with angels through His love. Hallelujah!

All this He did to show His grace
To our poor and sinful race;
For this let Christendom adore
And praise His name for evermore. Hallelujah!

MARTIN LUTHER

DECEMBER 26

JOY IN THE MORNING

Weeping may endure for a night, but joy cometh in the morning.
PSALM 30:5

Christian, if you are in a night of trial, think about tomorrow. Cheer your heart with the thought of the coming of your Lord and be patient for: Lo! He comes with clouds descending.

Be patient! The Vinekeeper waits until His harvest is ready to reap. Be patient! You know He said, "Behold, I come quickly; and my reward is with me to give every man according as his work" (Revelation 22:12).

If this morning is your low point, remember:

A few more rolling suns, at most,

Will land thee on fair Canaan's coast.

Today your head may be crowned with thorny troubles, but before long you will wear a starry crown. Your hand may be filled with cares, but it will soon sweep the harp strings of heaven. Your garments may be soiled with dust, but by and by they will be white. Wait a little longer. Your trials and troubles will seem as nothing when you look back. Looking at them here they may seem immense, but when you get to heaven you will:

With transporting joys recount,

The labours of our feet.

Our trials will then seem light and momentary afflictions. Press on boldly. If the night has never been so dark, still the morning is coming. This is more than those who are shut up in the darkness of hell can say.

Do you know what it is to live on the future, to live on expectation, to live on heaven? Believer, you have a sure and a comforting hope. It may be dark now, but it will soon be light. It may be all trial now, but it will soon be all happiness.

What difference does it make if weeping may endure for a night, because joy comes in the morning!

CHARLES H. SPURGEON

DECEMBER 27

THE DEATH OF OUR LORD JESUS

Father, into thy hands I commend my spirit.
LUKE 23:46

Like David (Ps 31:5), Christ had often committed His spirit into the hands of His Father for His daily life and need. But here is something new and very special. He gives up His spirit into the power of death, gives up all control over it, to sink down into the darkness and death of the grave where He can neither think, nor pray, nor will. He surrenders Himself to the utmost into the Father's hands, trusting Him to care for Him in the dark and in due time to raise Him up again.

If we have indeed died in Christ and are now in faith every day to carry about with us the death of our Lord Jesus, this word is the very one that we need. Just think once again what Christ meant when He said that we must hate and lose our life.

We died in Adam: the life we receive from him is death; there is nothing good or heavenly in us by nature. It is to this inward evil nature, to all the life that we have from this world, that we must die. There cannot be any thought of any real holiness without totally dying to this self or "old man". Many deceive themselves because they seek to be alive in God before they are dead to their own nature - a thing as impossible as it is for a grain of wheat to be alive before it dies. This total dying to self lies at the root of all true piety. The spiritual life must grow out of death.

And if we ask how we can do this, we find the answer in the mind in which Christ died. Like Him we cast ourselves upon God without knowing how the new life is to be attained; but as we in fellowship with Jesus say, "Father, into thy hands I commend my spirit," and depend simply and absolutely upon God to raise us up into the new life, there will be fulfilled in us the wonderful promise of God's Word concerning the exceeding greatness of His power in us who believe, according to the mighty power which He wrought in Christ when He raised Him from the dead.

This indeed is the true rest of faith that lives every day and every hour in the absolute dependence upon the continual and immediate quickening of the Divine life in us by God Himself through the Holy Spirit.

ANDREW MURRAY

DECEMBER 28

AT THE SAVIOUR'S FEET

Be ready in the morning, and come up ... unto mount Sinai,
and present thyself there to me.
EXODUS 34:2

The morning is the time fixed for my meeting the Lord. This very word morning is as a cluster of rich grapes. Let me crush them, and drink the sacred wine. In the morning! Then God means me to be at my best in strength and hope., I have not to climb in my weakness. In the night I have buried yesterday's fatigue, and in the morning I take a new lease of energy.

Sweet morning! There is hope in its music. Blessed is the day whose morning is sanctified! Successful is the day whose first victory was won in prayer! Holy is the day whose dawn finds Thee on top of the mount! Health is established in the morning. Wealth is won in the morning. The light is brightest in the morning. "Wake, psaltery and harp; I myself will awake early".

To Jesus every day I find my heart is closer drawn;
He's fairer than the glory of the gold and purple dawn;
He's all my fancy pictured in its fairest dreams and more;
Each day He grows still sweeter than He was the day before.

JOSEPH PARKER

DECEMBER 29

ALL THINGS NEW

The former things are passed away.
REVELATION 21:4

John is gazing into the perfected city of God. He is filled with intense surprise. It is not so much what he sees, as what he does not see, which holds him in fascinated wonder. It is the things that are missing which open his eyes in a wide surprise, the 'former things' that 'have passed away'. He discovers that many things, which he had regarded as essential and permanent portions of the structure, were only rough scaffolding, temporary expedients, which have no office in that perfected kingdom. In chapter after chapter we find him missing familiar things; scaffolding after scaffolding he finds removed, until at last, when, with one comprehensive vision, he contemplates 'the holy city, the new Jerusalem', 'prepared as a bride adorned for her husband', he puts his wondering sense of missing familiarities into this one pregnant phrase, 'the former things are passed away.'

Let us glance at two or three of these things that are missing in the perfected life.

'I saw no temple therein.' The temple is a temporary structure erected to serve the ends of the invisible Church. If I unduly exalt the scaffolding, if I regard it as an end, and not as a means, I throw my entire life into a false perspective, and I get astray from the pregnant truth. What remains in the life to come is the character the temple has helped to produce - the character of holiness, of fellowship, of praise; the character that apprehends the divine and loves it. Upon this I must place the emphasis, the spiritual internality, and not upon the temple externality, which will assuredly pass away.

J. H. JOWETT

DECEMBER 30

BELIEVE AND LIVE

The harvest is past, the summer is ended, and we are not saved.
JEREMIAH 8:20

Not saved! Dear reader, is this your situation? You know the way of salvation. You read it in the Bible. You heard it from the pulpit. It has been explained by friends. Yet you neglect it and are not saved. You will have no excuse when the Lord will judge the living and the dead (2 Timothy 4:1).

Years have followed one another into eternity and your last year will soon be here. Your youth has gone, life is going, and you are not saved.

Let me ask you, will you ever be saved? Is there any possibility? Already the most advantageous seasons have left you unsaved. Can other occasions change your condition? Affection and prosperity have failed to impress you. Tears, prayers and sermons have been wasted on your barren heart.

A convenient time never has come .Will it ever come? It is logical to fear that it never will arrive, and like Felix (Acts 24: 24-25), you will find no convenient season and find yourself in hell.

I want to startle you. Oh be wise. Be wise in time. Before another year begins, believe in Jesus who is able to save to the uttermost (Hebrews 7:25).

Consecrate these last hours of the year to private thoughts, and if deep repentance comes, it will be well for you. And if it leads to a humble faith in Jesus, that will be best of all.

Oh see to it that you are forgiven before this year passes away. Let not tomorrow's midnight celebrations sound on a joyless spirit. Now, now, now believe and live.

"Escape for thy life; look not behind thee, neither stay thou in all the plain; escape to the mountain, lest thou be consumed." (Genesis 19:17)

CHARLES H. SPURGEON

DECEMBER 31

WAITING AND WORKING

His wife hath made herself ready.
REVELATION 19:7

There is danger of becoming morbid even in preparing for the Lord's coming. We remember a time in our life when we had devoted ourselves to spending a month in waiting upon the Lord for a baptism of the Holy Ghost, and before the end of the month the Lord shook us out of our seclusion and compelled us to go out and carry His message to others; and as we went, He met us in the service.

There is a musty, monkish way of seeking a blessing, and there is a wholesome, practical holiness which finds us in the company of the Lord Himself not only in the closet and on the mountain-top of prayer, but among publicans and sinners, and in the practical duties of life.

It seems to us that the practical preparation for the Lord's coming consists, first, of a very full entering into fellowship with Him in our own spiritual life, and letting Him not only cleanse us, but perfect us in all the finer touches of the Spirit's deeper work; and then, secondly, getting out of ourselves and living for the help of others and preparation of the world for His appearing.

• • •

The year is dying but our God is living. Ring out the old year with praise! Ring in the new with confidence! The believers future is as bright as the promises of God and as secure as His throne.

A.B. SIMPSON